# CALIFORNIA WATERCOLORS
## 1850–1970

*An Illustrated History &*
*Biographical Dictionary*

*By Gordon T. McClelland*
*and Jay T. Last*

**HILLCREST PRESS**

Hillcrest Press, Inc.
3412 MacArthur Blvd., Unit G
Santa Ana, CA 92704
1-800-248-8057
hillcrestpi@earthlink.net
www.hillcrestpressinc.com

© Hillcrest Press, Inc. 2002

ISBN 0-914589-10-5

All rights reserved. No part of this book may be reproduced
without written permission from Hillcrest Press, Inc.

Preproduction, research and editing: Susan Wilden Baron
Design and production: G.S. Murray
Printed and bound in China by Dai Nippon

## *Table of Contents*

    4  INTRODUCTION

    6  CHAPTER ONE
*Traditional and Modern Realism
1850-1970*

  36  CHAPTER TWO
*The California Style
1930-1970*

  62  CHAPTER THREE
*Abstract and Non-Objective
1918-1970*

  78  CHAPTER FOUR
*Artist Biographies*

216  ARTIST INDEX AND
PHOTO GALLERY

230  GENERAL BIBLIOGRAPHY

232  ACKNOWLEDGEMENTS

WAYNE LA COM  *Avalon Casino, Catalina*  1955  15" x 22"  Private Collection

# Introduction

In the one hundred and twenty year period between 1850 and 1970, California has been the home to a large number of extremely talented and versatile watercolor artists. While some became nationally and internationally recognized, most were largely overlooked until recent years. Since the 1970s, art collectors and museum curators have developed a serious interest in California watercolors and have been seeking these works to collect and display.

Rather than discussing California watercolors on a strictly chronological basis, this book has been divided into three sections dealing with different stylistic approaches—traditional and modern realism, the California style, and, abstract and non-objective watercolors.

Traditional and modern realism had its roots in British, French, and early American watercolor styles, characterized by carefully rendered pictures which were developed from detailed pencil drawings. From the earliest watercolor depictions of California in the 1830s to a series of twentieth-century modern movements, realism has remained a popular form of California watercolor expression.

The California style of watercolor painting flourished between 1930 and 1970. The group of artists working in this style often chose to paint watercolors depicting scenes of everyday life in the cities and suburbs of California. They were considered an important part of the American Scene or Regionalist movement that swept across the United States during the mid part of the twentieth century. The best of their works were painted directly with little or no preliminary pencil drawing, had bold design, creative use of the white paper as a "color" and featured the transparency of this unique medium. With the increased popularity of watercolor painting in recent years, the innovations of the California style have become part of the mainstream of American art.

The third section, abstract and non-objective watercolor painting, deals with works produced by artists who chose to explore a wide variety of modern art approaches and techniques. Synchromism, cubism, surrealism, action painting, and figurative abstractionism were among the different approaches these artists employed. Although the roots of these abstract styles go back to 1918, works produced from 1946 to 1970 are featured. These achievements have laid the foundation for artists working in the last decades of the twentieth century who have continued to develop individual approaches to modern art.

A final chapter is an illustrated biographical listing of 555 California watercolor artists who were active in the period covered by this book.

MARION K. WACHTEL  *Sycamores*  22" x 30"  Buck Collection

JACK LAYCOX  *Feno*  1960s  30" x 36"  Private Collection

PAUL DARROW  *Untitled*  1957  18" x 24"  Claremont Fine Arts

WILLIAM KEITH  *Mountain Cascade*  1867  16" x 23"  North Point Gallery

CHAPTER ONE

# Traditional & Modern Realism
## 1850-1970

In the years prior to the Gold Rush of 1849, California had few, if any, professional resident artists. San Francisco, Los Angeles, and Monterey were small settlements, just beginning to develop. Periodically, survey crews or exploration parties visited the region and brought artists to visually document the trips by producing drawings and watercolors depicting landscape subjects.

Among the first were the English artists visiting the West Coast in the late 1830s and early 1840s. They painted watercolors which were used as illustrations in Alexander Forbes 1839 book titled *California: A History of Upper and Lower California*. This book was part of an effort to convince British citizens to immigrate and establish residence in California. Other works of merit were the watercolors produced for John C. Fremont's 1845 *Report of the Exploring Expeditions of 1842 and 1843-44*.

While these are above average works of art, it really wasn't until the 1849 Gold Rush that a number of well trained artists arrived and established residence in California. Some came to seek their fortune in the gold fields and others were sent by magazines to produce art for publication. One of these pioneer California artists was Harrison Eastman.

Eastman sailed from Boston to San Francisco on the ship *Rudolf,* arriving in September of 1849. After a brief stay at a gold mining camp, he took a job as a clerk at the newly opened post office in San Francisco. In his off time, he produced watercolors depicting everyday life in San Francisco and also worked as an engraver for local printing firms.

He was an expert watercolorist and did works that were reproduced as lithographs by Pollard and Britton, one of California's first lithographers. Other commissions included a portrait of James Marshall, the man who first discovered gold in California, and a well-known historical lithograph titled *Lombard, North Point,* on which he collaborated with friend Arthur Nahl. His art career blossomed quickly and from 1854 until the time of his death in 1862, Eastman produced watercolors, engravings and illustrations for *Hutchings Illustrated California Magazine.*

Two other watercolor artists who tried their hand at gold mining were George H. Goddard and George H. Burgess. Both of these men were from England, both arrived at the beginning of the Gold Rush, and both lived the remainder of their lives in California working full-time producing art. The lure of striking it rich initially enticed them to move to California. This was a story that played out in many lives. Once people realized how difficult it was and how great the odds were, they fell back on a trade or took advantage of a natural talent to earn a living.

A number of other talented watercolor artists arrived about the same time as Eastman, Goddard, and Burgess, but stayed on the West Coast for only a few years before moving on. Among them were William McIlvaine, Bayard Taylor, Cleveland Rockwell, Peter Petersen Toft and James Madison Alden. While none of these artists spent more than six years in California, the watercolors they produced depicting California subjects have become an important part of the region's art heritage.

**GEORGE BURGESS** *Merced River, Yosemite* 1883 13" x 10" Maxwell Galleries, Ltd.

**JAMES MADISON ALDEN** *Santa Barbara Channel* 1856 10" x 14" Braarud Fine Art

*Above is a rare example of a mid-nineteenth century California watercolor painting. It was produced by James Madison Alden during the time he was working as a topographer on the Pacific Coast Survey crew. As the survey crew sailed north through San Francisco, Mendocino and into the Pacific Northwest Alden painted similar works depicting coastal subject.*

CLEVELAND ROCKWELL  *The Willamette River*  1885  11" x 14"  Braarud Fine Arts

JUAN B. WANDESFORDE  *Mt. Shasta*  1880s  12" x 22"  Garzoli Gallery

CLEVELAND ROCKWELL  *Murder Cove, Admiralty Island*  1880s  14" x 20"  Braarud Fine Arts

During this era, art works were shown and occasionally sold through book stores, stationary stores and in hotel lobbies, but little attention was given to the art until 1857. That year, the Mechanics Institute Fair, which normally featured mining and agriculture exhibits, set up a special section for art. This is generally considered the first official art exhibition in California and the top prize went to Harrison Eastman for his watercolor titled *Scene on Montgomery Street, 1851*.

While San Francisco's art community developed slowly over the next 20 years, it was during this era that several very influential artists came to the West Coast. Juan Buckingham Wandesforde, Thomas Hill and William Keith settled and spent their lives building art careers and an art community in San Francisco. Albert Bierstadt and Thomas Moran spent less time in California, but helped to promote the natural beauty of this region waiting to be discovered by landscape painters.

All of these artists, except Bierstadt and Hill, were expert watercolorists and considered this medium an important part of their artistic output. An immigrant, Wandesforde studied with famed British watercolorist John Varley and applied his studies when producing works depicting the California landscape. William Keith was almost exclusively a watercolorist during the 1860s and continued to explore the medium throughout his career. Thomas Moran's watercolors are acknowledged as masterpieces of American art and are credited with helping to convince the United States Congress to declare Yellowstone our first National Park.

During this period, two art organizations were formed: the California Art Union in 1865 and the San Francisco Artists' Union in 1868. Both of these failed. Then in 1871, the highly successful San Francisco Art Association was established. Within three years, this art association was sponsoring exhibitions and was responsible for setting up the first art school on the West Coast; the San Francisco School of Design.

In addition to these efforts by local artists, other art patrons began to promote the arts in California. In 1872, the Bohemian Club was formed in San Francisco and became a showplace for art produced by local artists. In Sacramento, the E.B. Crocker Art Gallery was established in 1873. A number of commercial art galleries soon opened in San Francisco and one of the

PETER PETERSEN TOFT  *Seal Rocks / Cliff House*  1886  15" x 10"  Braarud Fine Arts

HERMAN HANSEN  *Race for the Chuckwagon*  1905  20" x 30"  Biltmore Galleries

HERMAN HANSEN  *The Attack*  1895  20" x 28"  Mackie Collection

most prominent was the Beaux Arts Gallery. The Snow and Roos Store had previously displayed only a small number of art works, but they expanded their business to include an art store and gallery.

Unfortunately, this boom of interest in art was somewhat short-lived. By 1880, San Francisco was experiencing a severe economic depression that had a negative effect on local art sales and caused a number of artists to move out of state. Many of those who chose to stay began seeking employment as art teachers or explored the possibility of letting their art be used for commercial purposes such as prints or posters.

Among the most successful color lithographers in San Francisco were Britton and Rey, Bosqui, A.L. Bancroft and the H.S. Crocker lithograph companies. These firms developed a steady business producing prints, posters, calendars, stationary, illustrated books, labels and other printed products. As their business grew, the demand for art increased. Although this was not considered a prestigious job for an artist, it did pay enough to support a family.

There were also newspapers and magazines reproducing art on the West Coast. Most issues of the *Examiner* and *Hutchings Illustrated* included reproductions of art and special commissioned illustrations. Arthur Mathews, Charles Graham and Alfred Farnsworth all contributed art to publications like these.

The process of reproducing a watercolor painting, using the lithographic technique of that era, was very complex. Rarely did the artist work directly on the Bavarian limestone plates from which the print was made. They usually supplied a finished watercolor, from which a master printer or engraver worked.

Thomas Moran's large, full color lithographs depicting Grand Canyon subjects were already available throughout America and in parts of Europe. Harrison Eastman and George Henry Goddard produced detailed views of San Francisco that were made available locally. H.W. Hansen's Western scenes, that often included advertising for beer or whiskey companies, were in nearly every saloon on the West Coast.

For many artists the teaching occupation was the most desirable choice. Often the teachers were able to do watercolors along with their students. This afforded them additional time to spend doing what they wanted to do and allowed them to reap the benefits of constant

JOHN REED DICKINSON  *Chinese Market, San Francisco*  1890s  6" x 7"
Maxwell Galleries, Ltd.

JOHN REED DICKINSON  *Friends*  1897  19" x 10"  Naim Farhat Collection

LORENZO P. LATIMER *Sunset* 20" x 30" North Point Gallery

LORENZO P. LATIMER *On the Fish Hatchery Road* 1890s 17" x 11"
North Point Gallery

interaction with enthusiastic young artists.

Two prominent teacher/watercolor artists of this era were Lorenzo Latimer and Christian Jorgensen. Latimer was born in Goldhill, California at the height of the Gold Rush and was the first native born watercolorist to gain prominence in the newly formed state. After studying at the School of Design, he became a teacher there while developing a market for his watercolors.

Christian Jorgensen was one of the finest watercolor artists on the West Coast in the 1880s, but could not make a living selling his works of art. To supplement his income he taught at the School of Design and worked for several years as a draftsman at an architectural firm. He later married Angela Ghiradelli, whose father owned Ghiradelli Chocolate in San Francisco. Historian Alfred C. Harrison wrote, "Their marriage in 1888 solved Jorgensen's financial problems, allowing the artist to follow his own genius unencumbered by the necessity of making a living."

As the turn of the century approached, San Francisco remained the center of California art. It hosted a major art exhibition in 1894, when the California Midwinter International Exposition took place. It had become a haven for artists interested in progressive art experimentation and home for a group of American Tonalist painters led by Arthur and Lucia Mathews and Xavier Martinez. Gradually art was being elevated to a place of some importance in San Francisco culture.

All of this changed in 1906 when the San Francisco earthquake and fire destroyed most of the buildings in the city. This included thousands of works of art and in some cases, the entire lifetime portfolio of some artists. It was a devastating blow to California art and is probably the primary reason why so few watercolors by early California artists exist today.

About the time San Francisco experienced this setback, other regions of California were beginning to flourish. Southern California had a rapidly growing citrus industry, a major tourist boom, and oil was discovered in a number of areas. The fishing industry in San Pedro was beginning to show promise and the release of Francis Boggs' film, *The Count,* became the first important movie to be filmed in California. The population of Los Angeles had grown from about 11,000 residents in 1880 to 102,000 in 1900, and

CHRISTIAN JORGENSEN  *Waterfall*  1916  15" x 11"  North Point Gallery

PAUL DE LONGPRE  *Peonies*  1902  38" x 16"  Joseph L. Moure Collection

business was good enough to support the establishment of a stock exchange in downtown Los Angeles.

Although Los Angeles could not boast of having a large number of professional watercolor artists at this time, it did have a few that were prominent including John Joseph Ivey, William Lees Judson, Paul De Longpre and Marion Kavanaugh Wachtel. Ivey, an English born watercolorist, arrived in Los Angeles in 1887. He became a professor of art at the University of Southern California and held that position until the mid-1890s. During his stay in Southern California, he painted views of the local landscape using a traditional English approach. In 1891, Fowler and Colwell, a Los Angeles publishing company, released Ivey's book *A Plain Guide to Landscape Painting and Sketching from Nature in Watercolor*. This was California's first "how to" art book on watercolor painting.

John Ivey then moved to Northern California and William Lees Judson, another English born watercolorist, became an art professor at the University of Southern California. Judson was a prolific artist and produced a large number of watercolors depicting landscape subjects. Most of them were done with transparent paints and often featured delicate washes with lost and found edges. Although he was an accomplished painter, Judson is best known for having founded the University of Southern California College of Fine Arts.

In 1898, Paul De Longpre settled in Los Angeles. He was a French born watercolor artist who established careers in Paris and New York City before choosing to move West. Once in Los Angeles, he built an elaborate mansion and planted extensive flower gardens on the surrounding acreage. The beauty of this estate attracted so much attention from tourists that a street was named after him.

De Longpre's most popular watercolors were his carefully rendered depictions of roses and other floral subjects. He found these subjects in his garden and painted pictures of them indoors in an elaborate studio decorated with Victorian objects and Oriental carpets. His watercolors were so popular during this era that publishing companies produced thousands of full color lithographs featuring De Longpre floral subjects. These lithographs were distributed in America, England, and France.

PAUL DE LONGPRE  *Untitled*  1902  10" x 22"  Joseph L. Moure Collection

PAUL DE LONGPRE  *Blackberries*  1890s  21" x 10"  DeRu's Fine Arts

MARION K. WACHTEL  *Untitled*  1920s  20" x 30"  David Tonnemacher Collection

MARION K. WACHTEL  *Santa Monica*  1930s  25" x 30"  Joan Irvine Smith Collection

MARION K. WACHTEL  *Ojai Valley*  1920s  13" x 19"  George Stern Fine Arts

Throughout this time, other artists including Benjamin Brown, Elmer Wachtel and Charles Stetson were using watercolors as a sketching medium. The art supplies were compact, and in the hands of a competent artist, could record enough visual information necessary to produce larger oil paintings when back at the studio. On occasion, the watercolor would turn out good enough to frame and sell as a finished work of art.

Also among the new arrivals in the Los Angeles area was Marion Kavanaugh Wachtel. She was already an accomplished watercolorist, having studied in Chicago under John Vanderpoel. She also studied in New York City with William Merritt Chase and in San Francisco with William Keith. Shortly after moving to Los Angeles, she married artist Elmer Wachtel and they settled in Pasadena.

From their Pasadena studio residence, the Wachtels traveled all over California. Marion Wachtel's watercolors from these painting excursions, and those done in the Arroyo Seco near her home, are among the finest watercolors produced in California during this era. Her ability to capture the unique atmospheric conditions and lighting found in the canyons and foothills of California brought her a great deal of attention during her lifetime. She was working exclusively with transparent watercolors and mastered the technique of building delicate layers of transparent washes from light to dark. She often blended or defined areas with a thin line of pastel chalk.

The Monterey Peninsula also became a haven for artists, especially those seeking refuge from the 1906 earthquake. Carmel and Pacific Grove were particularly favored since they were located on a rugged and picturesque section of coastline. Monterey, with its natural harbor and fishing industry, was also a well liked area, particularly for artists seeking those types of subjects to depict in their paintings. It was also one of the key resort areas in California, with the huge Del Monte Hotel being the main tourist destination.

In February of 1907, the hotel made a commitment to create the Del Monte Hotel Gallery, featuring art works by local artists. William Keith, Arthur Mathews and Xavier Martinez were asked to help and by late April, the gallery was ready to open. It soon became the focal point of art in Northern California and, through its sales, helped many artists financially recover

MARION K. WACHTEL  *Untitled*  1918  19" x 15"  Joan Irvine Smith Collection

WILLIAM WATTS  *Untitled*  1920s  29" x 23"  Courtesy Ken Cody

from their earthquake losses. About forty artists a year were able to have works exhibited and made available for sale through this gallery.

Tourists from all over America and Europe visited the gallery and purchased art to take home. Artists Sydney Yard, Mary DeNeale Morgan, William Ritschel, Francis McComas and William Watts all contributed watercolors to their shows.

Of this group, Sydney Yard was the first to settle in the area. In 1904, he moved his family from San Francisco to Carmel and established an art studio in what is now the downtown area. Early in his career, he traveled to the British Isles to study watercolor painting with Sutton Palmer and from that time forward he worked exclusively in the transparent medium. His paintings were usually small in size and featured beautifully rendered landscape subjects.

Ritschel and McComas also made their homes in this region, but chose to travel much of the time. Both had established credentials on the East Coast and continued to develop those connections for both sales and exhibition purposes. Ritschel sent works regularly to shows at the National Academy of Design, New York Watercolor Club and American Watercolor Society. McComas sent his works to the Salmagundi Club, the Philadelphia Watercolor Society, and in 1913 was one of only three California artists asked to participate in the Armory Show in New York City. To some extent they had become art ambassadors, representing the West Coast and in particular the art community developing on the Monterey Peninsula.

William Watts was primarily a watercolorist and also a world traveler. He grew up in Pennsylvania and studied art at the Pennsylvania Academy of Fine Arts. There he received instruction from Thomas Anshutz, an exceptional watercolor artist, and Robert Vonnoh, the teacher of many famous artists including Robert Henri, William Glackens and Maxfield Parrish.

As a youth, Watts studied color pigments and their chemical compounds in his father's factory and then began making his own watercolor supplies. He worked on a hard, hot press paper which caused the colors to remain vivid. It also made them pool up in unusual ways and created unique effects. Most of his subject matter was derived from scenes near his home in Carmel or from travels he took to Europe and India.

FRANCIS MCCOMAS *Canyon de Chelley* 22" x 28" George Stern Fine Arts

WILLIAM WATTS *Lobster Fishermen* 1920s 22" x 36" Claremont Fine Arts

FRANCIS MCCOMAS *California Oak & Carmel Mission* 28" x 35" William A. Karges Fine Art

SYDNEY YARD  *California Pastoral*  15" x 22"  North Point Gallery

PERCY GRAY  *Marin County*  1929  12" x 15"  Buck Collection

PERCY GRAY  *Field of Flowers*  1929  12" x 15"  Buck Collection

Another art colony that emerged at this time was in Laguna Beach. In 1900, it was a remote coastal community with only about ten year-round residents. This population swelled during the summer months when vacation-bound tourists arrived to enjoy California beach activities. They stayed in tents, rustic beach shacks, or in the Hotel Laguna which was built in 1889. When they weren't swimming or fishing, visitors could hike into the hills or canyons and find shade beneath the many eucalyptus trees planted by early settlers.

One of the original residents was artist Norman St. Clair. He was an English trained watercolorist who produced detailed paintings of local coastal scenes and hillside landscape subjects. These works were sold through galleries in Los Angeles and helped to create an awareness of how beautiful this region was. It is St. Clair who is credited with founding the Laguna art community and encouraging other artists to build studios there.

Within ten years, there were enough resident artists to consider this an art colony. William Wendt and Garner Symons, two of California's most admired landscape painters, had studios there. Others including Karl Yens, Edgar Payne, Elsie Palmer Payne and William Swift Daniell soon followed. While all of these artists are best known for their oil paintings, the latter four also produced and exhibited watercolor and gouache paintings.

The period between 1912 and 1920 was a rich time for the production of watercolors in California. Maynard Dixon returned to San Francisco after six years in New York City and began producing outstanding illustrations using gouache and watercolors. His depictions of American Indians and Western subjects on posters and billboards and in magazines helped to promote his name and art throughout the United States. The regular income from these commissions also afforded him the time to pursue the fine art paintings that ultimately made him famous.

Percy Gray, another San Francisco area artist, was producing exquisite transparent watercolors during this period. He was employed by the *Examiner* newspaper as an artist, but found plenty of time to paint depictions of local landscape subjects. While his approach to painting was based in the traditional English watercolor school, like all great watercolorists, his personal style emerged. Through numerous exhibitions of art in San

PERCY GRAY  *Monterey Oaks*  1930  15" x 20"  Buck Collection

PERCY GRAY  *Eucalyptus Grove*  1918  21" x 28"  George Stern Fine Arts

JOHN JAY BAUMGARTNER  *Laguna Beach*  1923  10" x 14"  North Point Gallery

JOHN JAY BAUMGARTNER  *Laguna Beach*  1922  10" x 14"  North Point Gallery

Francisco and Monterey, Gray established a reputation as one of Northern California's premier watercolorists of the era.

A variety of other outstanding watercolor artists also began working in the Bay Area. John Jay Baumgartner produced watercolors and gouache works often depicting figurative subjects in landscape settings. Francis Todhunter favored farm scenes and landscape subjects in Marin County. Frank Van Sloun did luminous gouache paintings depicting landscape subjects.

In Southern California, the art community was growing as well. John Hubbard Rich, an artist from Minnesota, moved to Los Angeles and along with William Cahill founded the School for Illustrating and Painting. Rich produced genre paintings and portraits using opaque watercolors and became an influential teacher.

Joe Duncan Gleason, a native Californian, returned to Los Angeles from his studies in Chicago and New York City. He used watercolor and gouache to produce commercial illustrations for magazines and advertising. Gleason had a love for sailing and became known for his depictions of marine and coastline subjects.

Colin Campbell Cooper, an accomplished American Impressionist painter, settled in Santa Barbara. Edouard Vysekal, a watercolorist and promoter of modern art, moved to Los Angeles. Stephen Seymour Thomas, a famed portrait artist and watercolorist, built a home in La Crescenta.

Of the new watercolor artists that moved to California, probably the most prolific was Donna Schuster. She was a student of William Merrit Chase and she had developed a very colorful, painterly style. She primarily used transparent watercolors and chose to paint while on location. Schuster became actively involved in many Southern California art associations and taught at the Otis Art Institute.

In 1915, Central America celebrated the completion of the Panama Canal, which allowed cargo ships from Europe and the Atlantic Coast to reach the Pacific Ocean without sailing around South America. This was a major event for California, especially San Francisco and San Diego, both of which were major seaports set up for cargo deliveries and tourist ships. To commemorate this accomplishment, both cities decided to host an international exposition.

JOHN JAY BAUMGARTNER *Tassajara* 1924 10" x 14" North Point Gallery

JOHN JAY BAUMGARTNER *Abalone Point* 1923 10" x 14" Buck Collection

JOHN JAY BAUMGARTNER *A Quiet Moment, Tassajara* 1925 10" x 14" Buck Collection

FRANCIS MCCOMAS *Cliff City* 1920s 22" x 28" Buck Collection

COLIN CAMPBELL COOPER *Magic City, San Diego* 1916 20" x 14" Buck Collection

San Francisco called its event the Panama-Pacific International Exposition. The city went to great lengths to feature art from all over the world and ended up exhibiting some 11,400 works of art. French painters Camille Pisarro, Claude Monet and Auguste Renoir were among the many European artists represented. John Singer Sargent, William Merrit Chase, Childe Hassam and John Marin were among the Eastern Americans represented. California had a section with key works by Guy Rose, William Keith, Clarence Hinkle, Maynard Dixon, William Wendt and Armin Hansen.

Although watercolors were not a major part of the art exhibit, the medium was well represented. Monterey artist Francis McComas had a featured section with ten works on display. Writer John E.D. Trask wrote "In considering landscape paintings in California, one necessarily thinks of Francis McComas, the watercolorist, who is one of the most distinguished workers in that medium to be found anywhere in the country." His large watercolors depicting southwestern mesa landscapes, with bold design and flowing wet washes, were particularly well received.

Other watercolorists were singled out for awards, special mention, or had watercolors reproduced in the books documenting this event: Marion Wachtel for her painting *Eucalyptus and Clouds,* Lucia Mathews for *Monterey Oak,* Percy Gray for *Live Oaks of California,* and Mary DeNeale Morgan for *Cypress Trees—Gray Day.*

San Diego's event was named the Panama-California Exposition. Although it was considerably smaller than its San Francisco counterpart, it was a major project for a city with fewer than 50,000 residents. The most celebrated art exhibition in this Exposition was the show assembled by Robert Henri, a well-known artist and teacher from New York City. He selected outstanding works by American Impressionists, Southwestern art by artists living in Taos, New Mexico, and he presented a special section of paintings by The Eight, a group of artists led by Henri. They often chose to paint depictions of slum areas and back alley city scenes, which led to them being dubbed the Ash Can School by Eastern art critics. William Glackens, John Sloan, George Luks and Maurice Prendergast, all important members of this group, had works on display.

COLIN CAMPBELL COOPER  *An Afternoon Stroll, Balboa Park*  1916  17" x 21"  Redfern Gallery

COLIN CAMPBELL COOPER  *Near Capistrano*  1916  5" x 7"  Joan Irvine Smith Collection

CARL OSCAR BORG  *The Prospector-Lake Tahoe*  1925  28" x 34"  Redfern Gallery

DUNCAN GLEASON  *La Jota*  1920s  12" x 14"  De Ru's Fine Arts

In 1917, America became involved in World War I. Many Californians participated in the war but the West Coast was a long way from Europe and in many ways was still isolated from eastern America where the war effort was centered. Most of the prominent artists were more than fifty years old and not able to serve. For them, this period became a time to organize groups of artists for the purpose of fellowship and art exhibition organization.

One of the most important art clubs to form in the post World War I era was the California Water Color Society. Originally it was a very small organization with only fourteen members. Dana Bartlett was the president and in a *Los Angeles Times* article stated that the goal of the Society was to set up high quality exhibitions of watercolors to help further the appreciation and understanding of work done in this medium. He also added that there would be no attempt to make it a large organization.

The first annual exhibition of the California Water Color Society was held at the Los Angeles Museum of History, Science and Art in September of 1921. It included works by Marion Wachtel, Carl Oscar Borg, William Ritschel, Donna Schuster, Dana Bartlett, Hanson Puthuff, John Cotton, Edouard Vysekal, Charles L.A. Smith, Henri De Kruif, Max Wieczorek, Karl Yens, Crafts Watson and Birger Sandzen. Newspaper reviews from that era indicate it was only moderately successful in attracting local residents, but art reviewers all seemed to give it plenty of press and favorable coverage.

During this early period, the jury which was set up to decide which watercolors would be included in the exhibitions was quite open-minded. Hanson Puthuff's works were done mostly with pastels adding just a bit of watercolor. Max Wieczorek, known for his portrait and figurative works, usually combined watercolor with charcoal and chalk line. William Ritschel's works were often mixed media paintings that included opaque paint, chalk and ink.

Marion Wachtel, Harry Law, John Cotton and Dana Bartlett contributed conservative works, almost always depicting pure landscape subjects. Henri De Kruif, Donna Schuster and Edouard Vysekal considered themselves progressive artists and exhibited modern works inspired by Fauvism and Cubism.

NORMAN ST. CLAIR *Laguna Coastline* c.1915 20" x 24" George Stern Fine Arts

DUNCAN GLEASON *Quiet Harbor* 1920s 10" x 14" Jeff Olsen Collection

HARRY LAW *Park in Pasadena* 1920s 12" x 16" Jeff Olsen Collection

GUNNAR WIDFORSS  *Death Valley*  1920s  20" x 16"  Knowles Collection

GUNNAR WIDFORSS  *The Ahwahnee & Half Dome*  1920s  22" x 28"
North Point Gallery

Carl Oscar Borg was one of the top Western artists of the era and frequently chose to show his luminous gouache paintings of Southwestern Indians and desert landscapes. Birger Sandzen produced vigorously designed, highly colored watercolors and Crafts Watson, from Milwaukee, sent abstract works based on still-life setups. The variety was pleasing to most art critics and the consistent choices of only top works by expert watercolorists made for high quality exhibitions.

Throughout the 1920s, the California Water Color Society grew in membership to just over 100 members. Most of the new watercolorists were accomplished artists and a few were becoming acknowledged on a national and international level. At the top of this category was Gunnar Widforss, a Swedish born watercolorist who took residence in San Francisco in 1921.

Widforss used his San Francisco address as a home base, but actually spent much of his time traveling throughout the Southwest painting watercolor depictions of landscape scenery. His early works of Yosemite captured the attention of several officials in the National Park Service and led to an open invitation for him to spend extended periods of time painting on location in Yellowstone, Bryce, Zion and throughout the Grand Canyon. He also traveled to Monterey, Catalina Island, San Juan Capistrano and Palm Springs where he produced watercolors that were exhibited on the West Coast, East Coast and in Europe.

Most of the artists who were contributing works to the annual exhibitions of the California Water Color Society were also represented by commercial art galleries. By the mid-1920s, tourism was the second largest industry in California and art was one of the most popular items purchased by tourists. A number of art galleries were established to supply the demand for high quality works of art.

Large luxury hotels were built in key locations throughout California. They primarily catered to affluent clients, who were often educated in the arts and were accustomed to purchasing art as part of their traveling experience. Many of the hotels, particularly those in Northern California, recognized this and arranged for regular art exhibitions in a hotel gallery.

In Southern California, there were small galleries at the Riverside Inn and a few other popular hotels, but it was not until 1921 that anyone seriously developed

GUNNAR WIDFORSS  *Canyon View*  1920s  24" x 16"  William Karges Fine Arts

MARION K. WACHTEL  *Women at the Fountain*  1935  28" x 22"  Buck Collection

the idea. At that time, Earl Stendahl, a thirty-three year old entrepreneur from Wisconsin, founded Stendahl Art Gallery at the Ambassador Hotel in Los Angeles. He quickly realized the market potential and expanded with additional galleries being set up at the Huntington Hotel in Pasadena, Vista del Arroyo Hotel, The Maryland Hotel and in San Diego, at the Hotel del Coronado. By the late 1920s, he was also promoting his interests by publishing *Stendahl's Quarterly Art Review*.

To a large degree, this growing art market was driven by the favorable economy that existed during this era. The excess of prosperity provided Californians and tourists from throughout America with enough extra money to purchase original works of art. This was a luxury that many Americans could not previously afford.

It also helped improve the lifestyle of California artists. Many were able to live in small communities like Laguna Beach, La Jolla, Carmel, Santa Barbara or Mill Valley. They sold their paintings through galleries in Los Angeles, San Francisco and San Diego. These larger cities were close enough to make deliveries of art reasonably easy, but far enough away to have little effect on the secluded lifestyle many of the artists preferred.

At the close of the 1920s the economy began to falter and in 1929 the stock market crash ended financial prosperity for many people. Most of the artists simply adjusted to the economic change and continued to produce art. Some had saved enough money to ride out the tough times ahead, while others took on outside work to help supplement the income derived from fine art sales.

With all things considered, the 1920s was a period of advancement for California watercolor painting. Francis McComas, Marion Wachtel, Gunnar Widforss and other outstanding watercolorists received acclaim and press coverage, both regionally and on a national level. The California Water Color Society was well established and provided an annual exhibition and membership meeting as a central gathering location for artists interested in this medium.

Prior to the 1930s, most of the successful watercolor artists in California were working in traditional styles that they learned from studying art produced in Europe and Eastern America. As the new decade unfolded, the art public's attention began rapidly shifting

EDGAR PAYNE *Sierra Sketch* 1930s 12" x 12" Joseph L. Moure Collection

EMERSON LEWIS *Golden Gate Exposition, San Francisco* 1939 14" x 10" Jeff Olsen Collection

GEORGE GIBSON  *Lojas Gossips*  1950s  22" x 30"  Courtesy George Gibson

JESSIE ARMS BOTKE  *Untitled*  1940s  15" x 21"  Sogliuzzo Collection

AIM MORHARDT  *Sierra Lake*  1950s  10" x 12"  Courtesy Ken Cody

to more modern works being produced by a group of young artists known as the "California Group."

This group of artists, led by Millard Sheets, Hardie Gramatky, Lee Blair and Barse Miller, quickly took over the California Water Color Society. Their actions were clearly unpopular with many of the elder watercolorists and, in protest, twelve long-time members including Carl Oscar Borg and Birger Sandzen dropped their memberships.

Throughout the 1930s, 1940s and early 1950s, the public interest in traditional style, representational watercolors continued to decrease. Most of the well established artists were able to sell works and teach art, but very few younger artists were interested in carrying on this tradition. It wasn't until the early 1960s that increasing numbers of California watercolor artists began to receive attention for the representational styles they were exploring and developing.

Donald Teague, a retired commercial illustrator living in Carmel, was among the first to receive attention. As a young man he had known Sir Frank Brangwyn, one of England's finest traditional watercolorists, and had been a student of Norman Wilkinson while living in London. Throughout his life, Teague traveled around the world and drew his subject matter from what he had seen. By the late 1950s, he was recognized as one of America's premier watercolorists and was a leading figure in the movement to revive interest in traditional watercolor painting.

In Southern California, there were a number of artists who were also producing outstanding representational style watercolors by the early 1960s. Among them were Joseph Henninger, Eileen Whitaker, Gerald Brommer, Diane La Com, George Gibson, Aim Morhardt, Jessie Arms Botke and Duncan Spencer. Each of these artists had a strong academic background and could apply his or her expert drawing and painting skills when producing works featuring figurative, landscape and cityscape subjects.

Throughout the post World War II years, the San Francisco art scene was heavily dominated by Abstract Expressionism, Figurative Abstraction, Geometric Abstraction and other forms of Modern Art. In the early 1960s, a small number of Bay Area artists began to react against these art forms. The direction they went became known as Photo Realism.

DONALD TEAGUE  *Don Quixote Country*  1960s  20" x 30"  Thomas Nygard Gallery

GERALD BROMMER  *Quiet Garden*  1960s  22" x 30"  Courtesy Gerald Brommer

ROBERT BECHTLE  *67 Polara*  1972  11" x 16"  O. K. Harris Gallery

RICHARD MCLEAN  *Spring Doe*  1974  9" x 10"  O. K. Harris Gallery

Robert Bechtle, a key innovator of this style, recalled that in school they were told not to work from photographs and to avoid letting their art become too realistic. Instead, he began producing representational art and frequently used photographs as a reference source. By 1964, he and artist Richard McLean were working from slides and sharing ideas about producing paintings derived from photographic images.

Bechtle was selecting suburban scenes of the Oakland area which often included cars, people and buildings bathed in the strong sunlight of midday. McLean did a series of works depicting horses and their owners. Ralph Goings, another California artist living in the Sacramento area, also began producing Photo Realist works featuring pickup trucks, roadside diners, and other images which were typical of the small farming communities near his home.

Their goals were never to simply copy the slide image they were working from. Bechtle stated that he would take a large number of slides at an event or location and carefully select scenes that might be interesting subjects for paintings. Often the scene or event was just moderately interesting or so common that most people would not take notice. When the slides of these images came back, occasionally they would capture something that attracted the artist to it. From there he would enhance the image by working the painted edges, bumping up contrast, or manipulating the overall feel to create a strong mood. The artist's goal was to create a work of art that made a more definitive statement than the photograph alone could express.

From the beginning, it was clear that certain images could be painted as watercolors and others were more suitable for large oils. Both mediums were of interest to these artists, although their most celebrated works have been large scale oils on canvas. By 1970, the O.K. Harris Gallery in New York City was showing works by Goings, McLean and Bechtle. Since that time, they have received international attention and their works have been the subject of several major publications.

The art created by representational watercolorists and Realists from the 1960s helped to re-establish the importance of that style. In addition, their influence helped spawn a new generation of artists who have since continued to develop styles based on what these artists did.

RALPH GOINGS *Yellow and White Pick Up* 1973 10" x 14" O. K. Harris Gallery

ROBERT BECHTLE *California Garden* 1973 11" x 16" O. K Harris Gallery

RALPH GOINGS *Dairy Delight* 1973 8" x 10" O. K. Harris Gallery

REX BRANDT  *On the Road to San Jacinto*  1938  21" x 29"  E. Gene Crain Collection

CHAPTER TWO

# *The California Style*

### 1930-1970

In the 1920s, Los Angeles experienced tremendous growth. The city's population grew from one million people to over two million people by 1930. Building was at a frantic pace. Gas stations, train stations, restaurants, high-rise buildings, the Red Car transportation lines, the monumental City Hall building and elaborate movie theaters were among the many construction projects. It was an exciting era for this city and Southern California in general.

During this period, a small group of young artists began producing watercolor paintings which pictorially captured what was happening around them. They often chose to paint depictions of cityscape subjects, with people, cars, buses and local scene activities. Barse Miller, Millard Sheets, Paul Sample, Charles Payzant, Phil Dike and Hardie Gramatky were key artists in this group.

The Chouinard Art Institute in Los Angeles was where most of the interaction between these artists took place. Miller and Sample were art teachers there and the others were advanced students. Frank Chamberlin, Clarence Hinkle and Lawrence Murphy were also key instructors at Chouinard.

While studying art with Chamberlin and Hinkle, the students were introduced to watercolors by Paul Cezanne, Winslow Homer, John Singer Sargent, Russell Flint, Frank Brangwyn, and other masters of the medium. In addition, they were shown ancient watercolors from Persia, China and Japan. This had a stimulating effect, especially on Sheets, Gramatky and Dike who were just teenagers when they began studying at Chouinard.

During this era, it was common practice to go painting on location with one or two other artists. Miller and Sample often painted together, as did Sheets and Dike, and Gramatky and Payzant. They used this time together to discuss painting problems and share advancements in painting technique. There was real comradery within this group that helped to stimulate their creative energy and advance each artist's abilities.

The watercolors they were producing weren't getting much attention until Arthur Millier, an art critic for the *Los Angeles Times* newspaper, began reviewing their shows. In May of 1930, he wrote an article after viewing a watercolor exhibit at the Dalzell Hatfield Gallery in Los Angeles. Millier wrote: "The watercolors in this exhibit indicate the presence of a rapidly growing school that requires only the encouragement of a moderate money shower to blossom into something fine and strong." He concluded the article by saying, "May it mark a new day for water colors in Southern California."

From all accounts the "money shower" was very moderate, due to the Depression, but it didn't seem to matter. The California Water Color Society, which held annual watercolor exhibitions, dramatically increased in membership as the news and excitement of a developing art movement got around. Lee Blair, Mary Blair, Milford Zornes, James Patrick, Emil Kosa, Jr., Tom Craig, Rex Brandt and Phil Paradise were among the new artists from Southern California who became affiliated with this group. From San Francisco came works by Stanley Wood, Maurice Logan, Dong Kingman and George Post.

BARSE MILLER  *Casino, Agua Caliente*  1929  11" x 15"  Jeff Olsen Collection

HARDIE GRAMATKY  *Bridge Construction*  1929  11" x 15"  Private Collection

STANLEY WOOD  *San Francisco*  1929  12" x 15"  California Art Gallery

PHIL DIKE  *Net Mending, Newport*  1935  15" x 22"  Phillip H. Greene Collection

MILLARD SHEETS  *Snow Day*  1936  22" x 30"  Claremont Fine Arts

BARSE MILLER  *Country Doctor, Night Call*  1934  15" x 22"
David Tonnemacher Collection

Over the next few years, several more important changes took place. Pruett Carter, a prominent American illustrator, moved to Los Angeles and became an influential art instructor at Chouinard. Most of the important 'second wave' California watercolor artists were directly influenced by his teaching. He was particularly adept at figurative painting and encouraged artists to include people in their works of art.

Another important change was the opening of the Art Center School in Los Angeles. Edward A. Adams founded the school in 1930 and hired Barse Miller and Stanley Reckless to teach. Watercolor painting was a priority class and many outstanding watercolorists came out of this school.

By the mid-1930s, Millard Sheets, Lee Blair, Hardie Gramatky and Barse Miller were in control of the California Water Color Society. They worked hard to organize and coordinate traveling shows and served on the board of directors throughout this era. It was an exciting period, as art critics throughout America began favorably reviewing the shows. To identify this group of artists, the critics gave them various names including: the "California School" and "California Style" watercolor artists.

One of the most important contacts the Society made was with the Riverside Museum in New York State. This institution began hosting biennial exhibitions of the California Water Color Society that generated a great deal of attention on the East Coast. As a result, the Metropolitan Museum, Whitney Museum of American Art, and other prominent museums purchased California watercolors for their permanent collections.

During this time, some of the California artists were elected into the membership of the American Watercolor Society and a few were asked to join the National Academy of Design. Both of these organizations held prestigious shows in New York City featuring some of the finest watercolors produced in the United States.

In Northern California, the San Francisco Museum of Art and the Oakland Art Gallery began hosting annual watercolor exhibitions in the mid-1930s. This brought attention to many outstanding local artists including Maurice Logan, George Post, Dong Kingman, John Haley, Alexander Nepote and Erle Loran. All of these artists also exhibited in the annual California Water Color Society shows, and in the case

MILLARD SHEETS  *San Dimas Train Station*  1933  15" x 22"  Hilbert Collection

MILLARD SHEETS  *Beer for Prosperity*  1933  15" x 21"  E. Gene Crain Collection

JOHN HALEY  *Gas, Eleven-Nine*  1942  17" x 22"  McClelland Collection

ERLE LORAN  *Beach Near Jenner*  1942  17" x 22"  Claremont Fine Arts

of Post and Kingman, became strongly affiliated with the watercolor group in Southern California.

Most of the Bay Area watercolorists of this era chose to depict cityscape subjects that were unique to their region. George Post was particularly interested in the construction projects surrounding the building of the Bay Bridge in 1936. This massive iron bridge links San Francisco to Oakland, with Treasure Island at about midpoint across the Bay. When the workers were digging up a portion of Rincon Hill to lay foundations for the bridge, Post was on location painting watercolors of the activity. As the bridge building progressed he continued producing works until the project was complete. These watercolors serve as an historical record as well as individual works of fine art.

Across the bay at the University of California, Berkeley, another group of artists, led by art professor John Haley, were also receiving acclaim for their watercolor paintings. Haley's works were "modern" by the standards of that period and were often designed using an open grid composition. He ground his own pigments to produce colors and used both transparent and opaque watercolors. The objects in the paintings were often defined by caligraphic drawing or outlined images.

Haley first learned the approach in the late 1920s from Cameron Booth, his instructor at the Minneapolis School of Art. Booth was an innovative watercolorist who had been winning prizes since the early 1920s. By the early 1930s, when Haley settled in Northern California, he had already taken this approach to another level and was producing outstanding works inspired by West Coast cityscape subjects.

When these works were exhibited in Bay Area shows, the local art critic, Alfred Frankenstein, gave them the name "Berkeley School Watercolors." Other artists who were known for producing this type of art include Erle Loran, Karl Kasten, John Ayres, Virginia Belle Gould, Miné Okubo, Leah Rinne Hamilton, Doris Miller Johnson and Worth Ryder.

Most of the California watercolor artists of this era were either employed as art instructors or worked in the motion picture industry. Hollywood production companies were very busy making and releasing motion pictures, news reels and animation films. All of these projects required various forms of art and provided a source of regular income for artists willing to work

GEORGE POST *Excavation on Rincon Hill* 1936 22" x 17"
Private Collection

GEORGE POST *Bay Bridge Under Construction* 1936
22" x 17" Private Collection

**MARY BLAIR** *Okie Camp* 1933 15" x 22" Studio 2 Antiques

**CHARLES PAYZANT** *Quiet Town* 1935 15" x 22" Courtesy Jessie Payzant

**ELMER PLUMMER** *Moving Day* 1936 13" x 19" Michael Johnson Collection

hard. For many, being involved in the development of animated films was as exciting as the growth of the watercolor movement.

In the early 1930s, many artists felt the most innovative animation art was being produced by the U.B. Iwerk Studios and the Harmon-Ising Studios (M.G.M.). Gradually, most of the key artists ended up at the Walt Disney Studios working on the first "Feature" animation films. Maurice Noble, Preston Blair, Lee Blair, Charles Payzant, Elmer Plummer, Hardie Gramatky, Mary Blair, Phil Dike, Art Riley and Ralph Hulett were some of the California Style watercolorists who also became important animation artists.

Some of the major feature film projects they worked on were *Snow White and the Seven Dwarfs, Pinocchio, Fantasia* and *Dumbo*. All of these films used watercolor backgrounds that allowed animated characters to move through the painted scenes. This was also true of the many thousands of cartoon shorts that came out of the Hollywood animation studios that featured Mickey Mouse, Woody Woodpecker, Daffy Duck, Foghorn Leghorn, Goofy, Donald Duck, Bugs Bunny and others.

Although the animation film business grew rapidly during this period, it represented only a small portion of the Hollywood area motion picture industry. By the mid-1930s, Metro-Goldwyn-Mayer, Columbia, Twentieth Century-Fox, Universal, Paramount and other motion picture studios were making large numbers of films and needed artists for many facets of the film making process.

Each company would normally assign an art director, set designer, sketch artist, scenic artist and special effects artist to each major movie production. The art director would work with a designer and a script to come up with plans for a set. This helped determine the costs involved in building the set. The sketch artist would then create watercolors depicting each major scene and continuity drawings to help visualize the action in the film sequences. These narrative illustrations would help the set builder, lighting crew, cameramen and scenic artist get a more complete idea of what they needed to do.

All of these procedures required skilled and talented artists. Emil Kosa, Jr., George Gibson, Herb Ryman, Joseph O'Malley, Ben Carre, Clem Hall, Duncan

LEE BLAIR  *San Francisco Cable Car Celebration*  1930s  15" x 22"  David & Sally Martin Collection

CHARLES PAYZANT  *Stormy Sunday*  1939  17" x 22"  McClelland Collection

EMIL KOSA, JR. *Close to L.A. Gaswork* 1930s 18" x 25" Private Collection

EMIL KOSA, JR. *A Little Corner Tucked Away* 1940s 22" x 30" Knowles Collection

Gleason, William Jekel and Duncan Spencer were all involved in this business and produced superb works of art for these purposes.

Another occupation that California watercolor artists pursued was commercial illustration. Maurice Logan, Donald Teague, Joseph De Mers, Alberto Vargas, Walton Titus, Nat Levy, Lonie Bee, Hardie Gramatky and Vernon Nye were successful in this field. Although their styles were very different, all of these artists used primarily watercolor or gouache to produce commercial works.

Maurice Logan was the head of Logan, Cox and Carey Advertisement Agency in San Francisco. His partners, Willard Cox and Paul Carey, were also watercolorists of note. Together they handled many California accounts including: Sunkist Growers, Standard Oil, *Sunset Magazine* and Southern Pacific Railway. Logan's many gouache paintings for these and other accounts rank as some of the finest commercial works ever produced on the West Coast.

Donald Teague received national acclaim for his Western illustrations. They were often published in the *Saturday Evening Post*. He also did a number of watercolor illustrations for *Collier's* magazine and signed them with the name Edwin Dawes. Most of Teague's accounts were on the East Coast and he served them by mailing the works.

Joseph De Mers taught illustration at Chouinard and had works published in *Fortune*. Nat Levy designed billboard art for Foster and Kleiser. Alberto Vargas did work for *Esquire*. Walton Titus did work for *Touring Topics* and *Sunset*. Vernon Nye worked with Harry Anderson producing art for children's books published by the Review and Herald Publishing Company.

Hardie Gramatky started out at *Fortune,* and then went on to do work for *Collier's, American, Woman's Day* and many other popular magazines. He also illustrated a number of children's books including his award winning best seller *Little Toot*.

To a lesser extent, artists Paul Sample, Millard Sheets, Phil Dike, Fletcher Martin, Rex Brandt and Ralph Hulett also did commercial illustration. Usually these were watercolors done for magazine covers or color illustrations for feature articles. *Fortune, Touring Topics* and *Sunset* were the main publishers.

**STANDISH BACKUS, JR.** *Buttresses of the Land* 1938 15" x 22" Jeff Olsen Collection

**STANDISH BACKUS, JR.** *Hoover Dam* 1938 15" x 22" Weare Collection

**HARDIE GRAMATKY** *Palms In Her Yard* 1935 15" x 22" Dillon Collection

MAURICE LOGAN  *Backbay*  1930s  22" x 30"  Claremont Fine Arts

LOUIS HUGHES  *Mitchell Hotel*  1940s  20" x 28"  Carlson Gallery

WILLARD COX  *Untitled*  1940s  22" x 30"  Knowles Collection

Throughout this era, artists had the opportunity to produce watercolors for president Franklin D. Roosevelt's New Deal Art Project. The artists would sign up for the program, then receive a small payment for each watercolor submitted. The art works were framed, then hung in schools, libraries, hospitals and other public buildings. Milford Zornes, George Post, Dong Kingman, Elmer Plummer, Joseph De Mers, and James Couper Wright were among the many artists who submitted works. On the West Coast, watercolor painting was not considered a particularly important part of the W.P.A. program, so most of these artists dropped out within a few months.

In the late 1930s, a group of artists from San Francisco formed the "Thirteen Watercolorists." The members worked in the commercial illustration field and produced fine art watercolors as well. Although the members changed from show to show, some of the regular exhibitors included Maurice Logan, Nat Levy, William Cameron, Paul Carey, Willard Cox, James Forman, Rene Weaver, Marshall Potter, Harold Gretzner, Francis Woodcock and Louis Hughes.

All of the artists in this group were expert watercolor painters and focused on producing California scene paintings with transparent watercolors. They exhibited mainly at the San Francisco Museum of Art and at the Bohemian Club where they were members.

Another small organization was also formed about this time and was given the name the "California Group." It was led by an art promoter and radio celebrity named Lawson P. Cooper. The artists involved were Lee Blair, Millard Sheets, Phil Dike, Rex Brandt, George Post, Milford Zornes, Paul Sample, Barse Miller, Tom E. Lewis, Everett Gee Jackson, Paul Mays and Tom Craig.

Cooper assembled a traveling exhibition of watercolors by these artists and set up shows across America. He had access to radio stations in each area and would present an on-the-air lecture to generate interest. This was a very successful venture and helped to introduce California Style watercolors to a national audience.

By the late 1930s, a number of individual California watercolor artists were being represented in leading New York art galleries and getting recognition from East Coast art circles. Phil Dike was showing at the Ferargil Gallery, Emil Kosa, Jr. at the MacBeth

NAT LEVY  *Sunday on the Farm*  1940s  20" x 27"  Private Collection

MILFORD ZORNES  *Downtown L.A.*  1939  15" x 22"  Courtesy Milford Zornes

PHIL DIKE  *Then It Rained*  1939  26" x 17"  McClelland Collection

Gallery, Millard Sheets at the Milch Gallery, Milford Zornes at the Walker Galleries, Barse Miller at the Rehn Gallery and Dong Kingman at the Midtown Galleries. This was a major boost for the artists, considering these galleries were also showing America's most prominent Regionalist artists including Grant Wood, Thomas Hart Benton, Charles Burchfield and Edward Hopper.

Additional attention was called to the artists when several nationally distributed art books were released in 1939 including: *Eyes on America* by Studio Publications and *Modern American Painting* by Dodd, Mead and Company. Paintings by Paul Sample, Barse Miller, Ben Norris, Millard Sheets and Milford Zornes were included to represent California Regionalist art. This recognition added to the building interest in West Coast watercolorists.

As the decade of the 1930s ended, two major art events took place. The New York World's Fair held an art exhibition titled *American Art Today* and the Golden Gate International Exposition featured *California Art Today* and *California Art in Retrospect*.

The New York exhibition focused on Regional art from all over the United States. The goal was to show how each area in America had its own indigenous art style and depicted subject matter unique to its region. California watercolor artists Rex Brandt, Millard Sheets, George Post, Barse Miller, Phil Paradise, Tom E. Lewis, Dan Lutz, Fletcher Martin and Tyrus Wong were among those chosen to represent the West Coast.

At the Golden Gate International Exposition in San Francisco, sixty-eight artists who were known as California watercolorists were included in the *California Art Today* section. Like the New York exhibition, this display featured Regionalist style art. When combined with the *California Art in Retrospect* show and art in other displays, over 600 works by California artists were on exhibit, making this the largest show of California art ever assembled.

By the end of the 1930s, the success of the California Style watercolor movement had far exceeded anyone's expectations. In 1940, *Art Digest* published the following statement while reviewing a one-man show by Emil Kosa, Jr. at the MacBeth Gallery: "Even though the Los Angeles Chamber of Commerce has not yet claimed it, California is, when viewed from the

LEE BLAIR  *Elevator*  1935  15" x 22"  Buck Collection

MILLARD SHEETS  *Paradise Cove*  1935  21" x 28"  E. Gene Crain Collection

EMIL KOSA, JR.  *Truckers' Gathering Spot*  1938  18" x 25"  Private Collection

ARTHUR BEAUMONT  *Bombardment (USS Wisconsin)*  1946  21" x 30"
Phillip H. Greene Collection

REX BRANDT  *Horsemen at Mission Beach*  1942  21" x 32"  David & Sally Martin Collection

JAMES PATRICK  *Tank Transport*  1940s  15" x 22"  Buck Collection

vantage point of New York's 57th Street, the land of watercolorists. From this sun flooded territory has come a steady stream of watercolorists to take prizes in Eastern group shows and to win acclaim in one-man shows."

On December 7, 1941, America entered World War II, an event that changed California forever. San Francisco, Long Beach and San Diego quickly became centers for producing and distributing war related materials needed in the Pacific. Trained ship builders and aviation industry workers moved to California by the thousands. Soldiers from all over the United States were sent to California to train. In a very short period of time, the population of California had more than doubled.

Most of the California art exhibitions were canceled or scaled down to moderate showings. The majority of watercolor artists were working full-time jobs that supported the war effort and had little or no time to paint. Those who became soldiers either quit painting or took sketching materials that they used occasionally. In just a few months, the focus and momentum of the California watercolor movement that had been generated in the previous decade had come to an abrupt halt.

Although there wasn't a great demand for war art, a few California watercolor artists became official war artists and produced paintings for the United States War Department Collection. Ed Reep was an official combat artist for the U.S. Army. He was sent to the front lines in Italy where he produced watercolor paintings of war activities while the fighting raged around him.

Milford Zornes also served in the U.S. Army as an official war artist and was sent to China, India and Burma. He produced watercolors of wartime activities throughout his time in the service. Arthur Beaumont served in the U.S. Navy and, throughout the 1940s and 1950s, painted watercolors depicting naval activities. Barse Miller, Millard Sheets, Fletcher Martin, Tom Craig, Watson Cross, Ben Norris, Lee Blair, Hubert Buel, and James Patrick also produced outstanding watercolors of war subjects. Some of their works were exhibited in recreation halls on military bases and others were reproduced in magazines including *Life*, *Fortune* and *National Geographic*.

Another viewpoint of the war years was depicted in watercolor paintings produced by Japanese American citizens who were put in internment camps

WATSON CROSS, JR. *Loading Planes* 1942 15" x 22" Studio 2 Antiques

MILFORD ZORNES *Revelie* 1943 22" x 30" Mike & Sue Verbal Collection

DONG KINGMAN  *Dockside, San Francisco*  1950s  15" x 20"  Courtesy Greg Young

during World War II. Artists Chiura Obata, Gene Sogioko, Kango Takamura and Miné Okubo were among the many outstanding watercolorists who produced works while in these camps. They depicted the daily activities of the people who were at the various locations and visually documented the conditions they were expected to endure.

After World War II, most of the California Style watercolorists returned to the West Coast. They continued to develop their individual approaches to painting with watercolors and many were hired to teach watercolor painting to classes that were filled with students on the G.I. Bill.

In Northern California, George Post, Maurice Logan, Dong Kingman, Daniel Mendelowitz and Alexander Nepote were among the key California Style watercolor teachers. They were expert painters and inspiring teachers. Their classes were often held at outside locations where they taught students to paint directly, while viewing a subject selected by the instructor. At the end of each session, the works were lined up and a discussion of their strengths and weaknesses would be carried out.

Some of the students of this era were well advanced painters and quickly received attention. Ken Potter, Horace Page, Jack Laycox, Robert Jensen and Marshall Potter were among them. By the early 1950s, all of these artists were exhibiting in Bay Area shows and working as professional artists.

During the post war years, much of the media attention in San Francisco was directed toward radical abstraction and non-objective painting. Both the San Francisco Museum of Art annual exhibition and the Oakland Art Museum exhibition were extremely modern and tried mixing all different types of art together. This didn't seem to please anyone. Many of the older, more conservative artists were very unhappy with this situation.

To help resolve this problem, they formed an art organization called the Society of Western Artists. They held annual exhibitions at the M.H. de Young Memorial Museum in San Francisco and had a special division for watercolors. This became the largest art organization on the West Coast and the annual shows were very successful.

In Southern California, the watercolor artists regrouped after the war and began rebuilding the

KEN POTTER *The Oregon Cafe (San Francisco)* 1960s 22" x 30" Courtesy Ken Potter

GEORGE POST *Southern Pacific at Julian Street* 1951 15" x 22" Hilbert Collection

GEORGE POST *Hunter's Point* 1950s 15" x 22" Dr. & Mrs. Larry Ho Collection

EMIL KOSA, JR. *Skyline Patterns* 1954 22" x 30" Philip H. Greene Collection

WILLIAM JEKEL *Packing House* 1940s 15" x 22" Courtesy William Jekel

ROGER ARMSTRONG *Taking Down Bunker Hill* 1950 16" x 21"
Courtesy Roger Armstrong

California Water Color Society. Emil Kosa, Jr. was the first to step forward and become president for a year. He was followed by Millard Sheets, Douglass Parshall and Rex Brandt.

The first post war exhibition was the Society's twenty-fifth annual show. Mr. Kosa arranged for eighty-six watercolors to travel to Chicago after being exhibited in Los Angeles. This was followed by an entirely new show of one hundred and twenty watercolors which opened at the Riverside Museum in New York a few months later. *New York Times* art critic Edward Alden Jewell gave this show a glowing review and hailed it as "One of the highlights of the season."

This was encouraging for California Style watercolor artists, but what most of them needed was some type of steady financial income. Fortunately there were many job openings for art instructors. Thousands of soldiers who visited California during the war decided to move there when they were discharged from active duty. Los Angeles was a popular destination and going to art school was an option for collecting money on the G.I. Bill.

Art classes at Chouinard Art Institute, Art Center School and Otis Art Institute filled up quickly. Art classes at the local colleges and universities were also full to capacity. The overflow went to new schools including the Jepsen Art Institute and the School of Allied Arts. Watercolor classes were especially popular, so the demand was high for skilled artists who could teach.

During this era, Los Angeles was really changing. The freeway systems were being built, the old Victorian houses on Bunker Hill were being torn down to build high rise office buildings and the suburbs were growing rapidly. Art students and professional artists took interest in these activities and they became subjects for numerous California Scene watercolors. Outstanding works were produced by Emil Kosa, Jr., Ralph Hulett, Ed Reep, Roger Armstrong and William Jekel.

As the interest in watercolor painting increased, the art schools and university art departments could not handle the demand. When the popular teachers realized this, they began holding private classes during the summer months. These offered one-on-one instruction in watercolor painting. Barse Miller, Phil Dike and Eliot O'Hara pioneered this concept. They held classes on the beach in Laguna.

EMIL KOSA, JR. *Freeway Beginning* 1940s 22" x 30" Buck Collection

ED REEP *Bunker Hill, L.A.* 1946 18" x 24" Private Collection

REX BRANDT *Summertime, Corona del Mar* 1957 16" x 12" Courtesy Rex Brandt

Rex Brandt took this idea and developed it into the Brandt-Dike Summer School of Painting. Classes were held at Brandt's Blue Sky Studio in Corona del Mar. The teachers were Phil Dike, Rex Brandt, Joan Irving Brandt and George Post. Guest instructors included: Millard Sheets, Emil Kosa, Jr., Barse Miller, Milford Zornes and other prominent watercolorists. Brandt wrote a number of books to help students advance their abilities and learn to see the world through the eyes of an artist. The school and his books were highly successful and became a model for watercolor workshops across America.

Hundreds of artists benefitted from these post war art classes. Robert E. Wood, Crandall Norton, Robert Perine, George James and Ritchie Bensen were among those who continued to use watercolor as their primary painting medium. All of these artists joined watercolor clubs and sent works out for exhibition. Wood and Perine also wrote art books and became well-known educators.

By the late 1950s, there were many more watercolor workshop opportunities available for those seeking instruction. Jade Fon and Harold Gretzner set up annual workshops on the Monterey Peninsula. Robert E. Wood established his school in the mountains of Southern California near Lake Arrowhead. Vernon Nye offered classes on the Northern California coast.

In addition, Therman Huett and Tony Van Hasselt organized international travel workshops with popular teachers. Milford Zornes, Millard Sheets, Dong Kingman, George Post and many other prominent artists were guest instructors for painting tours in Hawaii, Japan, Europe, South America and other areas of great beauty. Gerald Brommer was involved in similar excursions and wrote several books to supplement his teaching.

Most California watercolor workshops were held during the summer months, so the beach regions, where the weather was pleasant, often became the gathering spot of choice. As artists became more familiar with these locations, they continued to return to the beach seeking inspiring subjects. The expanded highway and freeway system made the coastline much more accessible at a time when the popularity of swimming, surfing, sailing, fishing, volleyball and sunbathing was increasing. The color, action and vitality of this thriving beach culture offered fresh new subjects for regional art.

**PHIL DIKE** *Summer Pageant* 1949  15" x 27"  E. Gene Grain Collection

**PHIL DIKE** *The Pink Beach House* 1940s  15" x 22"  McClelland Collection

**GEORGE JAMES** *Balboa Pavilion* 1955  18" x 18"  Courtesy George James

WAYNE LA COM  *Santa Monica Palisades*  1950s  15" x 22"  Jeff Olsen Collection

STANDISH BACKUS, JR.  *Goleta Beach*  1954  15" x 22"  Michael Johnson Collection

HUGH DUNCAN  *Harbor Reef, Catalina Island*  1950s  18" x 24"  Courtesy Hugh Duncan

Older paintings of the California coastline depict empty beaches and small villages along remote stretches of open land. As it became possible to live at the beach and commute inland to work, the coastal towns began to experience considerable growth. Santa Monica and Malibu were among the first beach regions to heavily develop and become home to those working in Los Angeles, Hollywood and Beverly Hills. Newport and Laguna also grew rapidly as the demand for housing grew to support the inland Orange County business community.

Artists Rex Brandt, Phil Dike and Robert E. Wood produced hundreds of watercolors documenting the activities in Newport Harbor during this era. Wayne La Com spent a great deal of time painting watercolors on location in the beach region between Santa Monica Pier and Point Mugu. Standish Backus, Jr., had a studio in Montecito, that was within walking distance of the beach. Hugh Duncan, an avid sailor, produced watercolors of sailing and harbor subjects in Long Beach, Catalina and other coastal areas.

It was apparent that the watercolor medium was perfect for capturing the realm of the casual beach lifestyle that was becoming so popular in Southern California. A number of magazine art directors picked up on this and began paying the artists for permission to print pictures of their watercolors in their publications. They would also write biographical information about the artists and include it within the publication.

*Westways,* published by the Southern California Automobile Club, was one of the main publications to feature watercolors on its covers. *Orange County Illustrated,* a popular local publication and *Ford Times,* a nationally distributed magazine, also incorporated California Style watercolors into their cover designs. This gave the artists and their art a great deal of exposure and helped to create a demand for their original works of art.

As coastal towns grew, they too became the target of redevelopment projects. Many of the landmark buildings were torn down or altered dramatically. The Long Beach Pike, Golden Bear night club, Laguna boardwalk, Rendezvous Ballroom and Pacific Ocean Park were all demolished. Fortunately, watercolor artists who were seeking classic regional subjects painted their creative interpretations of these historically important locations.

CRANDALL NORTON  *Snacks-Laguna Beach*  1960s  36" x 28"  Courtesy Crandall Norton

HORACE S. PAGE  *Fisherman's Galley*  1960s  22" x 30"  Courtesy Mrs. Horace Page

DON O'NEILL  *Mission Inn, Riverside*  1970s  22" x 30"  Courtesy Don O'Neill

In the early 1970s, the California Water Color Society changed its name to the National Watercolor Society, a move that accurately reflected what was happening. Their membership included artists from across the United States, and while the shows started in California, they traveled nationally and reflected what was happening with watercolor painting on a national level. The trend toward abstract and non-objective painting was particularly evident.

As these changes were implimented, it became clear that California Style watercolors depicting regional scene subjects would no longer dominate these shows. For many artists this marked the end of their involvement with this organization. A number of them continued to produce regional scene art well into the 1970s. Most of these artists had gallery representation on the West Coast and were not overly concerned with society exhibitions anyway.

In Northern California several artists who enjoyed painting together, formed the "Oakland Group" of watercolor painters. Maurice Logan, Harold Gretzner, Horace Smith Page, Jade Fon and Henry Doane were regular members. They continued the tradition of producing regionalist watercolors painted outdoors on location. Their works were featured in a number of exhibitions that took place in East Bay galleries.

In Central and Southern California, Milford Zornes, George Gibson, Robert E. Wood, Ken Potter, Robert Landry, Crandall Norton, Vernon Nye, Don O'Neill, Roger Armstrong, Wayne La Com, Bill Anderson and Hugh Duncan were among those who continued to develop this art form. While most of these artists received individual acclaim beyond the 1970s, it was during that decade that the organized group of California Style watercolor artists that had formed in the 1930 to 1960 era, finally disbanded.

JADE FON  *Surfers Near Pacifica*  1960s  22" x 30"  Claremont Fine Arts

KEN POTTER  *Trainyard, Rio Vista*  1960s  22" x 30"  Courtesy Ken Potter

BILL ANDERSON  *Golden Bear*  22" x 30"  Courtesy Anderson Art Gallery

STANTON MACDONALD-WRIGHT  *Santa Monica Canyon*  1918  14" x 19"  Goldfield Galleries Ltd.

Chapter Three

# Abstract & Non-Objective
## 1918-1970

The history of abstract and non-objective watercolor painting in California can be traced back to a small group of artists who were meeting at the Art Students League of Los Angeles in 1918. The group was being led by Stanton MacDonald-Wright. Among the students were Nick Brigante and Edouard Vysekal.

MacDonald-Wright previously lived in Europe and New York City. During the 1907 to 1917 era, he and Morgan Russell painted abstract and non-objective works they called Synchromist paintings, a term they derived from symphony and chromo (color). When the works were exhibited in Munich, Paris, and New York City, the response was positive enough to assure them a place in world art history. Shortly after his move to Santa Monica in 1918, MacDonald-Wright began instructing at the Art Students League and introduced modern art ideas to young students.

From early in his career, MacDonald-Wright was interested in watercolors. He purchased several of Cezanne's watercolor originals while living in France. His personal watercolors ranged widely from Synchromist abstractions to representational works done while traveling in Europe, Japan and other parts of the world.

Brigante and Vysekal were among his first students, and both began producing modernist watercolors about 1918. Los Angeles was a very conservative city at that time and for the most part, their works were either ignored or severely criticized.

Throughout the 1920s and early 1930s, abstract and non-objective watercolor paintings were included in group shows of Southern California modern art. Often the shows were presented by short lived art organizations like the Modern Art Workers, Progressive Painters of the Southland and the Group of Eight. Some of the modernist watercolor artists who were involved in these groups include Clarence Hinkle, Tom E. Lewis, Wilson Coles, Nick Brigante, Edouard Vysekal and Henri De Kruif.

In Northern California, especially San Francisco, there was a thriving modern art community, but only a few of the artists chose to paint with watercolors. Bernard Von Eichman and Selden Gile, both members of a modern art group known as the Society of Six, were among the few who were producing abstract watercolors. They were each given one man shows of their watercolors at the Oakland Art Gallery in 1928 and they usually included a few watercolors in each of the Society of Six exhibitions.

When the San Francisco Museum of Art opened in the mid-1930s, Grace Morley became the director. She brought world class shows to the museum which featured watercolors by Paul Cezanne, Vasily Kandinsky, George Grosz, Lyonel Feininger, Paul Klee and Arshile Gorky. In addition, she established an annual watercolor exhibition to feature watercolors by Bay Area artists.

One of the first watercolorists to receive attention from these annual exhibitions was Karl Baumann, a German immigrant who settled in San Francisco in 1920. He produced expressionist and non-objective works throughout the 1930s and was often singled out for special awards and attention in art reviews.

**NICK BRIGANTE** *Laguna Beach* 1917 7" x 9" Knowles Collection

**KARL BAUMANN** *Two Dimensional Still Life* 1939 22" x 30" Maxwell Galleries, Ltd.

**JULES ENGEL** *Brilliant Moves* 1946 12" x 16"  Courtesy Jules Engel

**JULES ENGEL** *Untitled* 1947 9" x 11"  Courtesy Jules Engel

**JULES ENGEL** *Pomp and Circumstance* 1940s 10" x 12"  Courtesy Jules Engel

In the late 1930s and early 1940s Abstract Surrealism was also being explored by artists living in the San Francisco area. Charles Howard, Clay Spohn and Gordon Onslow Ford were innovative artists, known for their surrealistic works that were often created using watercolors or gouache.

Across the bay in Oakland, James McCray, a graduate of the University of California, Berkeley, was experimenting with hard-edge, non-objective painting in the early 1940s. His colorful works were painted with opaque watercolors. These were well received paintings when shown in gallery and museum exhibitions.

After World War II, there was considerably more interest in exploring the idea of using watercolors to produce abstract and non-objective works of art. In Los Angeles, the Jepsen Art Institute was opened and some of the outstanding teachers were Rico LeBrun, Howard Warshaw, Francis de Erdely and William Brice. Warshaw was a student of Rico LeBrun and had developed a personal style based on Cubist ideas. His work titled *Wrecked Automobile* received national attention in 1949 and caused the art community to take notice of the artists from the Jepsen Art Institute and other watercolorists working with abstract and non-objective approaches to art.

Among those who began receiving acclaim were Ed Reep, Keith Crown, Leonard Edmondson, Paul Darrow, Clinton Adams, Jules Engel, Michael Frary, Robert McIntosh, Jan Stussy, James Strombotne and Lenard Kester. The emphasis during this period was on individualism. Most of the artists producing abstract watercolors were trying to develop highly personal styles and wanted to avoid being part of any "School" of art. In their search for new approaches to visual communication, some of them seriously studied world art history and developed their approach in a very calculated manner.

Ed Reep, a teacher at the Chouinard Art Institute and Emil Bisttram School of Art, began experimenting with the golden section and dynamic symmetry as a compositional tool for creating watercolor paintings. These composition formulas were developed by Euclid, the Greek mathematician of the third century B.C., and have since been used by artists as a way to bring structural authority to their art.

Another major source of modern art information

JAMES MCCRAY  *Attenuation*  1947  27" x 39"  Courtesy Virginia McCray

JAMES MCCRAY  *Painted and Jointed*  1945  16" x 20"  Courtesy Virginia McCray

RICHARD DIEBENKORN  *Untitled (Berkeley)*  1954  14" x 11"  Private Collection

was Erle Loran's book *Cezanne's Composition*. In this book, Loran reproduced pictures of Cezanne's paintings alongside photographs of the actual scene. He added diagrams explaining the process Cezanne used to compose each work. He did this in a way that showed the obvious influence on many outstanding artists including Pablo Picasso, George Braque and Lyonel Feininger. For many California watercolorists, this was both valuable and illuminating information.

The University of California, Berkeley, published *Cezanne's Composition* and their art department found notoriety for its commitment to teaching modern art ideas. Hans Hofmann, a well-known European modernist painter, taught on campus in 1930. Four of his loyal students, John Haley, Erle Loran, Worth Ryder and Margaret Peterson, were teachers at Berkeley and promoted Hofmann's modern art ideas for many years. Their lessons on the art of Giotto, Titian, El Greco and Picasso were considered essential studies. An understanding of Egyptian, Byzantine and Greek art was also viewed as very important information for artists who were choosing to pursue serious abstract painting.

Across the bay in San Francisco, there was another group of artists committed to producing abstract art using a much less structured approach. They were centered at the California School of Fine Arts. Their primary instructors were Clifford Still, David Park, Hassel Smith, Edward Corbett and Richard Diebenkorn. The works they produced received international recognition and the group became known as the San Francisco Abstract Expressionists.

Most of the artists from this group worked with oils on canvas. The thickness of the paint and the textures they achieved by building areas with overpainting were important elements in achieving the desired look. A few of these artists also achieved similar effects by using gouache and tempera paint.

Elmer Bischoff and Hassel Smith were teaching at the California School of Fine Arts in the 1940s, and exhibited watercolors in annual art exhibitions. John Grillo and George Stillman were students during that era and by the late 1940s were also exhibiting works which were painted with watercolors, gouache, tempera and poster paints.

In the early 1950s, Richard Diebenkorn did some abstract expressionist works using watercolor, gouache

JOHN HALEY *Yellow* 1952 16" x 22" Courtesy John Haley

LEAH R. HAMILTON *Untitled* 1948 15" x 22" Courtesy Steven Wolf

KARL KASTEN *Tango* 1952 16" x 20" Courtesy Karl Kasten

ED REEP  *Downtown L.A.*  1955  24" x 38"  McClelland Collection

KEITH CROWN  *Manhattan Beach*  1953  20" x 28"  Buck Collection

ROBERT MCINTOSH  *Building Materials*  1950  22" x 36"  Jim Waterbury Collection

and ink. He produced some of these works while living in Albuquerque, New Mexico, and others after he moved back to the Bay Area. Although the scale is smaller than most of his oil paintings, they stand out as important works from this exciting era in art exploration.

As California art exhibitions became increasingly receptive to modern art, some highly imaginative works were presented. Keith Crown developed a unique style that was more or less influenced by Expressionism and Abstract Surrealism. Crown used shapes, colors, symbols and abstract gestural passages to visually represent sounds, smells, wind and heat. These were combined with abstract interpretations of piers, boats, buildings and other structures near his beach-side home.

In Southern California, the most prestigious show for Modernist art was the annual exhibition at the Los Angeles County Museum. It was the *Artists of Los Angeles and Vicinity* show and included works by artists living within one hundred miles of Los Angeles. Each show featured up to 300 works of art including oil paintings, watercolors, sculpture, prints and drawings.

The California Water Color Society also hosted their annual show in Los Angeles and encouraged artists to submit abstract works for exhibition. By the early 1950s, there were increasing numbers of abstract watercolors in their shows. This led to many heated discussions, as some of the more conservative artists resisted the mixing of representational art with abstract and non-objective works. The Society held to their policy of welcoming all types of high quality art and gradually overcame any opposition.

Leonard Edmondson, Ynez Johnston and Jules Engel were consistently singled out for awards and mentioned in art reviews. Edmondson and Engel began exhibiting abstract works in the late 1940s and were among the first Modernists to have radical abstracts accepted for exhibition in California Water Color Society annuals. By 1951, Ynez Johnston, Hilda Levy, Sueo Serisawa, John Leeper and Gerd Koch were also exhibiting abstract or non-objective works.

As support for modern art increased, a large number of commercial art galleries opened in the Los Angeles area, especially along La Cienega Boulevard. This provided an outlet for many watercolor sales. The Felix Landau Gallery handled art by Keith Finch and

LEONARD EDMONDSON  *Arabesque*  1952  18" x 27"  Courtesy Leonard Edmondson

LEONARD EDMONDSON  *Meditation*  1952  19" x 28"  Courtesy Leonard Edmondson

NICK BRIGANTE  *Tidepool Grasses*  1963  35" x 22"  Knowles Collection

Clinton Adams. The Frank Perls Galleries represented James Strombotne, Rico Lebrun, Howard Warshaw and William Brice. John Altoon showed at the Ferus Gallery, Ed Reep and Keith Crown were with the Paul Rivas Gallery, Paul Darrow showed at the Camara Gallery and Jan Stussy exhibited at Esther Robles Gallery.

In Laguna Beach, an area known for art galleries and exhibitions, there was also an active group supporting progressive painting. Los Angeles artists Hans Burkhardt, Ynez Johnston, John Leeper and Edgar Ewing all showed in Laguna exhibitions. Local artists Roger Kuntz, John Severson and Earl Klein were showing abstract works in one-man exhibitions at commercial galleries. Although the winter season shows had rather low attendance, the *All California Exhibition of Art* drew record crowds to this beach community during the summer months and helped bring support to the commercial galleries.

For some of the pioneers of modern art in Southern California, this was a period when they finally received some long overdue credit for their lives' work. One of these artists was Nick Brigante. He, along with Rex Slinkard, Stanton MacDonald-Wright, Lorser Feitelson and Helen Lundeberg, quietly promoted Modernism as far back as the 1920s and 1930s. Of this group only Brigante chose watercolor as a primary painting medium.

As Brigante's art progressed, the paintings became radical abstractions and non-objective works. In the 1950s and 1960s, when his watercolors began to receive acclaim, he was producing some of the most innovative art of his career. Most of these watercolors started out as black and white paintings; some received coloration and others did not. He often produced individual works as part of a series or set. *Tide Pool Set, Cloud Lands of Abstractions, Rolling Waters, Burnt Mountain Series* and *Space Images,* were some of the titles.

Another established modernist painter who received attention in the 1950s was Alexander Nepote. He began producing modern works in the 1930s while attending the California College of Arts and Crafts in Oakland. Gradually his work became more abstract and by the 1950s, he was producing non-objective and abstract expressionist watercolors.

These works were often painted using a wet into wet technique. He would soak the paper overnight,

NICK BRIGANTE *Burning Rock* 1961 28" x 18" Knowles Collection

NICK BRIGANTE *Untitled* 1960s 24" x 12" Private Collection

JOHN KWOK  *Fugue*  1968  22" x 30"  Courtesy National Watercolor Society

ARTHUR KAYE  *Tableau Jaune*  1960s  20" x 29"  Courtesy Arthur Kaye

WAYNE LA COM  *Guardian Angel*  1960s  22" x 30"  Courtesy Wayne La Com

then while it was still saturated with moisture, he would apply sweeping strokes of transparent color. The success of his abstract expressionist works relied on his ability to control large areas of flowing color. These works were usually painted spontaneously in one session. The calligraphy was added when the paint was dry.

Both Nepote and Brigante exhibited their abstract expressionist works nationally in annual art shows. They, and other California abstract painters, were included in exhibitions at the Metropolitan Museum of Art in New York, Chicago Art Institute, Springfield Art Museum in Missouri, Virginia Museum of Fine Arts, Whitney Museum of American Art, Corcoran Gallery of Art and other prominent art institutions. These were juried shows featuring top artists from all over America.

On the West Coast, artists sent watercolors to the art divisions at the California State Fair in Sacramento and the Los Angeles County Fair in Pomona. The *California Art Exhibition* at the National Orange Show in San Bernardino also hosted a well-known art exhibition at the annual event. These shows, combined with the art show annuals at the San Francisco Museum of Art, Oakland Art Museum, Los Angeles County Museum of Art and the Pasadena Art Museum, made it possible for California watercolorists to have works on public display year round.

By the late 1950s, another art movement, known as Bay Area Figurative Painting, was receiving national recognition. David Park, Richard Diebenkorn, Elmer Bischoff, James Weeks, Nathan Oliveira, Theophilus Brown and Paul Wonner were some of the key artists whose works defined this movement. Paul Mills, curator at the Oakland Art Museum, assembled the first major show in 1957. Exhibitions in Los Angeles and New York City followed.

Clearly the most celebrated works from these artists were painted with oils on canvas, but most of the artists also produced watercolor and gouache paintings of similar figurative subjects. Diebenkorn and Oliveira produced many watercolor studies which were used for ideas when producing larger works. Park worked with gouache during the early part of his career, then during the final year of his life painted exclusively with opaque watercolors.

Paul Wonner, one of the youngest members in the group, probably produced the largest number of water-

ALEXANDER NEPOTE  *Traveling*  1955  22" x 30"  Courtesy National Watercolor Society

ALEXANDER NEPOTE  *Untitled*  1959  22" x 30"  Courtesy Hanne-Lore Nepote

PAUL WONNER  *Living Room at I's*  1964  12" x 18"  Courtesy Paul Wonner

JUNE FELTER  *Untitled*  1960s  16" x 24"  Buck Collection

color and gouache works. In the early 1960s, he had moved to Malibu and was teaching in Southern California. His works, shown at the Felix Landau Gallery on La Cienega Boulevard, influenced a number of young Los Angeles artists to pursue abstract figurative painting.

Throughout the 1950s and 1960s Los Angeles area artist James Strombotne also received acclaim for his abstract figurative works. Often the images in his paintings communicated his personal outrage with political corruption and social injustice. In 1956 Edward Kienholz arranged for a Strombotne show at the Coronet Louvre Gallery in Los Angeles. By 1958 he was showing at the Frank Perls Gallery and during the 1960s at the David Stuart Galleries.

Most of Strombotne's works on paper were painted with opaque watercolor and ink. By the late 1960s he was also incorporating photo collage. His oil paintings have similar imagery, but are much larger in scale.

As abstract figurative painting developed, a number of talented painters produced noteworthy works in the watercolor medium. Susan Hertel of Claremont, Roger Kuntz of Laguna and June Felter of San Francisco were among them.

By the early 1960s, abstract and non-objective watercolors dominated the California Water Color Society annual exhibitions. Each show had between one hundred and one hundred and thirty watercolors on display. These works were selected by a jury of five respected artists whose job it was to narrow the selection down from some eight hundred to a thousand entries.

Once the shows were organized, they traveled from Los Angeles to San Francisco, and then across America. Often two or three smaller shows were also assembled and sent out as the demand for exhibitions increased.

The Society prided itself in being open-minded. The directors encouraged diversity and allowed artists to submit works produced with watercolor, gouache, casein and collage-on-paper. In 1964, Howard Clapp, the Society president, wrote, "The jury is bound by no restrictions as to technique or style, but concerns itself solely with the qualities inherent in a work of art."

During this period, several of the established California Style representational watercolorists of the 1930s and 1940s began to exhibit abstract and non-objective works. They gradually moved in that direction

JAMES STROMBOTNE  *Untitled*  1960s  22" x 30"  Courtesy James Strombotne

JAMES STROMBOTNE  *Untitled*  1960s  22" x 30"  Courtesy James Strombotne

JAMES STROMBOTNE  *Untitled*  1960s  22" x 30"  Courtesy James Strombotne

PHIL DIKE  *Storm's Wake #5*  1962  22" x 30"  Weare Collection

REX BRANDT  *Our Blue Sky*  1967  22" x 30"  Courtesy Rex Brandt

ROBERT PERINE  *Untitled*  1964  22" x 30"  Courtesy Robert Perine

in the 1950s, and by the early 1960s were producing outstanding modern works. Rex Brandt, Phil Dike, Emil Kosa, Jr. and Robert Perine were among the most successful.

Brandt and Dike pursued styles inspired by Cubism and action painting. Kosa was a student of modern art pioneer Frank Kupka, and on occasion produced vital, non-objective paintings. Robert Perine, who entered the art scene as a California Scene watercolorist, received acclaim for his large non-objective watercolors featuring bold shapes, strong design and flowing washes.

In 1962 Sam Francis, a well established non-objective painter settled in Santa Monica, California. Prior to this, he studied in the San Francisco Bay area, then moved to Europe in the 1950s where he developed a reputation as a progressive modern artist. By the time Francis moved to Southern California he was frequently using watercolors and other water based mediums to produce art.

His early works in watercolor relied on the fluid nature of the liquid to create transparent pooling effects and flowing, organic forms. As his work progressed, he also developed techniques of dripping and flinging colors using gestural painting methods. Many of these works, especially those produced in the late 1960s and 1970s, received international acclaim and helped establish Francis as one of America's premier non-objective painters.

The period between 1918 and 1970 was a time of experimentation and discovery for California watercolor artists working with abstract and non-objective approaches to producing art. What they achieved laid a foundation for the generations of artists who have, since 1970, continued to develop individual approaches to modern art.

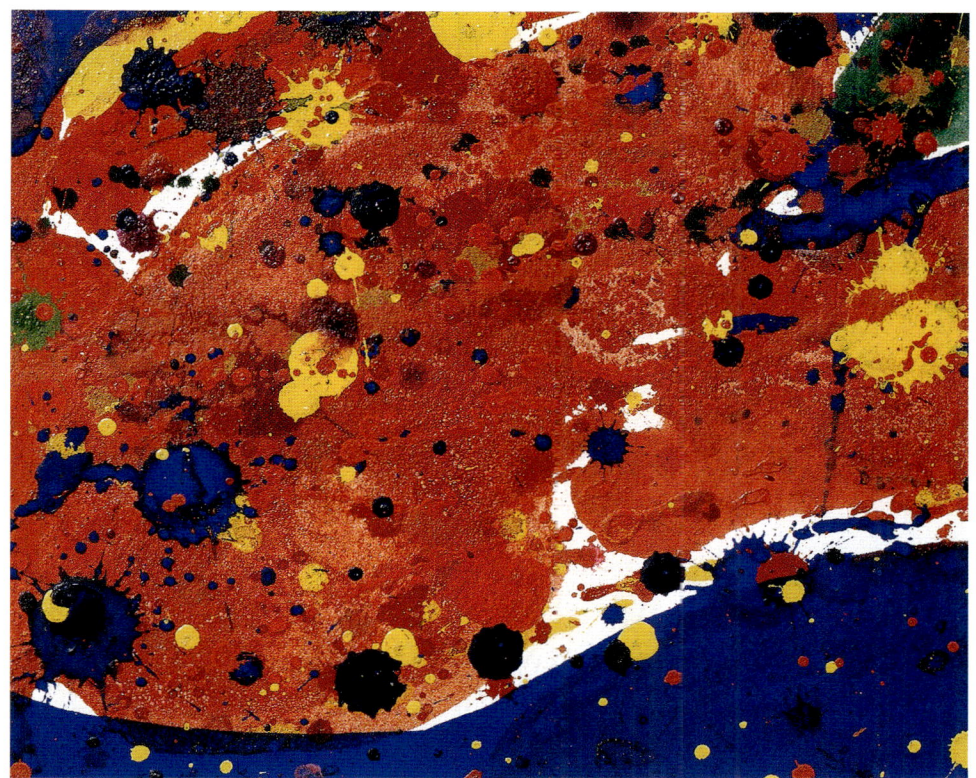

SAM FRANCIS  *Untitled*  1960s  9" x 12"  Martin Medak Collection

SAM FRANCIS  *Untitled*  1960s  9" x 12"  Martin Medak Collection

*Barse Miller doing a watercolor painting of a derailed train in Northern California, 1938.*   *Photographed by Rex Brandt*

## Chapter Four
# Artist Biographies

In this chapter are 555 biographies of artists who produced watercolors in California during the period between 1850 and 1970. Whenever possible the details of the artists lives and art careers were obtained through personal interviews with the artists themselves or with their relatives or friends. In other cases, the information was gathered from the references cited.

Many of the watercolors reproduced in this section are award-winning paintings and serve as exceptional examples of artworks produced by leading artists, active in California during the one hundred and twenty year period covered in this book. Below each painting is a caption crediting the artist, title of the work, date, size and source of the transparency used to make the reproduction.

**Rowena Meeks Abdy** (1887-1945) Born: Vienna, Austria; Studied: Mark Hopkins Institute of Art (San Francisco); Member: California Water Color Society, San Francisco Art Association, Carmel Art Association. Rowena Meeks Abdy spent her childhood in Europe and at age eleven, moved with her family to San Francisco where she received art instruction from Arthur Mathews and studied California history and geography. Throughout her career, she combined these interests by traveling extensively throughout the state painting depictions of unique landscapes and historically important subjects. She was an early member of the California Water Color Society and exhibited in annual museum shows in California. In addition, she illustrated several books and had a series of her watercolors reproduced as a fine art portfolio.
Biographical information:
*Who's Who in American Art*
*Women Artists of the American West.*

**Ben Abril** (1923-1995) Born: Los Angeles, CA; Studied: School of Allied Arts (Glendale), Art Center School (Los Angeles); Member: American Watercolor Society, California Water Color Society. Ben Abril grew up in California, produced art for the United States Navy during World War II, then studied art in Los Angeles after the war. Throughout his career as an artist, he worked with watercolors and exhibited them nationally. He is known for his paintings that depict historical California landmarks. Abril also taught painting and illustrated a number of books.
Biographical information:
Interview with Ben Abril, 1994.

**Frank Ackerman** (1933-1986) Born: Los Angeles, CA; Studied: Chouinard Art Institute (Los Angeles); Member: California Water Color Society. Frank Ackerman grew up in Glendale and studied art at Chouinard Art Institute while attending high school. He began painting with watercolors at Chouinard and by the early 1950s, was exhibiting with the California Water Color Society. After spending several years in the army, he studied further with Rex Brandt and Ed Reep.

After the mid-1950s, Ackerman worked regularly as an illustrator and graphic artist. Commissioned by the Navy to travel to New Zealand and the South Pole, he produced a series of paintings for the Naval History Art Collection. Ackerman served as president of the California Water Color Society in 1970 and he also taught watercolor painting.
Biographical information:
Interview with Frank Ackerman, 1984.

**Clinton Adams** (1918- ) Born: Glendale, CA; Studied: University of California (Los Angeles); Member: California Water Color Society. Clinton Adams received a Masters degree in 1942 and by 1946, was teaching art at the University of California (Los Angeles). He exhibited watercolors in the annual exhibitions of the California Water Color Society and the Los Angeles County Museum of Art. Although his watercolors produced in the 1940s and 1950s are expert works that received awards and notoriety, Adams is best known for his work in the field of lithography. In the early 1960s, he was the Associate Director of the Tamarind Lithography Workshop in Los Angeles. After 1970, he became the Director of the Tamarind Institute in Albuquerque, New Mexico. This institution was set up to train master printers and give artists the opportunity to explore this medium. Adams remains a key figure in this project. He is an acknowledged authority on the subject of lithography and authored the outstanding publication *American Lithographers, 1900-1960 - The Artists and Their Printers.*
Biographical information:
*Who's Who in American Art*
*American Lithographers, 1900-1960*
Tobey C. Moss Gallery, 1994.

**Karl Albert** (1911- ) Born: Halstead, KS; Studied: Art Center School (Los Angeles); Member: Laguna Beach Art Association. Karl Albert grew up in Southern California. After studying at the Art Center School, he took additional instruction from Edgar Payne and Sam Hyde Harris. Best known for his oil paintings of desert landscapes, Albert has also produced many watercolors. Most of these works were painted on location and depict California scene subjects.
Biographical information:
Interview with Karl Albert, 1985.

**James Alden** (1810-1877) Born: Portland, ME. James Alden served as an officer in the United States Navy during the mid-1800s. From 1857 to 1861, he produced watercolors for the Northwest Boundary Survey Report and became a San Francisco resident in 1873.
Biographical information:
*Artists of the American West.*

**James Madison Alden** (1834-1922) Born: Roxbury, MA. James Madison Alden sailed to San Francisco in 1853 to work as a topographer on the Pacific Coast Survey project. His uncle, James Alden was the commander of this survey crew. Between 1853 and about 1861 he documented his experiences by painting a number of important historical watercolors of California and the Pacific Northwest.
Biographical information:
*Artists in California, 1786-1940.*

**Anders Aldrin** (1889-1970) Born: Värmland, Sweden; Studied: Otis Art Institute (Los Angeles), Santa Barbara School of Fine Arts, California School of Fine Arts (San Francisco); Member: California Water Color Society. Anders Aldrin came to the United States from Sweden in 1911 and exhibited his watercolors with the California Water Color Society from 1930 to 1960. Many of his paintings depict city views, people and still life subjects done with expressive color and unique compositions. He is also well known for his color woodblock prints.
Biographical information:
*Anders Aldrin* (Catalog).

**Gladys Aller** (1915- ) Born: Springfield, MA; Studied: Art Students League (New York), Otis Art Institute (Los Angeles), Chouinard Art Institute (Los Angeles); Member: California Water Color Society. Gladys Aller received art instruction from George Grosz in the 1930s. She was a resident of Los Angeles and exhibited her watercolors locally.
Biographical information:
*Who's Who in American Art.*

**Ella Alluisi** (1912-1996) Born: Houston, TX; Studied: Smith College, University of California (Berkeley); Member: San Francisco Art Association. In the 1930s, Ella Alluisi studied art with pioneer modern artist Sonia Delaunay. By the 1940s, she was living on the West Coast and exhibiting watercolors in San Francisco area annual art exhibitions.
Biographical information:
Jan Holloway Gallery, San Francisco, 1992.

**John Altoon** (1925-1969) Studied: Otis Art Institute (Los Angeles), Art Center School (Los Angeles), Chouinard Art Institute (Los Angeles); Member: California Water Color Society. John Altoon grew up in Los Angeles and after graduating from high school, joined the United States Navy. He served as a radar technician during World War II and was stationed in the Pacific. When the war ended, he went to art school on the G.I. Bill. In the early 1950s, he lived in New York City, where he worked as a commercial illustrator for steady income, while developing connections for exhibiting his paintings. By 1956, he was living in Los Angeles and producing non-objective and radical abstractionist art works. His watercolors were exhibited in the California Water Color Society and Los Angeles County Museum of Art annual exhibitions. The Ferus Gallery in Los Angeles represented his works. Altoon is best known for his oil paintings and as an influential art instructor.
Biographical information:
*John Altoon* (Catalog)
California Water Color Society (Catalogs).

**Leon Amyx** (1908-1995) Born: Visalia, CA; Studied: Claremont College (California), University of California (Berkeley), California College of Arts and Crafts (Oakland); Member: California Water Color Society. Leon Amyx studied with Millard Sheets, Henry Lee McFee and Erle Loran. He taught art at Harnell College in Salinas from 1936 to 1972. During this period, he produced watercolors depicting local landscape subjects and was a prominent figure in the Central California art community.
Biographical information:
Interview with Leon Amyx, 1984.

**Bill Anderson** (1941-    ) Born: Mankato, MN; Studied: Mankato State University, California State University (Long Beach). Bill Anderson grew up in Minnesota, majored in art after high school, and began producing watercolors in the 1950s. By the early 1960s, he became a Southern California resident, exhibiting watercolors and prints and teaching art in Long Beach and Anaheim. In more recent years, he has operated the Anderson Art Gallery in Sunset Beach.
Biographical information:
Interview with Bill Anderson, 1995.

**Sidney Armer** (1871-1962) Born: San Francisco, CA; Studied: Mark Hopkins Institute of Art (San Francisco). Sidney Armer studied with Arthur Mathews in San Francisco and then began working as an artist at the Dickman-Jones Lithograph Company. He specialized in producing watercolor illustrations of California plants and flowers. These works were translated into color lithographs and were sold as fine art prints and advertisement illustrations. In the 1920s, he did calendar illustrations for Schmidt Litho Company and label designs for Traung Label and Lithograph Company.
Biographical information:
Interview with Hubert Buel, 1983.

**Roger Armstrong** (1917-    ) Born: Los Angeles, CA; Studied: Pasadena City College, Chouinard Art Institute (Los Angeles); Member: California Water Color Society. Roger Armstrong studied art with Phil Dike, Dan Lutz and Rex Brandt in the 1940s, and during this time, produced a number of watercolors depicting construction workers on Bunker Hill and other locations around Los Angeles. In the 1950s, he became a well-known cartoonist and has since received acclaim for his work in the field of animation. Armstrong is still producing transparent watercolor paintings, exhibits in Laguna Beach and is a well-known watercolor teacher.
Biographical information:
Interview with Roger Armstrong
and Dorothy Hurford, 1995.

**Samuel Armstrong** (1893-1977) Born: Denver, Colorado; Studied: School of Industrial Art (Philadelphia), Mechanics Art Institute (New York). Samuel Armstrong studied art with Jean Leon Ferris and Albert Herter. By 1918, he was living in Tacoma, Washington, and in 1923, he opened the Armstrong School of Art in Tacoma. In the 1930s, he lived in Santa Barbara, then moved closer to Los Angeles. He produced watercolor illustrations for many publications including *Sunset Magazine* and worked at the Walt Disney Studios producing watercolor backgrounds for animated films. Some of the key films he worked on were; *Snow White and the Seven Dwarfs*, *Fantasia*, *Dumbo* and *Bambi*.
Biographical information:
*The Disney Films*
*Artists in California, 1786-1940*.

**Victor Arnautoff** (1896-1979) Born: Mariupol, Ukraine, Russia; Studied: Russian Junior College, Cavalry Academy, California School of Fine Arts (San Francisco); Member: Artist Guild of San Francisco. Victor Arnautoff settled in the San Francisco area in 1931. From the 1930s until the 1950s, he exhibited watercolors in annual Bay Area art exhibitions. He was an art teacher at the California School of Fine Arts between 1933 and 1938, and then taught at Stanford University from 1937 until the early 1960s.
Biographical information:
*Who's Who on the Pacific Coast*.

**Irma Attridge** (1894-1978) Born: Chicago, IL; Studied: Chouinard Art Institute (Los Angeles); Member: California Water Color Society. Irma Attridge began exhibiting watercolors in the Southern California area in 1943. She was a resident of Beverly Hills and in 1966, served as president of the California Water Color Society.
Biographical information:
*Who's Who in American Art*.

**John Ayres** (1914-    ) Born: Modesto, CA; Studied: University of California (Berkeley); Member: San Francisco Art Association. John Ayres began producing watercolors in the 1930s while studying art with John Haley and Erle Loran.

LEON AMYX  *Range Cattle*  1940  22" x 27"  Buck Collection

LOREN BARTON  *Untitled*  1930s  22" x 30"  Courtesy Pomona College

STANDISH BACKUS, JR. *Selz Brothers' Circus* 1938 15" x 22" Knowles Collection

STANDISH BACKUS, JR. *San Bernardino Trainyard* 1938 15" x 22" Knowles Collection

His early works were in the classic Berkeley School style. In the mid-1950s, he produced a number of non-objective works, then went back to abstract and representational styles. Since World War II, he has taught art history and painting classes at Chico State College.
Biographical information:
Interview with John Ayres and Raymond Wilson, 1994.

**Robert Otto Bach** (1917- ) Born: San Francisco, CA; Studied: California School of Fine Arts (San Francisco); Member: San Francisco Art Association. Robert Bach worked in San Francisco as a commercial artist in the late 1930s. After serving in World War II and working in Hawaii, he returned to the Bay Area and stayed until 1957, when he moved to Philadelphia. He exhibited watercolors while in California and was a member of the Thirteen Watercolorists.
Biographical information:
*Artists in California, 1786-1940.*

**Standish Backus, Jr.** (1910-1989) Born: Detroit, MI; Studied: Princeton University, University of Munich (Germany); Member: American Watercolor Society, California Water Color Society. Standish Backus, Jr. grew up in Michigan and first started painting with watercolors while studying architecture at Princeton University. He continued his art education in Europe and then settled in Santa Barbara. For a brief period in the mid-1930s, he took further instruction in watercolor painting from Eliot O'Hara and then opened a studio and painted full time.

Backus served as an official war artist during World War II and produced watercolors depicting naval battles. He also taught art, produced murals and served as the official naval artist for Admiral Byrd's 1955 Antarctic expedition.
Biographical information:
Interview with Standish Backus, Jr., 1983.

**William S. Bagdatopolous** (1888-1965) Born: Zante, Greece; Studied: Rotterdam Art Academy (Holland), Athens Academy (Greece); Member: California Water Color Society. William S. Bagdatopolous grew up in Holland, studied in Europe and traveled extensively before moving to California in 1932. He settled in Santa Barbara and for several years and exhibited his works with the California Water Color Society. In addition, a collection of his watercolors was exhibited at the National Gallery of Art in Washington, D.C. in 1930.
Biographical information:
*Southern California Art.*

**Ralph Baker** (1908-1976) Born: Deckard, TN; Studied: Mark Hopkins Institute of Art (San Francisco), California College of Arts and Crafts (Oakland); Member: Society of Western Artists. Ralph Baker came to California as a young man and after studying art in the Bay Area, became a commercial illustrator. His watercolor illustrations were reproduced as magazine illustrations and pictorial label designs. From the 1930s until the 1970s, he also painted fine art watercolors depicting landscape, cityscape and mining camp scenes. Baker taught art in the Sonora area.
Biographical information:
Interview with Ralph Baker, 1975.
*California Orange Box Labels: An Illustrated History.*

**Helen Balfour** (1847-1925) Born: London, England; Studied: Chicago Art Institute; Member: California Water Color Society, Laguna Beach Art Association. Helen Balfour immigrated from England to America with her family in the early 1850s. She studied painting with her mother, who was an accomplished artist, and continued her studies at the Chicago Art Institute. In 1910, she moved to the Los Angeles area and settled there. She was Marion Wachtel's aunt, so occasionally they went on painting excursions. Balfour exhibited watercolors in the annual shows at the Chicago Art Institute, in early California Water Color Society annuals and had several one-woman shows in Los Angeles area art galleries.
Biographical information:
*Women Artists of the American West*
California Water Color Society (Catalogs).

**Olive Barker** (1885-1961) Born: Chicago, IL; Studied: New York School of Fine and Applied Art; Member: California Water Color Society. After moving to California in the early 1930s, Olive Barker studied with F. Tolles Chamberlin, Millard Sheets and Paul Sample. She began exhibiting her work at this time. Many of her paintings depict street scenes in the Los Angeles area.
Biographical information:
*Who's Who in American Art.*

**Dana Bartlett** (1882-1957) Born: Ionia, MI; Studied: Art Students League (New York); Member: California Water Color Society. Dana Bartlett studied with William Merritt Chase in New York, and worked as a commercial artist for the Foster and Kleiser Company in Oregon before moving to Los Angeles in 1915. He was one of the original fourteen artists to exhibit in the first California Water Color Society show in 1921 and was the Society's first president. Many of his watercolors were decorative in design, sometimes incorporating pastels to give unusual effects. He taught at the Chouinard Art Institute and owned an art gallery that featured watercolors, sketches, etchings and small paintings.
Biographical information:
*Plein Air Painters of California.*
California Water Color Society (Catalogs).

**Loren Barton** (1893-1975) Born: Oxford, MA; Studied: University of Southern California; Member: New York Water Color Club, American Watercolor Society, California Water Color Society. Loren Barton grew up in Southern California and studied art with William L. Judson in Los Angeles. She began exhibiting with the California Water Color Society in 1924 and continued to do so until the mid-1950s.

While living in Europe in the 1930s, she painted landscape and cityscape scenes of Spain, Italy and England. After returning home in the late 1930s, she did a number of American Scene paintings depicting working-class people in various industrial environments.

For many years she taught watercolor painting at the Chouinard Art Institute and helped promising students begin exhibiting their artworks on a professional level. She also produced book illustrations, textile designs and prints.
Biographical information:
California Water Color Society (Catalogs).

**Jack Rivera Bates** (1907-1990) Born: San Luis Potosi, Mexico; Studied: Chicago Art Institute, Art Students League (New York), Columbia University (New York). Jack Rivera Bates was born in Mexico during a period when his American parents were living there. He studied art in San Miguel de Allende and traveled to the United States, where he received further education. He was an active artist, inventor and design engineer. During World War II, he was a Captain, sailing for the Military Sea Transport Service. He exhibited watercolors in art gallery showings in Mexico City, Hawaii, California, Texas and New York.
Biographical information:
Anderson Art Gallery.

**Karl Baumann** (1911-1984) Born: Leipzig, Germany; Member: San Francisco Art Association. Karl Baumann grew up in Germany and immigrated to California in 1929. After settling in the San Francisco area, he worked for about ten years as a commercial artist at a large lithography company. In the late 1930s, he began to pursue a full time career in fine art.

Throughout his career, he focused on painting bold, colorful, expressionistic watercolors of still life and cityscape subjects. He also produced oil paintings of similar subjects, designed large murals, worked as a printmaker and taught for several years at the California College of Arts and Crafts in Oakland.
Biographical information:
Interview with Mrs. Karl Baumann, 1984.

**John Jay Baumgartner** (1865-1946) Born: Milwaukee, WI; Member: Bohemian Club. John Jay Baumgartner, a self-taught artist, was active as a watercolorist in San Francisco from 1894 to 1946. He primarily produced works depicting landscape subjects.
Biographical information:
*Artists in California, 1786-1940.*

**Arthur Beaumont** (1890-1978) Born: Norwich, England; Studied: Mark Hopkins Institute of Art (San Francisco), Chouinard Art Institute (Los Angeles), Los Angeles School of Art, Slade School of Art (London), Académie Julian (Paris); Member: New York Water Color Club, American Watercolor Society, California Water Color Society. Arthur Beaumont grew up in England then immigrated to America via Canada when he was nineteen years old. He studied art with Stanton MacDonald-Wright in Los Angeles, William Russell Flint and Frank Brangwyn in London and Jean-Paul Laurens in Paris. In the late 1920s, he taught at the Chouinard Art Institute and operated a freelance commercial art business. In the 1930s, he became a Lieutenant in the United States Naval Reserve and began producing the first of many watercolors depicting battle ships and other naval subjects.

During World War II, he was a war artist, documenting naval battles. A series of these works were published in *National Geographic* magazine. After the war he continued producing watercolors of naval activities in China, Japan, Guam, Vietnam and the Antarctic. Although he painted depictions of landscape and figurative subjects and worked as a commissioned portrait artist, Beaumont is best known for his watercolors of ships and harbor scenes.

Throughout his career, he exhibited in California on a regular basis. His works were very popular, especially in the 1940s and 1950s, with articles about his works appearing in many newspapers and magazines. In 1989, a book titled *Arthur Beaumont, Naval Artist*, which documented his life and art, was published in conjunction with a retrospective exhibition at the Laguna Art Museum.
Biographical information:
Interview with Dorothy Beaumont, 1982
*Arthur Beaumont, Naval Artist.*

**Robert Bechtle** (1932- ) Born: San Francisco, CA; Studied: California College of Arts and Crafts (Oakland), University of California (Berkeley). Robert Bechtle grew up in the East Bay and studied art in Oakland and Berkeley during the late 1950s. His works from this period were mostly expressionistic in style with figurative subjects. In the early 1960s, he lost interest in painting abstractions and began working in a representational style, which led to the photo realist paintings he became known for. Bechtle has been a leading figure in the photo realist movement and works with both oils on canvas and watercolor on paper. His works are in numerous museum collections including the Whitney Museum of Art, Museum of Modern Art, Guggenheim Museum and San Francisco Museum of Art. He has taught art at the California College of Arts and Crafts and since 1968, has taught at San Francisco State University. The O.K. Harris Gallery in New York City has handled sales of his works since the early 1970s.
Biographical information:
Interview with Robert Bechtle, 1998.

**Rick Beck-Meyer** (1930- ) Born: Van Nuys, CA; Studied: Glendale College (California), California College of Arts and Crafts (Oakland), San Jose State College (California); Member: California Water Color Society, Carmel Art Association. Rick Beck-Meyer grew up in Burbank and became interested in watercolor painting in the late 1940s. While studying art in Oakland on a scholarship, he became interested in theater, film and teaching. Since the 1950s, he has worked in all of these fields in both Northern California and Hollywood. All of his watercolors are signed "Rick".
Biographical information:
Hauk Fine Arts, Pacific Grove, 1996
Interview with Rick Beck-Meyer, 1996.

**Lonie Bee** (1902-1995) Born: Santa Rosa, CA; Studied: University of California (Berkeley), California School of Fine Arts (San Francisco), California College of Arts and Crafts (Oakland); Member: Society of Illustrators. Lonie Bee is best known for his many commercial illustrations which were featured on prominent magazine covers beginning in the 1930s. He has also painted and exhibited watercolors and worked as a portrait painter.
Biographical information:
*The Illustrator in America, 1880-1980.*

**Carl Beetz** (1911-1974) Born: San Francisco, CA; Studied: Art Students League (New York), California School of Fine Arts (San Francisco), Chouinard Art Institute (Los Angeles); Member: California Water Color Society. Carl Beetz studied with George Bridgman in New York City, Spencer Macky in

ARTHUR BEAUMONT  *The Fish Cannery*  1939  18" x 24"  Courtesy John Moran Auctions

ARTHUR BEAUMONT  *Bikini*  1946  18" x 24"  Ken Blackburn Collection

MARY BLAIR  *Laundry Day*  1935  17" x 21"  Michael Johnson Collection

RITCHIE A. BENSEN  *Lake Union Boat Works*  1960s  18" x 24"  Michael Johnson Collection

San Francisco and Pruett Carter in Los Angeles. Many of his works depict poor people in depressing, run-down environments. They were done in a Regionalist style with the human figure as the focal point. He taught at the Chouinard Art Institute, the California College of Arts and Crafts, the Academy of Advertising Arts and San Francisco City College. He lived in Los Angeles during the 1940s and 1950s and then settled in San Francisco.
Biographical information:
Interview with Brigitta Beetz, 1983.

**Alvin J. Beller** (1902-1968) Born: Michigan; Studied: Detroit Commercial Art School, Art Students League (New York); Member: California Water Color Society. Alvin Beller moved to California in 1928 and received painting instruction from Dong Kingman, Arthur Beaumont and Noel Quinn. He was a resident of Carmel in the 1930s and moved to Downey after the late 1940s.
Biographical information:
*Artists in California, 1786-1940*.

**Ritchie A. Bensen** (1941-1996) Born: Los Angeles, CA; Studied: Art Center School (Los Angeles); Member: American Watercolor Society, California Water Color Society. Ritchie A. Bensen grew up in the Los Angeles area during the World War II era. By the late 1950s, he was studying watercolor painting and by the 1960s was exhibiting on a national level. He spent a great deal of time painting along the California coast and was most interested in producing works which pictured boats and harbor scenes. His watercolors were sold through the Challis Gallery in Laguna Beach and through art association exhibition sales. Although he continued to paint occasionally in Southern California, most of Bensen's later works were done in Mendocino, California, or farther north in Washington state where he spent a lot of time painting on the beaches and in the harbors.
Biographical information:
Interview with R.A. Bensen, 1994
Esther Wells Gallery, Laguna Beach, 1993.

**Franz Bergman** (1898-1970) Born: Dimling, Austria; Studied: National Academy of Fine Arts (Vienna); Member: San Francisco Art Association. By the late 1930s, Franz Bergman was a resident of Mill Valley, and was exhibiting his watercolor paintings in annual museum shows in the San Francisco area. He worked as an art instructor at the California School of Fine Arts and also as a mural artist, author and illustrator of children's books.
Biographical information:
*Who's Who in American Art*.

**Jane Berlandina** (1898-1970) Born: Nice, France; Studied: Ecole National des Arts Decoratifs (Paris). Jane Berlandina studied art in France with Raoul Dufy. She moved to San Francisco in the 1930s and began showing her works in local exhibitions, including the Fourteen Bay Area Watercolorists show at the San Francisco Museum of Art in 1939. She was a jury member in many museum shows, painted murals and was a costume designer for the San Francisco Opera.
Biographical information:
*Who's Who in American Art*.

**William Beynon** (1917-  ) Born: Springfield, OH; Studied: University of Southern California; Member: California Water Color Society. William Beynon worked in the Los Angeles area as a commercial artist and exhibited his watercolors on the West Coast and in Hawaii during the 1940s and 1950s.
Biographical information:
*Who's Who in American Art*.

**Jules Billington** (1900-1972) Born: Meadville, MO; Studied: University of Missouri, Chicago Art Institute, Art Students League (New York); Member: California Water Color Society. Jules Billington taught art at the Grand Central School of Art in New York during the late 1920s and early 1930s. He moved to Los Angeles in the mid-1930s where he taught art privately and exhibited with the California Water Color Society.
Biographical information:
*Who's Who in American Art*.

**Elmer Bischoff** (1916-1991) Born: Berkeley, CA; Studied: University of California (Berkeley); Member: San Francisco Art Association. Elmer Bischoff grew up in Northern California. He graduated from college in the late 1930s and by the early 1940s, was exhibiting in annual watercolor shows at the San Francisco Museum of Art. After World War II, he continued exhibiting watercolors for a few more years then devoted the rest of his art career to painting oils and acrylics on canvas. He was an active participant in the San Francisco Abstract Expressionist group, and then became a major force in the Bay Area Figurative group in the 1950s. Bischoff was an influential art instructor in the San Francisco area. His works are in numerous, major museums including the Metropolitan Museum of Art, the Whitney Museum of American Art and the Museum of Modern Art.
Biographical information:
*Who's Who in American Art*.

**Lee Blair** (1911-1993) Born: Los Angeles, CA; Studied: Chouinard Art Institute (Los Angeles); Member: New York Water Color Club, American Watercolor Society, California Water Color Society. Lee Blair was born and raised in Southern California. He attended art school in Los Angeles and studied with Pruett Carter, Millard Sheets, Lawrence Murphy and briefly with Mexican artist David Alfaro Siqueiros. While attending art school he won several major awards for his watercolor paintings, including a gold medal in the art division of the 1932 Los Angeles Olympics. He became president of the California Water Color Society in 1935, and it was largely through his efforts that the Society shows began traveling nationally and internationally.

Throughout his life, Blair produced California Style watercolors. In the 1930s, he was one of the key artists who helped develop this approach to watercolor painting and was a prominent award winner in many art exhibitions. He had a unique sense of wit and humor which often came through in his art works and usually determined the subjects he chose to paint.

Blair is also known for his innovative work in animated films. He began working at the famed U.B. Iwerk Studio, producing art for *Flip the Frog* cartoons in the early 1930s. He then went on to the Harman-Ising Studios where he worked on *Bosco* and other innovative cartoon shorts. In 1938, he switched to the Walt Disney Studios, where, over the next few years, he worked on *Pinocchio*, *Fantasia* and *Saludos Amigos*.

During World War II, Blair served in the United States Navy and for a time produced animated training films for the government. While in the navy, he continued to paint watercolors of wartime activity. After the war, he and his wife Mary, who was also an artist, moved to New York where they started Film Graphics, Inc. and T.V. Graphics, Inc. Both companies produced animated films; some for training and education, others for television commercials. Their clients included General Motors, American Iron and Steel, the United States Navy, Army Signal Corps, Walt Disney Educational Films, Lockheed Missiles and Space Co. and many others. The latter years of his career were spent near Santa Cruz, where he sailed, painted watercolors and worked on animated films.
Biographical information:
Interview with Lee Blair, 1983.

**Mary Robinson Blair** (1911-1979) Born: McAllister, Oklahoma; Studied: San Jose State College (California), Chouinard Art Institute (Los Angeles); Member: California Water Color Society. Mary Blair came to California when she was seven years old. She attended college in San Jose and then art school in Los Angeles, where she took instruction from Pruett Carter.

Throughout the 1930s, she painted and exhibited watercolors depicting Regional subjects and worked full time as a color stylist and designer for the Walt Disney Studios. She also produced tile murals for Disneyland and Disney World and designed several of their rides.

After World War II, she and her husband, Lee Blair, settled in New York where she developed a highly successful commercial art business producing magazine covers, children's book illustrations and theatrical stage settings.
Biographical information:
Interview with Lee Blair, 1983.

**Preston Blair** (1908-1995) Born: Los Angeles, CA; Studied: Los Angeles Art Institute, Chouinard Art Institute (Los Angeles); Member: American Watercolor Society, California Water Color Society. Preston Blair grew up in Southern California and studied art with Roscoe Shrader and Pruett Carter during the early 1930s. In the following years, he began a long career in the animation art business. His first job was at Universal drawing *Oswald the Rabbit*, then at the Charles Mintz Studio working on *Krazy Cat* cartoons. By the mid-1930s, he was working for the Walt Disney Studios producing art for *Pinocchio* and *Fantasia*, and then in the 1940s, worked on Tex Avery's masterworks of animation art at M.G.M. Studios. He wrote two books for Walter Foster Art Books respectively titled *How to Animate Film Cartoons* and *Animation*. He also produced animated television commercials in the 1950s and 1960s, then in the 1970s and 1980s created and designed interactive video games. Throughout his career Blair painted and exhibited fine art watercolors in the annual American Watercolor Society shows.
Biographical information:
Interview with Preston Blair, 1985.

**David Blower** (1901-1976) Born Fontanet, IN; Studied: Wicker School of Fine Arts (Detroit), Académie de la Grande Chaumiere (Paris), Académie Colarossi (Paris). David Blower began exhibiting his watercolors on a professional level about 1933. His California paintings depict farm scenes, cityscapes of Los Angeles and beach scenes painted along the Pacific Coast. He worked with transparent watercolors in a loose, bold style. He also worked as a commercial illustrator from 1930 to 1960.
Biographical information:
Michael Kizhner Fine Art, Los Angeles, 1992.

**Lester Bonar** (1896-1973) Born: Phoenix, AZ; Studied: University of California (Los Angeles); Member: Laguna Beach Art Association. Lester Bonar was raised in Arizona and moved to California in the 1920s. In the early 1930s, he took private painting instruction from Sam Hyde Harris and began painting with transparent watercolors. He exhibited these works locally through the 1960s.
Biographical information:
Interview with Claire Bonar, 1984.

**Sergei Bongart, A.N.A.** (1918-1985) Born: Kiev, Russia; Studied: Kiev Art Academy; Member: National Academy of Design (Associate), American Watercolor Society. Sergei Bongart spent his childhood in a small village in the Ukraine. He studied art in Kiev with Michael Yarovoy and Peter Kotov. Both were well-known Russian artists. After leaving Russia, he lived in various places in Europe and in the 1940s, moved to the United States, settling in Santa Monica.

His style of painting with both watercolors and oils received immediate recognition and his works were regularly exhibited in galleries and museums in America and Europe. He wrote art books, articles for art publications and poetry. In addition, he taught art in California and Idaho.
Biographical information:
Interview with Sergei Bongart, 1984.

**Cora Boone** (1871-1953) Born: St. Louis, MO; Studied: Mark Hopkins Institute of Art (San Francisco), Central Arts and Crafts School (London); Member: San Francisco Society of Women Artists. Cora Boone's family came to California in 1876 and settled in San Francisco. After studying locally, she traveled to France and England for additional art education. By 1915, she returned and settled in Northern California. She painted, exhibited watercolors and was an art instructor for many years.
Biographical information:
*Artists in California, 1786-1940*.

**Edward Borein** (1873-1945) Born: San Leandro, CA; Member: Santa Barbara Art Club. Edward Borein grew up in Northern California and taught himself to draw and paint while working as a cowboy. Most of the watercolors he produced throughout his career depict western subjects; usually cowboys and ranch animals. He worked as a commercial illustrator, print maker and painted fine art oil paintings. Borein resided in Santa Barbara from the early 1920s until the mid-1940s.
Biographical information:
*Southern California Art*.

LEE BLAIR  *Pacific Coast Narrow Gauge*  1938  16" x 21"  McClelland Collection

LEE BLAIR  *Untitled*  1930s  16" x 20"  Buck Collection

REX BRANDT  *Lido Bridge*  1970s  20" x 30"  Stary-Sheets Fine Arts

REX BRANDT  *Lakeside Camp*  1938  11" x 15"  Hilbert Collection

**Carl Oscar Borg, A.N.A.** (1879-1947) Born: Grinstad, Sweden; Studied: Stockholm and Paris, National Academy of Design (New York); Member: California Water Color Society, National Academy of Design (Associate), San Francisco Art Association. Carl Oscar Borg worked his way from Europe to California as a seaman in 1903. He found work as an interior decorator and scenic painter for the theater while he established himself as a fine art painter. Beginning in the 1920s, he concentrated on Indian, Western and historical subjects that established his reputation. He painted with both watercolors and oils and also produced etchings. His works were in the first California Water Color Society show in 1921, and he continued to be in the annual exhibitions until the mid-1930s.
Biographical information:
*Southern California Art.*

**Dorr Bothwell** (1902-2000) Born: San Francisco, CA; Studied: California School of Fine Arts (San Francisco), Rudolph Schaeffer School of Design (San Francisco); Member: San Francisco Art Association, Society of Women Artists. Dorr Bothwell actively exhibited her watercolors in Bay Area museum shows during the 1940s. She was an art instructor at both the Parsons School of Design in New York and at the California School of Fine Arts and received recognition for her fine art prints.
Biographical information:
*Who's Who in American Art.*

**Cornelis Botke** (1887-1954) Born: Leevwarden, Holland; Studied: School of Applied Art (Holland), Member: California Water Color Society, Carmel Art Association. Cornelis Botke immigrated to the United States when he was nineteen and lived in the Midwest for twelve years. He and his wife, Jessie Arms Botke, moved to California and lived in Carmel for several years before settling in near Santa Paula in 1927. His works were primarily landscapes of the rural areas near his home, painted in a representational style. He was an accomplished oil painter and received many awards for etchings and block prints.
Biographical information:
*Southern California Art.*

**Jessie Arms Botke** (1883-1971) Born: Chicago, IL; Studied: Chicago Art Institute; Member: American Watercolor Society, California Water Color Society, Carmel Art Association. Jessie Arms Botke grew up and was educated in the Midwest. During the 1920s, she moved to the West Coast and settled near Santa Paula.

Although Botke painted and exhibited many watercolors and worked prolifically as a printmaker, she received national recognition for the production of murals and decorative oil paintings of exotic birds. Many of these paintings were reproduced by the New York Graphic Society and distributed world wide.
Biographical information:
*Southern California Artists (1890-1940).*

**Howard Bradford** (1919- ) Born: Toronto, Ontario, Canada; Studied: Chouinard Art Institute (Los Angeles), Jepson Art Institute (Los Angeles); Member: Carmel Art Association. Howard Bradford studied with Rico Lebrun in the late 1940s. By the 1950s, he was exhibiting large abstract watercolors in Southern California art shows. In the 1970s, he was listed as a resident of Monterey and director of the Serigraphs Ltd. Gallery.
Biographical information:
*Who's Who in American Art.*

**Alexandra Bradshaw** (active in 1950s) Born: Nova Scotia, Canada; Studied: Stanford University, University of California (Los Angeles), Columbia University; Member: California Water Color Society. Alexandra Bradshaw studied art with Hans Hofmann, Rex Slinkard and Andre L'Hote in the late 1930s and early 1940s. She was an art instructor at Fresno State College and had a second residence in South Laguna.
Biographical information:
*Who's Who in American Art.*

**Rex Brandt, N.A.** (1914-2000) Born: San Diego, CA; Studied: Chouinard Art Institute (Los Angeles), University of California (Berkeley); Member: National Academy of Design, American Watercolor Society, California Water Color Society, Philadelphia Water Color Club. Rex Brandt was a native Californian artist. He was raised in Southern California and in 1928, while still attending junior high school, began studying art at the Chouinard Art Institute. After a few years at Riverside Junior College, he continued his art education at the University of California (Berkeley), studying with John Haley.

By the time he returned to Southern California, the core group of California watercolor artists was already forming. Although Brandt was still quite young, the more established artists immediately recognized his artistic talent and readily accepted him into the group. Within a few years he was winning awards from art shows throughout Western America.

For a brief period, he was involved with the P.W.P.A. Art Project and in 1939 was selected as one of the premier California watercolorists to exhibit in the New York World's Fair art exhibition, *American Art Today*. In the 1940s, 1950s and 1960s he refined his skills and developed the style of painting which would bring him international recognition.

Teaching art was also an important aspect of Brandt's career. In the early 1940s, he promoted watercolor workshops in San Diego. After World War II, he and Phil Dike formed the Brandt-Dike Summer School of Painting in Corona del Mar. This became one of the most successful watercolor schools in California during the 1950s era. From 1947 to 1952, he taught watercolor painting and composition classes at the Chouinard Art Institute. Through these classes and his eleven instructional books on watercolor painting, Brandt educated and inspired a large number of professional watercolor artists.

In addition, he has produced murals, made six educational films and painted a number of architectural renderings. His watercolors have been printed on a variety of magazine covers and his story illustrations have appeared in *Fortune*, *Life* and *Westways* magazines. He was president of the California Water Color Society in 1948 and is considered one of the most important and influential California watercolor artists.
Biographical information:
Interview with Rex Brandt, 1983.

**Arnold Franz Brasz** (1888-1966) Born: Polk County, WI; Studied: Minneapolis School of Fine Arts; Member: California Water Color Society. Arnold Franz Brasz studied art in Minneapolis, and then with Robert Henri in New York. He became a member of the California Water Color Society in 1926 and served as its president in 1933. He lived in Glendale and produced etchings and commercial illustrations in addition to his watercolors.
Biographical information:
*Who's Who in American Art.*

**William Brice** (1921- ) Born: New York City, NY; Studied: Art Students League (New York), Chouinard Art Institute (Los Angeles); Member: Artists Equity Association. William Brice's works began receiving awards in the late 1940s and have since been added to the permanent collections of the Metropolitan Museum of Art, Whitney Museum of American Art and other prominent American museums. He has produced and exhibited watercolors since the 1940s and has taught art at the University of California (Los Angeles).
Biographical information:
*Who's Who in American Art.*

**Nicholas Brigante** (1895-1989) Born: Padua, Italy; Studied: Art Students League (Los Angeles); Member: California Water Color Society. When Nicholas Brigante was two years old, his family emigrated from Italy to the United States and settled in Los Angeles. About 1914, he began studying with Rex Slinkard. Together they reviewed world art from ancient cultures right up to modern art. In addition, they studied poetry, literature and the philosophies of artists and their contemporaries. These studies helped Brigante develop his very personal approach to art and living.

After serving in the Army during World War I, he studied painting with Stanton MacDonald-Wright in Los Angeles, and then spent a year in New York City. In the 1920s and early 1930s, he worked as a sign painter in Los Angeles. He left that profession in 1936 to work full time as a fine art painter. During the late 1930s, he produced a number of outstanding watercolor paintings that visually represent historical events. His masterwork, *Nature and Struggling, Imperious Man*, is painted on nine large panels and measures nearly twenty-one feet long, and was produced during this time. Gradually his works became increasingly abstract. By the early 1960s, he was producing non-objective art.

Throughout his career, Brigante used watercolor as his primary painting medium. He felt strongly that it was an under valued medium and championed it by producing major works which were accepted as important contributions to American art.
Biographical information:
Interview with Nick Brigante, 1983.

**Morris Broderson** (1928- ) Born: Los Angeles, CA; Studied: University of Southern California, Jepson Art Institute (Los Angeles). Morris Broderson was a student of Francis de Erdely and by the 1950s was exhibiting in the Los Angeles area. In the 1960s, he received national attention for his art and was featured in an article in *Time Magazine*.
Biographical information:
*Who's Who in American Art.*

**Gerald Brommer** (1927- ) Born: Berkeley, CA; Studied: Concordia Teachers College (Nebraska), University of Nebraska, Chouinard Art Institute (Los Angeles), Otis Art Institute (Los Angeles), University of California (Los Angeles), University of Southern California; Member: California Water Color Society, West Coast Watercolor Society. Gerald Brommer grew up in Northern California then studied to be an educator in Nebraska where he earned a Master's degree. After moving to Southern California, he received instruction in watercolor painting from Watson Cross, Noel Quinn and Robert E. Wood. At the beginning of his career he taught geography and painted whenever possible. Gradually, he phased out the geography classes to allow more time to paint and teach art.

Since the 1950s, he has produced watercolors on a regular basis. Many of his early works were very carefully planned and executed watercolors. On occasion, he added paper collage to give added textures. Recently he has been painting on location and works more spontaneously, responding directly to the subject he is viewing.

The subjects he has chosen to paint vary widely from California coast views, to desert landscapes and European city scenes. Throughout his life he has been interested in geology and rock formations that are often included in his work. He finds their varied textures and unique shapes particularly interesting as subject matter.

Brommer has also become an internationally recognized teacher of watercolor painting and is the author of eighteen art instruction books and numerous articles in art magazines. He served as president of both the California Water Color Society and West Coast Watercolor Society. Through the years he has actively exhibited watercolors, holding 110 one-man shows and having his works displayed in 204 group exhibitions. Since the 1960s, he has been in demand as an instructor of watercolor workshops and has traveled all over the world conducting these classes.
Biographical information:
Interview with Gerald Brommer, 1984.

**Benjamin Brown** (1865-1942) Born: Marion, KS; Studied: St. Louis School of Fine Arts, Académie Julian (Paris); Member: Pasadena Society of Artists, California Art Club. Benjamin Brown was a resident of St. Louis in the 1880s, but in 1885, he visited Southern California where he painted and sketched. After studying art in St. Louis and with Laurens and Constant in Paris, Brown moved to Pasadena in 1896. He produced watercolors throughout his career, but remains best known for his oil paintings and etchings.
Biographical information:
*Artists in California, 1786-1940.*

**Dorothy Brown** (1899-1973) Born: Houston, TX; Studied: Stanford University, University of California (Los Angeles); Member: California Water Color Society. Dorothy Brown exhibited her watercolors in the late 1940s and the 1950s, and was president of the California Water Color Society in 1958. She was an instructor at the University of California (Los Angeles) and served as the director of the campus art gallery.
Biographical information:
*Who's Who in American Art.*

GERALD BROMMER  *Streamside, China*  1970s  22" x 30"  Courtesy Gerald Brommer

GERALD BROMMER  *Santa Cruz Harbor*  1970s  15" x 22"  Courtesy Gerald Brommer

JOHN BURGESS  *Route 1*  1950s  15" x 22"  Courtesy Mrs. John Burgess

HUBERT BUEL  *Saint Peter and Paul*  1950  15" x 22"  David Howard Fine Arts

**Everett Bryant** (1864-1945) Born: Galion, OH; Member: California Water Color Society, Philadelphia Water Color Club. Everett Bryant studied art in Paris, London and Philadelphia with a number of important artists including William Merrit Chase. He was a resident of Los Angeles in the 1930s.
Biographical information:
*Who's Who in American Art.*

**Hubert Buel** (1915-1984) Born: Sacramento, CA; Studied: Fresno State College (California), University of California (Los Angeles); Member: California Water Color Society. Hubert Buel was born and raised in central California. In the early 1930s, he studied watercolor painting with Alexandra Bradshaw at Fresno State College then continued his art education at the University of California, Los Angeles. He worked briefly at the Walt Disney Studios and taught at Long Beach City College until 1940.

During World War II, he served as a United States Naval Officer in the South Pacific. He took painting supplies with him and produced a number of watercolors depicting island life and military involvement. After the war, he worked at Twentieth Century-Fox Studios as a set designer and then took a permanent job as art director at the *San Francisco Chronicle* newspaper.

Buel was a prolific watercolorist for fifty years. He often selected Bay Area subject matter near his home in San Francisco, but also painted in Hawaii, Mexico and Europe. The majority of his works were produced on location and were painted with transparent watercolors. He was a founding member of the West Coast Watercolor Society and became president of that organization in 1974.
Biographical information:
Interview with Hubert Buel, 1983.

**Conrad Buff** (1886-1975) Born: Switzerland; Member: California Art Club. Conrad Buff immigrated to the Los Angeles area in 1906. He worked as a painter, book illustrator and muralist. Although he is best known for his large oil paintings of southwestern subjects, Buff produced many opaque watercolors, painted on illustration board.
Biographical information:
*Six Decades* (Catalog).
George Stern Fine Arts (Catalog)

**George Henry Burgess** (1831-1905) Born: London, England; Studied: Somerset School of Design (England); Member: San Francisco Art Association. George Henry Burgess grew up in England and studied art there in the early 1840s. When he and his brother William heard about the Gold Rush, they sailed immediately for San Francisco. In 1849, a lithograph was produced by the H.S. Crocker Company from a watercolor Burgess painted that depicted the city of San Francisco. He produced additional works for Britton and Rey, the largest producer of lithographs in California. His watercolors depicting landscape and cityscape subjects were exhibited in Bay Area exhibitions starting in 1858.
Biographical information:
*California on Stone*
*Artists in California, 1786-1940.*

**John Burgess** (1911-1993) Born: Boston MA. John Burgess grew up in Boston. His early art education came from Harndon Foster, art director of the *National Sportsman* magazine. Additional instruction came from working as an apprentice under the celebrated naval architect, L. Francis Herreshoff. By 1929, Burgess was building race cars for the dirt track circuit, and for most of his life, documented the development of car racing in America. He is the only automotive artist of his stature in America who actually built and raced cars. Burgess also produced a series of art works depicting the railroads, sailing ships and Mohave Desert mining sites. He also helped design superchargers and jet engine housings. For twenty years he was the director for the Briggs Cunningham Automotive Museum.
Biographical information:
Interview with Glen Knowles, 1995.

**Hans Burkhardt** (1904-1994) Born: Basel, Switzerland; Studied: Cooper Union School of Art (New York), Grand Central School of Art (New York); Member: California Water Color Society. Hans Burkhardt immigrated to the United States in 1924 and lived in New York for 12 years. There, he studied with Arshile Gorky and became part of the modern art movement. In 1936, he moved to California. His paintings, particularly those from the 1930s and 1940s, are cubistic works often based on figurative subjects. He exhibited works with the California Water Color Society during this period.
Biographical information:
*The Art of California.*

**Jane Burnham** (1913-1997) Studied: University of California; Member: West Coast Watercolor Society, American Watercolor Society. Jane Burnham attended university, but primarily studied watercolor painting with Eliot O'Hara. She was a resident of San Jose and exhibited her works regionally. She also taught art in Northern California.
Biographical information:
West Coast Watercolor Society (Catalogs).

**Flavio Cabral** (1916-1990) Born: New York City, NY; Studied: Los Angeles State College; Member: California Water Color Society. Flavio Cabral, an artist of Portuguese descent, was largely self-taught. He exhibited watercolors in Southern California from the 1940s through the 1960s and was a resident of Hollywood. In addition, he taught art and art history in Los Angeles.
Biographical information:
*Contemporary American Painting and Sculpture.*

**William Ross Cameron** (1893-1971) Born: New York City, NY; Studied: California College of Arts and Crafts (Oakland); Member: Society of Western Artists, West Coast Watercolor Society. William Cameron worked for many years as a staff artist and art director for various San Francisco newspapers. He began exhibiting his watercolors in the 1930s and was one of the Thirteen Watercolorists. He painted small works, usually 12" x 16", featuring California and European scenes. He also illustrated several books, wrote articles on watercolor painting and taught art.
Biographical information:
Interview with Hubert Buel, 1983.

**Robert Caples** (1918-1996) Born: Los Angeles, CA; Studied: Chouinard Art Institute. Robert Caples grew up in Southern California and after graduating from high school in the mid-1930s, he attended art school in Los Angeles. He then went to work for the Walt Disney Studios producing watercolor background paintings for animated films.

In the 1950s and 1960s, he also did background painting for animated films produced by Warner Brothers Studios and Hanna-Barbera Studios. Throughout his career, and after retiring in the early 1970s, Caples also produced fine art and commercial illustrations painted with watercolors and gouache.
Biographical information:
Vi Caples courtesy of California Art Gallery,
Laguna Beach.

**Paul Carey** (1904-  ) Born: Palo Alto, CA; Studied: University of Oregon, California School of Fine Arts (San Francisco); Member: California Water Color Society. Paul Carey studied art in the mid-1920s and has exhibited watercolors in the Bay Area since that time. He was a partner in the commercial illustration business of Logan, Cox and Carey, was a founding member of the Thirteen Watercolorists, and was an assistant art professor at the California College of Arts and Crafts.
Biographical information:
David Howard Fine Arts, Mill Valley, 1991.
California Water Color Society (Catalogs)

**Jae Carmichael** (1925-  ) Born: Hollywood, CA; Studied: University of Southern California, Claremont College (California), Mills College (Oakland); Member: American Watercolor Society, California Water Color Society. Jae Carmichael studied art with; Francis de Erdely, Millard Sheets, Phil Dike, Dong Kingman and William Gaw. In 1953, she became a member of the California Water Color Society and has exhibited in the annual shows since that time.

In addition to painting and exhibiting her watercolors on a national level, Carmichael has produced sculpture, murals, oil paintings and films. She was a director of the Pasadena School of Fine Arts, president of the Pasadena Society of Artists and a director of the California Water Color Society. She is currently an Adjunct Professor of Cinema at the University of Southern California.
Biographical information:
Interview with Jae Carmichael, 1984.

**Ben Carrè** (1883-1978) Born: Paris, France; Member: Painters and Sculptors Club (Los Angeles). Ben Carrè was an art director in the motion picture industry in Hollywood. He came to Southern California in 1912 and by the 1930s, was painting and exhibiting watercolors depicting regional cityscape scenes of Los Angeles.
Biographical information:
*Scenes of California Life* (Catalog).

**Albert Ross Carter** (1909-1982) Born: Murphysboro, IL; Studied: University of Illinois, Syracuse University; Member: Philadelphia Water Color Club, Ohio Watercolor Club. Albert Carter moved to California from the Mid-west after World War II. While stationed at Fort Ord in the 1940s, he painted watercolors of the Monterey Peninsula and then settled in Marin County. He primarily worked with transparent watercolors and exhibited with the Thirteen Watercolorists through the 1950s and at annual art exhibitions in California and the Mid-west.
Biographical information:
Carlson Gallery, Carmel, 1997.

**Pruett Carter** (1891-1955) Born: Lexington, MO; Studied: Art Students League (Los Angeles); Member: Society of Illustrators. Pruett Carter spent his childhood living on an Indian reservation in Wyoming and his teenage years in Los Angeles. After studying art in California, he went to New York, took further studies with Walter Biggs, and became an art editor and illustrator for Hearst Publications. His paintings appeared in numerous, major magazines including *McCall's*, *Woman's Home Companion* and *Good Housekeeping*. He taught art at the Grand Central School of Art during the 1920s. In 1930, he moved back to Los Angeles, continued to produce magazine illustrations and taught at the Chouinard Art Institute.

His style of painting with both watercolors and oils influenced many West Coast artists and his teaching helped elevate the quality of commercial illustration done in Los Angeles.
Biographical information:
*The Illustrator in America, 1880-1980.*

**Roscoe Carver** (1896-1982) Studied: University of Washington (Seattle), California School of Fine Arts (San Francisco); Member: Santa Barbara Art Association. Roscoe Carver was raised in Washington State. After graduating from college, he moved to Northern California and studied art with Rudolph Schaeffer in San Francisco and Armin Hansen in Monterey. From the 1930s to the 1950s, he produced fine art watercolor paintings done in a representational style and worked as an art director at the McCann-Erickson Advertising Agency in San Francisco. After this, he lived near Santa Barbara and exhibited his watercolor paintings locally.
Biographical information:
Studio 2 Antiques, Santa Barbara, 1983.

**Frank Tolles Chamberlin** (1873-1961) Born: San Francisco, CA; Studied: Wadsworth Athenaeum (Connecticut), Art Students League (New York), American Academy (Rome); Member: California Art Club. Frank Tolles Chamberlin studied art with Dwight Tryon in Connecticut, George Bridgman in New York City and Frank Millet in Italy. He taught art in New York City until 1920, then moved to the West Coast and settled in Pasadena. Within a year, he became co-founder of the Chouinard Art Institute and was a key instructor at the school. Many of the finest painters discussed in this book took art instruction from Chamberlin and most credit him with having a profound influence on their art careers. His watercolors fall into two categories; some were sketches done on location or preliminary works for mural projects, others are carefully rendered paintings done in the classic English tradition.
Biographical information:
*Plein Air Painters of California*
Interview with Millard Sheets, 1983.

WILLIAM ROSS CAMERON  *From My Studio Window*  1930s  16" x 12"  Piedmont Lane Gallery

CLAUDE COATS  *Circus*  1930s  11" x 15"  Private Collection

DOROTHEA COOKE  *A Visit To Santa*  1943  15" x 22"  Tina O'Shea Collection

**Howard Clapp** (1920-1991) Born: Reedley, CA; Studied: University of California (Los Angeles); Member: California Water Color Society. While in college, Howard Clapp developed an abstract painting style based on architectural subjects. He exhibited with the California Water Color Society in the 1950s and served as the Society president three times. He taught watercolor painting in the Los Angeles area and lectured on art history.
Biographical information:
Interview with Howard Clapp, 1983.

**Homer Clark** (1921-   ) Born: Provo, Utah. Studied: Art Students League (New York); Homer Clark grew up in Utah and attended Brigham Young University. While studying in New York to be a physician, he received art instruction from Kenneth Hayes Miller and Reginald Marsh. After serving in the U.S. Navy, Clark lived in San Francisco. He received additional instruction from Millard Sheets, Barse Miller and Milford Zornes. Since the 1960s he has resided in Utah where he has worked as a doctor and artist.
Biographical information:
Interview with Homer Clark, 1998.

**Ted Clark** (1904-   ) Born: Bristol, England. Ted Clark came to San Francisco in 1922 and worked there as a commercial illustrator until the late 1960s. He produced thousands of watercolor, tempera and gouache paintings for use on fruit box labels, posters and magazine advertisements. He was primarily employed by Traung Label and Lithograph Company and the Carton Label and Lithograph Company.
Biographical information:
Interview with Ted Clark, 1978.

**Walter Clark** (1897-1981) Born: Bristol, England. Walter Clark studied art in England before moving to San Francisco about 1921. He worked for several years at the Traung Label and Lithograph Company, then set up a freelance commercial art studio, that he operated until the early 1960s. He primarily painted with watercolors and gouache, producing magazine advertisements, poster designs and fruit box label illustrations.
Biographical information:
Interview with Walter Clark, 1978.

**Samuel Clayberger** (1926-   ) Born: Kulpmont, PA; Studied: Chouinard Art Institute (Los Angeles), Jepson Art Institute (Los Angeles); Member: California Water Color Society. After serving in World War II, Samuel Clayberger moved to California where he studied art with Tom Craig, Don Graham, Rico Lebrun and Richard Haines. He has primarily painted figurative works, often placed in natural landscape settings. Throughout the 1950s, he worked in the animated film industry and pursued a fine art career as well. Since the early 1960s, he has taught at the Otis Art Institute and has continued to exhibit his paintings.
Biographical information:
Interview with Samuel Clayberger, 1984.

**John Coakley** (1918-1970) Born: New York City, NY; Studied: Chouinard Art Institute (Los Angeles); Member: California Water Color Society. When John Coakley was a teenager, his family moved to Southern California. After studying art in Los Angeles, he worked as an artist at the M.G.M. Studios and the Twentieth Century-Fox Studios. From the mid 1930s until the late 1960s, he exhibited watercolors locally.
Biographical information:
Interview with Marie Coakley, 1996.

**Claude Coats** (1913-1992) Born: San Francisco, CA; Studied: University of Southern California; Member: California Water Color Society. Claude Coats was raised in California where he studied watercolor painting with Paul Sample and Dan Lutz. After graduating in 1934, he began exhibiting with the California Water Color Society and for approximately ten years, was active as a watercolor artist. Coats worked for many years as an artist at the Walt Disney Studios, where he painted elaborate, colorful watercolor backgrounds for many classic animated feature films including *Pinocchio, Dumbo, Snow White and the Seven Dwarfs, Cinderella, Fantasia* and *Peter Pan*.
Biographical information:
Interview with Claude Coats, 1983.

**Lois Green Cohen** (1919-   )Born: Chicago, IL; Studied: Carnegie Technical (Pittsburgh), Chouinard Art Institute (Los Angeles), University of California (Los Angeles); Member: California Water Color Society. Lois Green Cohen studied art in Pennsylvania and then moved to Los Angeles in 1939, and continued her art education by studying with Pruett Carter and Herbert Jepson. Her many watercolors, depicting Los Angeles cityscape views, were regularly exhibited throughout the 1950s. In addition to her fine art painting, Cohen has produced illustrations and production art works for commercial accounts and the motion picture industry.
Biographical information:
James Snidle Fine Arts, 1995.

**Eleanor Colborn** (1866-1939) Born: Dayton, OH; Studied: Chicago Art Institute; Member: California Water Color Society, Laguna Beach Art Association. Eleanor Colborn attended the Chicago Art Institute and after graduation became an art instructor there. In the early 1920s, she moved to Laguna Beach, built a studio, taught, painted and exhibited her works. Many of her watercolors depict figurative subjects; particularly mothers and children. She was a director of the Laguna Beach Art Association from 1926 to 1929 and exhibited with the California Water Color Society in the 1930s.
Biographical information:
*Southern California Art.*

**Sam Colburn** (1909-1993) Born: Denver, CO; Studied: Chouinard Art Institute (Los Angeles); Member: Carmel Art Association. In the mid-1930s, Sam Colburn studied art in Los Angeles and then moved north and settled in Carmel. Throughout the 1940s and 1950s, he produced transparent watercolors of the Monterey Peninsula region and occasionally went on painting excursions to other states and Mexico. Colburn was an active member of the Carmel art community and taught painting classes for many years.
Biographical information:
William A. Karges Fine Art, Los Angeles, 1995.

**Gale Cole** (1914-  ) Born: San Diego, CA; Studied: California School of Fine Arts (San Francisco), Stanford University; Member: California Water Color Society, San Francisco Art Association. After attending Stanford, Gale Cole lived in San Francisco and exhibited with the California Water Color Society in the 1940s and 1950s. She was also an art instructor in the Bay Area.
Biographical information:
*Who's Who in American Art.*

**Dorothea Cooke** (1908-2001) Born: Hollywood, CA; Studied Chouinard Art Institute (Los Angeles). Dorothea Cooke grew up in Southern California where she studied art with F. Tolles Chamberlin and Pruett Carter. She worked as an illustrator and printmaker. In 1936 she and her husband, Hardie Gramatky, moved to New York. There she continued to do illustration and fine art watercolors.
Biographical information:
Interview with Dorothea Cooke Gramatky, 1983

**Colin Campbell Cooper, N.A.** (1856-1937) Born: Philadelphia, PA; Studied: Pennsylvania Academy of Fine Arts, Académie Julian (Paris); Member: National Academy of Design, New York Water Color Club, American Watercolor Society. Colin Campbell Cooper resided in Pennsylvania for most of his life, working full time as a fine art painter. He traveled all over the world and many of his watercolor paintings depict scenes from these travels. He moved to California in 1921 and until 1937, lived in Santa Barbara where he served as Dean of Painting at the Santa Barbara Community School of Arts.
Biographical information:
*Southern California Art.*

**Mario Cooper, N.A.** (1905-1995) Born: Mexico City, Mexico; Studied: Otis Art Institute (Los Angeles), Chouinard Art Institute (Los Angeles), Grand Central School of Art (New York); Member: American Watercolor Society, California Water Color Society. Mario Cooper studied art with F. Tolles Chamberlin, Harvey Dunn and Pruett Carter. He worked as an illustrator in Los Angeles during the 1930s and exhibited his watercolors in local Los Angeles exhibitions. By the 1940s, he was living in New York where he established a reputation as a prominent illustrator. He repeatedly served as president of the American Watercolor Society.
Biographical information:
*Who's Who in American Art.*

**Earl Cordrey** (1902-1977) Born: Piru, CA; Studied: Chouinard Art Institute (Los Angeles), Grand Central School of Art (New York); Member: California Water Color Society, Society of Illustrators. Earl Cordrey was a prominent West Coast commercial artist from the 1930s to the 1960s. His works appeared in numerous national magazines as story illustrations and in advertising art. Cordrey frequently used watercolors for commercial art works and for exhibition paintings. Prior to World War II, he lived in the Los Angeles area and later moved to Palm Springs.
Biographical information:
*Who's Who in American Art*
Interview with Mrs. Earl Cordrey, 1983.

**John Cotton** (1868-1931) Born: Toronto, Canada; Studied: Chicago Art Institute; Member: California Water Color Society. After attending the Chicago Art Institute, John Cotton studied art in London with E. Marsdon Wilson. He lived in Southern California in the 1920s and exhibited in the first nine annual shows of the California Water Color Society. Cotton was president of the Society in 1925.
Biographical information:
*Southern California Art.*

**Merle Cox** (1896-1949) Born: Indiana. Merle Cox began working in motion picture studio art departments in Los Angeles around 1928. By the mid-1930s, he was employed by the Walt Disney Studios as an artist; producing watercolor backgrounds for animated films. Some of the major animated film projects he produced watercolors for include; *Snow White and the Seven Dwarfs, Pinocchio, Fantasia, Saludos Amigos, Make Mine Music* and *Cinderella*.
Biographical information:
*The Disney Films*
*Artists in California 1786-1940.*

**Whitson Cox** (1921-  ) Born: Nebraska; Studied: University of Oregon; Member: West Coast Watercolor Society. Whitson Cox grew up in Oregon and attended college in Eugene. In 1947, he moved to the San Francisco area to pursue a career in architecture and then settled in Sacramento. He took further painting instruction from George Post and began exhibiting his abstract watercolors that were usually based on landscape subjects.
Biographical information:
Interview with Whitson Cox, 1996.

**Willard Cox** (1902-1974) Born: Wichita, KS; Studied: California College of Arts and Crafts (Oakland); Member: Bohemian Club, Puget Sound Group. From 1930 through the late 1960s, Willard Cox worked as a commercial art illustrator in San Francisco. He produced fine art watercolors which were exhibited in the Bay Area shows of the Thirteen Watercolorists, in Seattle with the Puget Sound Group and at the annual Oakland Art Gallery exhibitions. He usually worked with transparent watercolors and often chose to depict small town scenes of Northern California.
Biographical information:
Puget Sound Group Catalog.

**Thomas Craig** (1909-1969) Born: Upland, CA; Studied: Pomona College (California), University of California (Berkeley), University of Southern California; Member: California Water Color Society, Philadelphia Water Color Society. Thomas Craig was born and raised near Los Angeles. After studying botany at the University California (Berkeley), he received art instruction from F. Tolles Chamberlin, Clarence Hinkle and Millard Sheets in Southern California.

His innovative watercolors helped earn him a Guggenheim Fellowship in the early 1940s, which supported a painting trip across America. After serving as a war artist in World War II, Craig stopped painting and went back to his botanical interests.

Although he actively painted and exhibited for only about twenty years, he played an important role in the development

TOM CRAIG  *Near San Simeon*  1930s  15" x 22"  David Tonnemacher Collection

TOM CRAIG  *Los Angeles, Downtown*  1939  15" x 22"  Calvert Collection

WATSON CROSS, JR. *Trailer Camp* 1946 15" x 22" Courtesy Watson Cross Jr.

WATSON CROSS, JR. *Country Church* 1945 15" x 22" Courtesy Watson Cross Jr.

of the California Style of watercolor painting. His works were exhibited in many important shows including the California Group traveling exhibitions.
Biographical information:
Interview with Mrs. Thomas Craig, 1983.

**Watson Cross, Jr.** (1918- ) Born: Long Beach, CA; Studied: Chouinard Art Institute (Los Angeles); Member: California Water Color Society. Watson Cross, Jr. grew up in Long Beach. He studied with James Patrick, Phil Paradise, Henry Lee McFee and Rico Lebrun in Los Angeles during the 1930s and early 1940s. During this period, he began exhibiting California Style watercolors, which usually depict cityscape subjects. Works from the World War II era often include war related activities in Southern California. In the late 1950s and 1960s, his watercolors became abstract and often included figures.

Cross exhibited in many annual museum exhibitions and was president of the California Water Color Society in 1953. He has been an influential art instructor at a number of schools including Chouinard Art Institute, Otis Art Institute and Art Center School.
Biographical information:
Interview with Watson Cross, Jr., 1983.

**Keith Crown** (1918- ) Born: Keokuk, IA; Studied: Chicago Art Institute; Member: California Water Color Society. Keith Crown was raised in Gary, Indiana and studied art in Chicago from 1936 to 1940. During World War II, he was in the United States Army and was stationed throughout the Pacific theater. He became a field correspondent and produced art for *Yank Magazine*. After the war, he continued his education in Chicago and then became an art instructor at the University of California (Los Angeles). He lived in Manhattan Beach and drew inspiration for his colorful, abstract works from local coastline subjects. Most of these paintings were produced using opaque watercolors.

Between 1945 and 1970, he had forty-four one-man shows and was a key figure in bringing post war modern art to Southern California. Crown served on the board of the California Water Color Society several times and was president in 1959. In the early 1960s, his works became radical abstractions and were often produced using transparent watercolors. He received numerous awards, had a variety of one-man exhibitions and taught at universities throughout America and Canada. In 1986, a book titled *Keith Crown Watercolors* by Sheldon Reich was published by University of Missouri Press.
Biographical information:
Interview with Keith Crown, 1982.

**Leonard Cutrow** (1911-1992) Born: Russia; Studied: Art Center School (Los Angeles); Member: California Water Color Society. Leonard Cutrow received a Huntington Hartford Residence Fellowship to study at the Art Center School. He exhibited his watercolors with the California Water Color Society in the 1940s and 1950s. He also taught art at the Art Center School and the University of Southern California School of Architecture.
Biographical information:
*Who's Who in American Art.*

**David Cytron** (1901-1983) Studied: University of Southern California; Member: California Water Color Society. David Cytron, a watercolorist, exhibited in Southern California from 1944 until about 1965. He was a Long Beach resident and in 1949 and 1950 served on the board of directors for the California Water Color Society.
Biographical information:
California Water Color Society (Catalogs).

**Lois Cytron:** (active in 1950s) Member: California Water Color Society. From the early 1940s until the mid-1960s, Lois Cytron exhibited in Southern California and in 1951 served on the board of directors for the California Water Color Society. She lived in Long Beach and was active in local art circles.
Biographical information:
California Water Color Society (Catalogs).

**Robert W. Daley** (1922- ) Studied: Art Center School (Los Angeles). Robert W. Daley grew up in San Bernardino, California, and received a scholarship to study at Art Center School. During World War II, he was a combat artist for the United States Coast Guard and produced a series of watercolors depicting war activities in the South Pacific. After the war, Daley worked as a commercial artist and operated an art gallery in San Bernardino.
Biographical information:
*Widening Horizons*, 1949.

**William Swift Daniell** (1865-1933) Born: San Francisco, CA; Studied: Académie Julian (Paris), Académie Delecluse (Paris); Member: Laguna Beach Art Association, California Art Club. William Swift Daniell studied art in Boston and Paris before moving to Southern California in the early 1900s. He was primarily a watercolorist, painted landscapes, and was an early artist and art teacher in Laguna Beach.
Biographical information:
*Six Decades* (Catalog).

**Frode Dann** (1892-1984) Born: Jelstrup, Denmark; Studied: Royal Academy (Copenhagen); Member: California Water Color Society, Pasadena Society of Artists. Frode Dann began exhibiting his art work in Southern California during the early 1930s, and served as president of the California Water Color Society in 1943 and 1944. He and his wife, Katherine Skeele, directed and taught at the Pasadena School of Fine Arts in the 1950s and early 1960s.
Biographical information:
*Who's Who in American Art.*

**William S. Darling** (1882-1963) Born: Sandorhaji, Hungary; Studied: Royal Academy of Art (Budapest), Ecole des Beaux Arts (Paris); Member: Laguna Beach Art Association. William Darling was born Wilmos Bela Sandorhaji. In 1910, he immigrated to America and by the early 1920s, had changed his name to Darling, his wife's maiden name and settled in Southern California. Throughout the 1920s and 1930s, he produced watercolors and gouache paintings depicting local scenes and also worked as an artist for Twentieth Century-Fox Studios. During the 1950s, he became a well-known figure in the Laguna Beach

and Palm Springs art communities. His works from this era primarily depict coastal views and desertscapes, painted with watercolor or oil on canvas.
Biographical information:
Bluebird Gallery, Laguna Beach, 1989.

**Paul Darrow** (1921- ) Born: Pasadena, CA; Studied: Colorado Springs Art Center (Colorado), Claremont Graduate School (California); Member: California Water Color Society. Paul Darrow grew up in Southern California and after serving in World War II, studied art with Millard Sheets, Phil Dike, Phil Paradise and Milford Zornes. During the 1950s, he produced and exhibited abstract paintings, that were often done with transparent and opaque watercolors. Recently he has focused on paper collage and mixed media. Darrow taught art at the Scripps College in Claremont, Brigham Young University in Utah, Otis Art Institute and Laguna Beach School of Art. He also illustrated several books, produced murals and worked as a cartoonist.
Biographical information:
Interview with Paul Darrow, 1985.

**Don David** (1906- ) Born: Springberg, OR; Studied: Art Center School (Los Angeles), Chouinard Art Institute (Los Angeles); Member: California Watercolor Society. Don David attended Fresno State College in 1927 and received watercolor instruction from Alexandra Bradshaw. He continued his studies in Los Angeles with Barse Miller in the 1930s and produced California Style watercolors until the early 1950s. He then moved to New York, studied with Hans Hofmann and has since focused on painting abstract art.
Biographical information:
Michael Johnson Fine Art
Interview with Don David, 2000.

**Ken Decker** (1926-1994) Born: St. Louis, MO; Studied: Portland School of Art (Oregon). Ken Decker grew up in Southern California and after high school went into the United States Navy. He served in the Asian Pacific theatre during World War II and then attended art school on the G.I. Bill after the war. While working as an illustrator in Southern California, he became interested in watercolor painting. Gradually, he developed into a professional watercolorist and art instructor. Although he taught and exhibited all over Western America, he is best remembered in Northern San Diego County.
Biographical information:
Interview with Sue Decker, 1998.

**John De Cuir** (1918-1991) Studied: Chouinard Art Institute (Los Angeles); Member: Society of Motion Picture Art Directors. John De Cuir attended art school in Los Angeles during the 1930s. In the 1940s, he served in the United States Navy and worked in the art department of Universal Studios. After 1950, he was employed as an art director at Twentieth Century-Fox Studios. Throughout his career in motion pictures De Cuir produced elaborate watercolors which were used in the production of major motion pictures.
Biographical information:
*Production Design Magazine*, 1952
Interview with John De Cuir, Jr., 1999.

**Francis de Erdely** (1904-1959) Born: Budapest, Hungary; Studied: Royal Academy of Art (Budapest), Academy of San Fernando (Madrid), Sorbonne (Paris), School of the Louvre (Paris); Member: American Watercolor Society, California Water Color Society. Francis de Erdely grew up in Europe and became a well-known artist throughout the continent.

Just prior to World War II, he moved to the United States and settled in Los Angeles. He exhibited with the California Water Color Society and the American Watercolor Society from 1945 to 1955. The works he showed were masterfully rendered pencil, ink, crayon or charcoal drawings with watercolor washes.

De Erdely was an art instructor from 1944 until 1959, teaching classes at the University of Southern California, Pasadena Art Museum School and Jepson Art Institute. His teaching, as well as his paintings, drawings and lithographs, influenced many Southern California artists from that period.
Biographical information:
California Water Color Society (Catalogs).

**Stephen De Hospodar** (1902-1959) Born: Hungary; Studied: National Academy of Design (New York). Stephen De Hospodar was a student of Robert Henri, George Bellows and Charles Hawthorne. In the 1920s and 1930s, he lived in Los Angeles. During this period, he exhibited watercolors in Southern California art shows.
Biographical information:
*Who's Who in American Art*.

**Henri De Kruif** (1882-1944) Born: Grand Rapids, MI; Studied: Chicago Art Institute, Art Students League (New York); Member: California Water Color Society. Henri De Kruif was one of the fourteen artists to exhibit in the first annual show of the California Water Color Society in 1921 and served as the Society president in the 1920s. He was a modernist painter and produced colorful expressionist works, usually based on landscape subjects. During the late 1920s and early 1930s, he promoted transparent watercolors and encouraged artists to use them as a primary medium.
Biographical information:
*Southern California Art*.

**Annita Delano** (1894-1979) Born: Hueneme, CA; Studied: University of California (Los Angeles); Member: California Water Color Society. Annita Delano became a teacher at the University of California (Los Angeles) in 1918 and exhibited her paintings with the California Water Color Society from 1924 to 1954. She taught at the Otis Art Institute from 1944 to 1946.
Biographical information:
*Who's Who in American Art*.

**Paul De Longpre** (1855-1911) Born: Lyons, France. Paul De Longpre was born in central France and grew up in Paris. As a child, he began drawing flowers and birds, and then at the age of twelve, became employed as an artist painting floral designs on fans. In 1890, he moved to New York City and established a reputation for his exquisitely rendered watercolors of floral subjects. Many of these were reproduced by lithographic process and sold all over America. In the late 1890s, he moved to California, built a beautiful home in

DON DAVID  *Los Angeles Alley*  1945  15" x 22"  Michael Johnson Fine Arts

JOSEPH DE MERS  *Downtown Diner*  1930s  15" x 22"  Private Collection

JOSEPH DE MERS  *Ham and Eggs*  1930s  20" x 16"  Private Collection

Hollywood and surrounded it with flower gardens. His artistic talent, posh lifestyle, and stature as a famous French artist drew the interest of many Southern California publications and before long, he found celebrity status. His home became a regular tourist attraction and De Longpre Avenue, which runs parallel to Sunset Boulevard in Hollywood, was named after him.
Biographical information:
*Who's Who in American Art*
*Southern California Art.*

**Joseph De Mers** (1910-1984) Born: San Diego, CA; Studied: Chouinard Art Institute (Los Angeles); Member: California Water Color Society. After studying with Pruett Carter and Lawrence Murphy, artist Joseph De Mers went on to become an internationally recognized magazine illustrator. He lived in Southern California, taught art at Chouinard, and exhibited watercolors locally until the late 1930s. Later, he moved to the East Coast where he exhibited in major museum shows during the 1950s and 1960s.
Biographical information:
*The Illustrator in America, 1880-1980.*

**Al Dempster** (1911- ) Born: Atlantic City, NJ; Studied: Art Center School (Los Angeles). Al Dempster grew up in Southern California and enrolled at the Art Center School in the early 1930s. There, he studied with Barse Miller, Stanley Reckless and Joseph Henninger. He worked as a background painter for animated films at the Walt Disney Studios after finishing art school. His first major film project was to produce backgrounds for *Pinocchio*. Over the next thirty years, he worked on many of Disney's most famous animated films and produced illustrations for a number of children's books. In addition to his studio art, Dempster painted and exhibited fine art watercolors.
Biographical information:
Interview with Al Dempster, 1996.

**Albert De Rome** (1885-1959) Born: Cayucos, CA; Studied: Mark Hopkins Institute of Art (San Francisco); Member: Carmel Art Association. Albert De Rome grew up in California and began his art career doing commercial art. He was equally adept at working in watercolors or oils and spent his entire career working on the West Coast. His paintings depict California landscape subjects and seascapes done near Carmel.
Biographical information:
*Albert T. De Rome.*

**Harry Diamond** (1913- ) Born: Los Angeles, CA; Studied: Chouinard Art Institute (Los Angeles). Harry Diamond grew up in Southern California. He attended art school in Los Angeles and worked in the animation film business. In 1938, he moved to New York City and became art editor for *Scribner's* magazine. During this period he also was an art director for several advertising agencies. In 1948, he returned to Los Angeles and became an art instructor at the Chouinard Art Institute. His classes were on design and illustration. As a freelance commercial artist, he continued to produce illustrations for many magazines including *Vogue*, *Holiday*, *Good Housekeeping*, *American* and *Westways*. Throughout his career, Diamond painted with watercolors, gouache, tempera, casein and other water based media.
Biographical information:
Interview with Harry Diamond, 1998.

**John Reed Dickinson** (1844- ) Born: London, England; Member: San Francisco Art Association. John Reed Dickinson studied art in Europe before moving to San Francisco in 1879. He produced beautifully rendered watercolors of landscape and figurative subjects, that were exhibited in Bay Area art shows. He lost a great many of his works when the 1906 earthquake and fire destroyed his studio.
Biographical information:
*Artists in California, 1786-1940.*

**Charles J. Dickman** (1863-1943) Born: Germany; Studied: Académie Julian (Paris), California School of Design (San Francisco); Member: San Francisco Art Association. Charles Dickman was born in Europe and raised in eastern America before moving to San Francisco in 1883. Until 1896, he produced watercolors that were translated into commercial advertisements for the Dickman-Jones Lithograph Company. After selling this business, he continued his art studies in France and Germany and then returned to establish a career as a fine art painter.
Biographical information:
*Who's Who in American Art.*

**Eva Dickstein** (active in 1950s) Studied: Art Center School (Los Angeles); Member: California Water Color Society. Eva Dickstein, a resident of Los Angeles in the 1940s and 1950s, worked as a commercial artist and exhibited watercolors depicting regional California subjects.
Biographical information:
California Water Color Society (Catalogs).

**Phil Dike, N.A.** (1906-1990) Born: Redlands, CA; Studied: Chouinard Art Institute (Los Angeles), Art Students League (New York), American Academy (France); Member: National Academy of Design, American Watercolor Society, California Water Color Society, Philadelphia Water Color Club. Phil Dike was born and raised in Southern California. In 1923, he was awarded a scholarship to study at the Chouinard Art Institute and received instruction from F. Tolles Chamberlin and Clarence Hinkle. He continued his art education in New York City studying with George Bridgman, Frank Vincent DuMond and George Luks. After returning to California in 1929, he began teaching at the Chouinard Art Institute and was one of the first artists to develop what became known as the California Style of watercolor painting.

In the early 1930s, he continued teaching and painting and took further studies in Paris. His watercolors were being exhibited in museum shows throughout America and he was receiving wide acclaim and numerous awards. By 1935, he was also working at the Walt Disney Studios where he taught art and color theory while working on animated films. Among the many classic films he worked on were *Snow White and the Seven Dwarfs*, *Fantasia* and *The Three Caballeros*. In 1938, Dike served as president of the California Water Color Society.

After World War II, Dike left Disney and went back into

teaching and painting full time. He and Rex Brandt formed the highly successful Brandt-Dike Summer School of Painting and during regular school months, he taught at the Chouinard Art Institute. It was at this time that Dike's watercolors became more modern looking. He began using calligraphy in very creative ways and incorporating geometric-abstractionist ideas into his work.

Through the 1950s and 1960s, he was a Professor of Art at Scripps College and Claremont Graduate School. He was an inspiration to many well-known artists who came out of these schools, and was honored with the title of Professor Emeritus when he retired. In addition to living in Claremont and painting at Balboa Bay, Dike also built a second home in Cambria on the central California coast. Harbors, driftwood, figures on the beach and dramatic rock formations all became subjects for his many abstract watercolors of this era. Dike is remembered as a thoughtful, caring teacher and is one of the main innovators in the development of the watercolor painting movement in California.
Biographical information:
Interview with Phil Dike, 1983.

**James Budd Dixon** (1908-1967) Born: San Francisco, CA; Studied: University of California (Berkeley), Mark Hopkins Institute of Art (San Francisco), California School of Fine Arts (San Francisco); Member: San Francisco Art Association. James Budd Dixon exhibited watercolors depicting regional Bay Area subjects during the 1930s and early 1940s. In the mid-1940s, he began producing abstract oil paintings and taught modern art at the California School of Fine Arts.
Biographical information:
*Regionalism: The California View* (Catalog).

**L. Maynard Dixon** (1875-1946) Born: Fresno, CA; Studied: California School of Design (San Francisco); Member: San Francisco Art Association. Maynard Dixon was a native California artist. Born and raised in Fresno, California, he studied briefly at the California School of Design in 1893, but he was primarily a self-taught artist. Early in his career, he produced transparent watercolors depicting landscape subjects and local scenes including livestock and cowboys. He also did watercolor washes on his drawings and sketches that were reproduced as illustrations in the *Land of Sunshine* magazine and the *Overland Monthly*.

Throughout his career, Dixon worked simultaneously as a commercial artist and fine art painter. In both fields of art, he established a reputation for integrity and excellence. His fine art works were usually painted with oils on canvas, but occasionally he worked with watercolor or gouache. The art work for posters, billboards, magazine illustrations and mural studies were often produced using gouache or watercolors. These works, particularly the ones painted in the 1920s, were among the finest commercial art works produced on the West Coast during this era.

His paintings of Indian and cowboy subjects helped establish Dixon as one of California's most important artists of the early twentieth century. He was a resident of San Francisco much of his life, but also spent time in San Diego, Arizona and Utah.
Biographical information:
Interview with Edith Hamlin Dixon, 1984.

**Henry Doane** (1905- ) Born: Cambridge, MA; Studied: California College of Arts and Crafts (Oakland), Rudolph Schaeffer School of Design (San Francisco); Member: Society of Western Artists, San Francisco Art Association. Henry Doane began exhibiting his watercolor paintings in the 1940s. He also worked as a commercial display artist in San Francisco for many years, served as the president of the Society of Western Artists and taught watercolor painting.
Biographical information:
Interview with Henry Doane, 1983.

**Arthur Dodge** (1863-1952) Born: Providence, RI; Member: California Art Club. Arthur Dodge grew up in Northern California. After studying art in New York City, he moved to San Francisco and worked as a newspaper illustrator until 1901. At that time, he moved to Los Angeles, worked for the *Los Angeles Times* and produced watercolors depicting local scene subjects.
Biographical information:
*Artists in California, 1786-1940.*

**Richard Dodge** (1918-1974) Born: Sacramento, CA; Studied: Art Center School (Los Angeles), Cincinnati Art Academy (Ohio). Richard Dodge was raised in Northern California and studied art in Los Angeles during the mid-1930s. By the late 1930s, he was exhibiting watercolors in the Sacramento and San Francisco areas and producing illustration art.
Biographical information:
*Artists in California, 1786-1940.*

**William Dole** (1917-1983) Born: Angola, IN; Studied: Olivet College (Michigan), University of California (Berkeley); Member: California Water Color Society. William Dole began exhibiting his watercolors with the California Water Color Society in the late 1940s. He worked mainly in the abstract style, but in later years, added paper collage to his watercolors. He taught art in Indiana, Washington state, the University of California (Berkeley) and after the late 1940s, at the University of California (Santa Barbara).
Biographical information:
Interview with William Dole, 1983.

**Helen Dooley** (1907-1994) Born: San Jose, CA; Studied; Chouinard Art Institute (Los Angeles), Claremont College (California), California School of Fine Arts (San Francisco), University of California (Berkeley); Member: West Coast Watercolor Society; Carmel Art Association. Helen Dooley studied with Maurice Sterne and Millard Sheets, and began exhibiting her watercolors in the early 1950s. She also taught art and wrote a book titled *Art for Elementary Schools*.
Biographical information:
Interview with Helen Dooley, 1984.

**Jack Dudley** (1918-1996) Born: Sonora, CA; Studied: Art Center School (Los Angeles); Member: California Water Color Society, Laguna Beach Art Association. Jack Dudley grew up in Southern California and after serving in the United States Army during World War II, studied art with Barse Miller and Lorser Feitelson. After a short career in the commercial art field, he moved to Laguna Beach and began

PHIL DIKE  *Corona del Mar*  1940s  22" x 30"  Courtesy Rex Brandt

PHIL DIKE  *Elysian Park*  1930s  22" x 30"  Mike and Sue Verbal Collection

RICHARD DODGE  *Morning Walk, L.A.*  1938  18" x 24"  Ray Sahranavard Collection

HUGH DUNCAN  *Yellow House*  1950  15" x 22"  Courtesy Hugh Duncan

painting, selling and exhibiting fine art. Dudley often traveled to Mexico and drew much of his subject matter from that country.
Biographical information:
Interview with Jack Dudley, 1996
Esther Wells Gallery, Laguna Beach, 1990.

**Darwin Duncan** (1905- ) Born: St. James, MN; Member: Laguna Beach Art Association. Darwin Duncan studied painting with Edgar Payne and Sam Hyde Harris. Since the 1930s, he has produced oil paintings and watercolors depicting landscape subjects. Duncan is also well-known in Southern California as an art instructor.
Biographical information:
Interview with Darwin Duncan, 1978.

**Hugh Duncan** (1924-2001) Born: Glendale, CA; Studied: School of Allied Arts (Glendale), Art Center School (Los Angeles), Chouinard Art Institute (Los Angeles); Member: Watercolor West. Hugh Duncan grew up in Southern California and studied watercolor painting with Charles Payzant, Ralph Hulett, Arthur Beaumont and Rex Brandt. After World War II, he began exhibiting his fine art watercolors and working as a commercial illustrator in the Los Angeles area. Duncan was an avid sailing enthusiast most of his life and his watercolors often depict sailboats racing offshore or cruising in California harbors. In addition, he taught watercolor painting at workshops in Southern California since the 1970s.
Biographical information:
Interview with Hugh Duncan, 1996.

**Eyvind Earle** (1916-2000) Born: New York, NY; Member: California Water Color Society. Eyvind Earle was born in the United States, raised in France and studied art with his father, Ferdinand Earle. In the 1930s, he moved back to New York and painted watercolors for exhibitions and illustrations for commercial use. After serving in the United States Navy he moved to California and worked at the Walt Disney Studios. He formed his own production company to release animated cartoons, commercials and other products. In recent years, he has received international acclaim for his oil paintings and screen prints of highly stylized landscape subjects.
Biographical information:
Interview with Eyvind Earle, 1987.

**Harrison Eastman** (1823-1886) Born: New Hampshire. Harrison Eastman came to San Francisco in 1849 and eventually established an engraving company after working in that field for about ten years. He was an accomplished watercolorist, produced illustrations for local California magazines and is considered an important pioneer California artist.
Biographical information:
*Artists in California, 1786-1940.*

**Leonard Edmondson** (1916- ) born: Sacramento, CA; Studied: University of California (Berkeley); Member: California Water Color Society, San Francisco Art Association, Los Angeles Printmaking Society. Leonard Edmondson attended college in Northern California and in 1942, achieved a Master of Fine Arts degree. He served in the United States Army during World War II and afterwards, settled in Pasadena. By 1947, he was teaching art at Pasadena City College and exhibiting watercolors in California Water Color Society shows and in the Los Angeles County Museum of Art exhibitions. His paintings were among the first radically modern works to be accepted for these annual shows. Most of his watercolors were produced using transparent and opaque paints and he occasionally added paper collage.

By the mid-1950s, he was receiving national recognition for his watercolors and colored etchings. Major museums, including the Metropolitan Museum of Art, the Museum of Modern Art and the Brooklyn Museum, purchased his works for their collections. He became president of the California Water Color Society and in 1966, served as the president of the Los Angeles Printmaking Society. Edmondson taught art at the Otis Art Institute and at the California State University (Los Angeles), and was particularly influential as an instructor of printmaking.
Biographical information:
Interview with Leonard Edmondson, 1983.

**Duval Eliot** (1909-1990) Born: Arkansas; Studied: Art Center School (Los Angeles); Member: Pasadena Society of Artists, Women Painters of the West. In the mid-1930s, Duval Eliot studied watercolor painting with Barse Miller, Hardie Gramatky and Joseph Henninger while continuing her career as a professional fashion illustrator. Throughout this period, she also produced and exhibited watercolors. Of special interest to her were subjects of Los Angeles and the surrounding areas. The latter part of her life was spent teaching art and giving painting demonstrations.
Biographical information:
Interview with Robin Fuld and Karen Hackett, 1996.

**J. Milford Ellison** (1909-1989) Born: Sioux City, IA; Studied: Chouinard Art Institute (Los Angeles), Chicago Academy of Fine Arts, San Diego State College, University of Southern California; Member: San Diego Watercolor Society, Carmel Art Association. J. Milford Ellison moved to San Diego in the late 1920s and established a commercial art business. By the 1930s, he was exhibiting watercolors in annual art exhibitions and teaching art in the San Diego area.
Biographical information:
Stewart Galleries, Palm Springs, 1988.

**Jules Engel** (1915- ) Born: Budapest, Hungary; Studied: Chouinard Art Institute (Los Angeles); Member: California Water Color Society. Jules Engel moved from Europe to Southern California in 1938 and by the late 1940s, was exhibiting in annual art shows. Most of his works are nonobjective or abstracts, painted with transparent watercolors or gouache. Since 1970, he has taught experimental animation classes at the California Institute of the Arts.
Biographical information:
Interview with Jules Engel, 1995.

**Verna Scott Evans** (1905-1979) Born: Northern California; Studied: Scripps College (Pomona); Member: Laguna Beach Art Association. Verna Scott Evans grew up in San Francisco, then moved to Southern California. In the early 1930s, she attended college in Pomona and studied watercolor painting

with Millard Sheets. She received additional instruction from Rex Brandt, James Patrick and George Post. From the 1940s and into the 1960s, she actively exhibited California Scene watercolors that she painted on location.
Biographical information:
Doug Freeman.

**Edgar Ewing** (1913- ) Born: Hartington, NE; Studied: Chicago Art Institute; Member: California Water Color Society. Edgar Ewing moved to Los Angeles after World War II and began exhibiting with the California Water Color Society in the 1950s. He was the Society president in 1954. His watercolors are bold and abstract, depicting subjects from all over the world and often drawn from his extensive travels in North Africa and Europe. He taught art at the Chicago Art Institute and the University of Southern California.
Biographical information:
Interview with Edgar Ewing, 1983.

**Justin Faivre** (1902-1990) Born: Matthews, IN; Studied: Portland Art Gallery; Member: Society of Western Artists. Justin Faivre studied art in Oregon and then in 1923, moved to Los Angeles. By the late 1920s, he was a Bay Area resident and continued to exhibit there throughout his life.
Biographical information:
*Artists in California, 1786-1940.*

**Edward M. Farmer** (1901-1980) Born: Los Angeles, CA; Studied: Stanford University, Rudolph Schaeffer School of Design, Art Students League (New York); Member: California Water Color Society. Edward Farmer was a resident of Palo Alto and worked as a teacher at Stanford University starting in 1923. In the 1930s and 1940s, he exhibited watercolors in California and New York.
Biographical information:
*Who's Who in American Art.*

**Alfred Villiers Farnsworth** (1858-1908) Born: England. Alfred Farnsworth moved to San Francisco in 1892 and worked as a staff artist for the *Examiner* newspaper. Primarily a watercolorist, Farnsworth produced numerous works for his newspaper job and for sale as fine art at Bay Area galleries.
Biographical information:
*Artists in California, 1786-1940.*

**June Felter** (1919- ) Born: Oakland, CA; Studied: California College of Arts and Crafts (Oakland), California School of Fine Arts (San Francisco), Oakland Art Institute. June Felter studied art in the 1930s and then took further instruction from Richard Diebenkorn in the early 1960s. In addition to exhibiting watercolors, she has worked as a portrait painter and has taught art at the University of California in San Francisco.
Biographical information:
*Who's Who in American Art.*

**Eva Scott Fenyes** (1846-1930) Born: New York City, NY. Eva Scott Fenyes moved to California in the 1890s. Charles Lummis, founder of the Southwest Museum, encouraged her to paint watercolors of historically important buildings that included missions and adobe houses. She traveled throughout California and produced three hundred and one watercolors which were donated to the museum in the 1930s.
Biographical information:
*Artists of the American West.*

**Blair Field** (active in 1940s) Studied: Chouinard Art Institute (Los Angeles); Member: California Water Color Society. Blair Field studied with Millard Sheets during the 1930s in Los Angeles. She has exhibited watercolors in the Los Angeles and Orange County areas since the late 1930s and has worked as an art teacher. She often signed her early works "Blair".
Biographical information:
California Water Color Society (Catalogs).

**Keith Finch** (1920- ) Born: Holyoke, CO; Member: California Water Color Society. Keith Finch, a resident of Southern California in the 1950s and 1960s, exhibited watercolors on a national level during that period. His works in the California Water Color Society annual shows were abstract. He also worked as an art instructor in the Los Angeles area.
Biographical information:
*Who's Who in American Art*
California Water Color Society (Catalogs).

**Mary L. Finley** (1908-1964) Born: San Francisco, CA; Studied: University of California (Berkeley); Member: California Water Color Society. Mary L. Finley studied with Hans Hofmann and then worked as an illustrator and designer in Southern California. She exhibited her watercolors with the California Water Color Society from 1939 to 1953 and taught art at the University of California in 1948. Later works were signed with her married name of Mary Finley Fry.
Biographical information:
*Who's Who in American Art.*

**Mary Stevens Fish** (1842-1894) Born: Sidney Plains, NY. Mary Stevens Fish studied art in New York and moved to California in 1875. She continued studying art with New Yorker Henry Chapman Ford and eventually set up a studio in Santa Barbara where she produced watercolors and taught art. From 1886 to 1893, she worked out of Los Angeles, before retiring to the Santa Barbara area.
Biographical information:
*Artists in California, 1786-1940.*

**Hugo Anton Fisher** (1854-1916) Born: Kladno, Czechoslovakia; Member: San Francisco Art Association. Hugo Anton Fisher studied art in Prague before immigrating to America in 1874. By 1886, he was living in Northern California and had a studio in San Francisco. Fisher was primarily a watercolorist and often painted landscape subjects.
Biographical information:
*Artists in California ,1786-1940.*

**James Fitzgerald** (1899-1971) Born: Milton, MA; Studied: Massachusetts School of Art, Boston Museum School of Art; Member: California Water Color Society, Carmel Art Association. James Fitzgerald lived in Monterey from the early 1930s to the mid-1940s. His watercolors depict the Monterey Peninsula area and were exhibited with the California Water Color Society. He was involved with a number

EYVIND EARLE *Industry* 1960s 30" x 22" Private Collection

JADE FON  *Sunday on the Bay*  1960  22" x 29"  Pam Della Collection

JADE FON  *China Town*  1950s  22" x 29"  Diane Dodds Collection

of W.P.A. projects, including a large mural for the Los Angeles County Fairgrounds. He moved to Monhegan Island off the coast of Maine in the 1940s and continued to paint both watercolors and oils.
Biographical information:
*Monterey: The Artist's View* (Catalog).

**Jade Fon** (1911-1983) Born: San Jose, CA; Studied: University of Arizona, Art Students League (Los Angeles); Member: American Watercolor Society, California Water Color Society. Jade Fon grew up in Winslow, Arizona. During the 1930s, he moved to Los Angeles where he continued his education at the Art Students League and exhibited his paintings as a member of the California Water Color Society.

After the mid-1940s, he lived in the San Francisco area. Between 1940 and 1955, he also worked as a night club entertainer and occasionally produced commercial illustrations. In the 1970s, he was an art instructor and founder of a highly successful watercolor workshop in Asilomar.
Biographical information:
Interview with Jade Fon, 1982.

**Henry Chapman Ford** (1828-1894) Born: Livonia, NY. After studying art in Europe, serving in the Civil War and developing an art career in Chicago, Henry Chapman Ford moved to Santa Barbara in 1875. During the last twenty years of his life he traveled to Mission sites in California and produced watercolors and drawings depicting each site. These were also translated into etchings and serve as important historical documents of California's history.
Biographical information:
Studio 2 Antiques, Santa Barbara, 1983.

**James Harrison Forman** (1910-1969) Born: San Francisco, CA; Member: San Francisco Art Association. James Forman was raised in San Francisco and received art instruction from Frank Van Sloan, Maynard Dixon and Charles Henry Grant.

After art school, he began working as a commercial illustrator. During the 1930s, he worked out of a studio in San Francisco. In the early 1940s, he was employed by the Lawrence Studio in New York City producing illustrations for major magazines. In the mid-1940s, he returned to the West Coast and settled in San Francisco. After setting up a freelance commercial art business, he began producing watercolor illustrations for *Woman's Home Companion*, *American Home* and *Parents* magazines. Other prominent accounts included Chevrolet, Pan American Airways and Pacific Gas and Electric.

Throughout his life, Forman also painted fine art watercolors that he exhibited in the Bay Area. He was a founding member of the Thirteen Watercolorists and occasionally taught painting. Most of his watercolors were Regionalist style works depicting cityscape, industrial and landscape subjects.
Biographical information:
David Howard Fine Arts, Mill Valley, 1990
Jessica H. Fullmer, 1998.

**Erwin J. Fox** (1928- ) Born: Chicago, IL; Studied: Chicago Art Institute, Bradley University, University of Illinois; Member: Laguna Beach Art Association. Erwin Fox grew up in Chicago. After serving in the United States Marine Corps, he moved to Southern California. He worked as an architect and after receiving watercolor instruction from Rex Brandt in the 1950s, began exhibiting watercolors in Laguna Beach.
Biographical information:
Interview with Erwin J. Fox, 1996.

**Robert Frame** (1924-1999) Born: San Fernando, CA; Studied: Pomona College (California), Claremont Graduate School (California). Robert Frame was a student of Henry Lee McFee in the late 1940s. Early in his career he produced gouache paintings of still life subjects. Since the 1960s, he has been primarily known as an oil painter, exhibiting on a national level. Frame taught art at a number of schools including Otis Art Institute, University of Southern California, Scripps College, Claremont College and Santa Barbara City College.
Biographical information:
Stary-Sheets Fine Art Galleries, Laguna Beach, 1997.

**Sam Francis** (1923-1995) Born: San Mateo, CA; Studied: University of California, (Berkeley), Académie Fernand Léger (Paris). Sam Francis grew up in Northern California and at the age of eighteen began attending the University of California, Berkeley. In 1943, he went into the United States Army Air Corps and during World War II, injured his spinal cord. During his recovery, he became interested in producing art. Upon his release in 1945, Francis studied with David Park for a while and then went on to earn a Masters of Fine Art degree from the University of California, Berkeley. He spent the early 1950s studying in Paris at the Académie Fernand Léger and traveling through the Orient. After this, he settled in Santa Monica, California.

Prior to 1961, the majority of his works were oils on canvas. Gradually he began using gouache and watercolors on paper. As the years went by, he began to use this medium on a regular basis. His works are non-objective art and he was not affiliated with any art groups or organizations. Instead he chose to quietly pursue his individual approach to modern art and send out works to be shown in museums and galleries throughout the world.

After the 1960s, he was one of the most famous California artists regularly using the watercolor medium. His works of art are in the permanent collections of numerous museums and galleries including the Guggenheim Museum, the Museum of Modern Art, the Albright Art Gallery in New York City and the Tate Museum in London.
Biographical information:
*Art USA Now*.

**Marshall Frantz** (1890- ) Born: Kiev, Russia; Studied: Philadelphia Museum School of Industrial Art; Member: Society of Illustrators. Marshall Frantz received his art education in Pennsylvania and then settled in Van Nuys, California. He was primarily known for his watercolor and gouache illustrations, that often depicted people. His works were reproduced in many well known magazines including *The Saturday Evening Post*, *Cosmopolitan*, *Harper's Bazaar*, *Collier's*, *Liberty* and *The Delineator*.
Biographical information:
*Who Was Who in American Art*.

**Michael Frary** (1918- ) Born: Santa Monica, CA; Studied: University of Southern California, Chicago Art Institute, Académie de la Grande Chaumiére (Paris); Member: California Water Color Society, Southwestern Watercolor Society, Texas Watercolor Society. Michael Frary became interested in watercolor painting after meeting Dan Lutz, who was an art teacher at the University of Southern California. By 1941, when Frary earned his Master of Fine Arts degree in painting, he was already exhibiting watercolors. After a summer of study in Chicago, he returned to Los Angeles and worked as an art director in the motion picture industry. Frary taught landscape painting at the Chouinard Art Institute and in the late 1940s, he traveled to France for an additional year of study.

Throughout this period he was producing watercolors which were mostly abstractions, based on cityscape and still life subjects. He also did some non-objective works featuring opaque watercolors. These works were among the first abstract paintings to be accepted for exhibition in the California Water Color Society and other Southern California annual art shows.

In the 1960s, he continued to exhibit in California, but was living in Texas and teaching at the University of Texas in Austin. He became one of that states premier watercolorists and has written and illustrated three books based on his impressions of Texas landscape subjects. Frary has presented 202 one-man shows and received some 150 awards for his paintings.
Biographical information:
Interview with Michael Frary, 1983.

**Will Frates** (1893-1969) Born: Hayward, CA; Member: Society of Western Artists. Will Frates lived in Hayward during the 1940s and 1950s and exhibited his transparent watercolor paintings with the Society of Western Artists. He was also on the jury for those shows. Many of his works were American Scene paintings, that often included views of old houses in small towns and villages.
Biographical information:
Society of Western Artists (Catalogs).

**Priscilla Frazer** (1907-1973) Born: Battle Creek, MI; Studied: Académie de la Grande Chaumiére (Paris); Member: California Water Color Society. Priscilla Frazer lived in South Laguna and became a member of the California Water Color Society in 1930. She was an active member of the Laguna Beach Art Association and taught art at Orange Coast College.
Biographical information:
*Who's Who in American Art.*

**James Fuller** (1927- ) Born: Pierre, SD; Studied: University of California (Berkeley); Member: California Water Color Society. James Fuller began exhibiting abstract watercolors in the 1950s and has since been included in important museum shows on a national level. He has taught art at the University of California campuses at Berkeley and Davis, California State University, Los Angeles, and at Scripps College in Claremont.
Biographical information:
*Southern California 100* (Catalog).

**Karoly Fulop** (1893-1963) Born: Czabadka, Hungary; Member: California Water Color Society. Karoly Fulop studied art in Budapest, Munich and Paris before immigrating to New York in the 1920s. By the 1930s, he was a Los Angeles resident. Fulop produced watercolors with a flat pattern, Byzantine style. He exhibited on the West Coast through the 1950s.
Biographical information:
*Artists in California, 1786-1940.*

**Jane Greene Gale** (1898-1987) Born: Leipzig, Germany; Studied: Minneapolis School of Art, Art Students League (New York), Columbia University; Member: California Water Color Society. Jane Gale studied art with Hans Hofmann, Jean Charlot and Dong Kingman. She taught art in Florida and Ohio in the 1920s and early 1930s and then became a teacher at Fresno State College in 1935. She exhibited her watercolors in the annual California Water Color Society shows until the mid-1950s.
Biographical information:
*Who's Who in American Art.*

**John Gamble** (1863-1957) Born: Morristown, NJ; Studied: California School of Design (San Francisco), Académie Julian (Paris); Member: San Francisco Art Association, Santa Barbara Art Association. John Gamble grew up in New Zealand. At the age of twenty, he moved to San Francisco. He received art instruction from Virgil Williams and Emil Carlsen and continued his studies in Paris, France with Laurens and Constant. In the 1890s and early 1900s, he exhibited watercolors on a regular basis in San Francisco art exhibitions. After his studio and contents were burned and destroyed in the 1906 earthquake and fire, he exhibited oil paintings featuring landscape subjects and produced commissioned portraits.
Biographical information:
*Artists in California, 1786-1940.*

**Bernard Garbutt** (1900-1975) Born: Ontario, CA. Bernard Garbutt was born in Southern California and grew up in the Los Angeles area. After finishing high school, he was hired as a staff artist for the *Los Angeles Times* to cover county fairs, horse races and farming events to produce drawings for the Sunday supplements.

Garbutt was an extremely versatile artist. He wrote and illustrated a number of children's books, including *Timothy the Deer*. The Walt Disney Studios employed him to work on the animated film productions of *Snow White and the Seven Dwarfs* and *Bambi*. During World War II he was an artist for Screen Gems Productions in Hollywood and during the 1950s and 1960s, he taught at the Chouinard Art Institute.
Biographical information:
Interview with Janice Lovoos Garbutt, 1983.

**Julian E. Garnsey** (1887-1969) Born: New York City, NY; Studied: Harvard University, Art Students League (New York), Académie Julian (Paris); Member: California Water Color Society, California Art Club, Architectural League of New York. Julian E. Garnsey grew up on the East Coast and by the age of eighteen, was assisting his father Elmer on commissioned mural projects. He attended Harvard University

FRANK J. GAVENCKY  *The Stairs*  1930s  18" x 24"  Michael Johnson Fine Arts

FRANK J. GAVENCKY  *Market Scene*  1940s  16" x 24"  Michael Johnson Fine Arts

**GEORGE GIBSON**  *Toward Bunker Hill*  1946  22" x 30"  Michael Johnson Collection

**GEORGE GIBSON**  *Soledad Crossing*  1950s  22" x 30"  Knowles Collection

studying Architectural Design and then continued his art studies in Paris, France with Jean Paul Laurens and Richard Miller. Upon his return to New York City, he attended the Art Students League from 1915 to 1917 and became president of that art school.

During World War I, he served as Captain of Field Artillery and was awarded for his war efforts. After the war, he moved to Los Angeles where he worked for M.G.M. Studios and exhibited watercolors. He also produced murals and decorative art in public and private buildings.

In the late 1920s, he became an active member of the California Water Color Society and served as president in 1929. By the late 1930s, he was back in New York City supervising color schemes and decoration for the World's Fair. In the 1940s, he was an Associate Professor in Princeton University's School of Architecture. While living in California and later in Princeton, Garnsey produced watercolors depicting subjects ranging from local landscapes to European scenes.
Biographical information:
*Who's Who in American Art*
Century Association Memorial.

**Frank Gavencky** (1888-1966) Born: Chicago, IL; Studied: Chicago Academy of Fine Art; Member: Palette and Chisel Club, Bohemian Club. After developing a successful art career in Chicago, Frank Gavencky began spending extended periods of time in California. His opaque watercolors from the 1930s and 1940s depict a wide variety of subjects, including pastoral settings, cityscapes and marketplace scenes around Los Angeles. In the late 1940s, he settled in Southern California and spent the remainder of his life producing large scale oil paintings.
Biographical information:
*Who's Who in American Art.*

**William Gaw** (1891-1973) Born: San Francisco, CA; Studied: Mark Hopkins Institute of Art (San Francisco); Member: California Water Color Society, San Francisco Art Association, Bohemian Club. William Gaw began exhibiting his paintings with the California Water Color Society in the late 1920s. His paintings were bold and colorful modern works that were influenced by the European Cubists and Expressionists. He was acting director of the California School of Fine Arts in the 1940s and chairman of the art department at Mills College in the 1940s and 1950s.
Biographical information:
*William Gaw* (Catalog).

**Robert George** (1928-1999) Born: Chino, CA; Studied: University of Redlands (California), Harvard University, Claremont Graduate School (California); Member: California Water Color Society. Robert George grew up in Southern California and studied art with Millard Sheets and Henry Lee McFee. In the late 1940s, he began exhibiting watercolors and received notoriety for his colorful abstract and non-objective works. George taught art in the 1950s and has served as President of the Pomona Valley Art Association and Director of the Chaffey Community Art Museum.
Biographical information:
Interview with Robert George, 1995.

**Milton Gershgoren** (1909-1989) Born: Russia; Studied: Pennsylvania Academy of Fine Arts, Otis Art Institute (Los Angeles), Jepson Art Institute (Los Angeles); Member: California Water Color Society. Milton Gershgoren settled in California in the late 1930s. While serving in the United States Army, he produced a series of watercolors depicting military life. After that he worked in more abstract and expressionistic styles, using transparent watercolors. Gershgoren also worked as a commercial illustrator, printmaker and art teacher.
Biographical information:
Interview with Milton Gershgoren, 1984.

**George Gibson, N.A.** (1904-2001) Born: Edinburgh, Scotland; Studied: Edinburgh College of Art, Glasgow School of Art, Chouinard Art Institute (Los Angeles); Member: National Academy of Design, American Watercolor Society, California Water Color Society. George Gibson grew up in Northern Scotland. In 1930, he emigrated from Scotland to the United States and settled in Los Angeles where he continued his art education with F. Tolles Chamberlin. After serving in the United States Marine Corps in World War II, he began to exhibit his watercolor paintings on a professional level. Since then, he has taken painting trips to many remote areas of the state and become nationally recognized for his representational depictions of the California landscape.

Gibson worked as an artist in the motion picture industry for thirty-five years. He started as a painter of storyboard illustrations and eventually became head of the scenic art department at M.G.M. Studios. In the late 1940s, he was on the board of the California Water Color Society and in 1951 was the Society's president.
Biographical information:
Interview with George Gibson, 1983.

**Robert Gilberg** (1911-1970) Born: Oakland, CA; Studied: Sierra College; Member: California Water Color Society. Robert Gilberg began exhibiting watercolors during the early 1940s in shows throughout California. He also produced illustrations for books and taught art classes in Northern California.
Biographical information:
*Who's Who in American Art.*

**Selden Conner Gile** (1877-1947) Born: Stowe, ME; Studied: California School of Arts and Crafts (Oakland); Member: Oakland Art League. Selden Gile moved to Northern California in 1903 and worked as a bookkeeper until 1927. From the late 1920s until the early 1940s, he was the leader of a Bay Area group named the Society of Six that included Maurice Logan among its members. He painted landscapes that usually included buildings, animals or figures. He exhibited with "The Six" and at local San Francisco art galleries.
Biographical information:
*Society of Six* (Catalog).

**John Giuliani** (1909- ) Born: San Francisco, CA; Studied: California School of Fine Arts (San Francisco), Academy of Advertising Art (San Francisco); Member: Marin Society of Artists. John Giuliani grew up in San Francisco and from 1927 until 1942, was employed as an artist at Traung Label

and Lithograph Company. From 1942 until the mid-1970s, he worked as a freelance commercial illustrator in the Bay Area and occasionally produced works for exhibition. Throughout his career, Giuliani worked primarily with watercolor and gouache.
Biographical information:
Interview with John Giuliani, 1978.

**J. Duncan Gleason** (1881-1959) Born: Watsonville, CA; Studied: University of Southern California, Mark Hopkins Institute of Art (San Francisco), Chicago Art Institute, Art Students League (New York); Member: California Art Club, Painters and Sculptors Club. Duncan Gleason was raised in Los Angeles. After receiving formal art instruction from Frank Vincent DuMond and John H. Vanderpoel in New York City, he moved back to Southern California and began producing illustrations for nationally distributed magazines including *Ladies Home Journal*, *Cosmopolitan*, *Good Housekeeping* and *Motor Boating*. He often used watercolor and gouache to produce these and other book illustrations. In addition to producing commercial art and studio art for Warner Brothers Studios and M.G.M. Studios, Gleason received numerous awards for his easel paintings and was an active leader in the Los Angeles area art community. He was also a well-known author of books relating to California sailing history.
Biographical information:
Interview with Dorothy Gleason, 1978.

**Gerald Gleeson** (1915-1986) Born: Providence, RI; Studied: Rhode Island School of Design, Mexico City College, California College of Arts and Crafts (Oakland); Member: Allied Artists of America. Gerald Gleeson grew up in Rhode Island and attended art school there in the late 1930s. After serving in World War II, he studied art with Jerry Farnsworth in Massachusetts and spent a year in Mexico before settling in Berkeley, California.

His watercolors from the 1940s and 1950s depict city street scenes, wharfs and bridges in the Oakland area. In addition to painting and exhibiting on a regular basis, Gleeson taught painting and drawing in the Bay Area.
Biographical information:
Interview with Gerald Gleeson, 1983.

**George Henry Goddard** (1817-1906) Born: Bristol, England; Studied: Oxford University. George Goddard immigrated to Northern California to join the Gold Rush of 1850. He ended up applying his art background as a map maker and watercolorist depicting mining camps and rural towns. Many of his works were destroyed in the 1906 earthquake and fire.
Biographical information:
*Artists in California, 1786-1940*.

**Ralph Goings** (1928- ) Born: Corning, CA; Studied: California College of Arts and Crafts (Oakland), Sacramento State College. Ralph Goings studied art in Oakland during the early 1950s and then took a teaching job in Crescent City. In 1959, he became chairman of the art department at La Sierra High School in Carmichael and in the mid-1960s, earned a Master's degree from Sacramento State College.

During the 1960s, he produced photo realist works. Some were painted with watercolors, others were oils on canvas. In 1970, he began receiving international recognition for these works after exhibiting at the O.K. Harris Gallery in New York City. His works are in numerous museum collections including the Museum of Modern Art in New York, the Museum of Contemporary Art in Chicago and the Kunstverien in Germany. Goings taught art at California State University, Sacramento and University of California, Davis, in the early 1970s. Since then he has resided in New York.
Biographical information:
*Who's Who in American Art*.

**Leon Goldin** (1923- ) Born: Chicago, IL; Studied: Chicago Art Institute, University of Iowa. Leon Goldin lived in California during the 1950s and taught at the California College of Arts and Crafts in Oakland. During this period, he exhibited gouache paintings with abstract subject matter at the Los Angeles County Art Museum and at the Oakland Art Museum. In addition, he had several one-man exhibitions at the Felix Landau Gallery in Los Angeles.
Biographical information:
*Who's Who in American Art*
Los Angeles County Art Museum (Catalogs).

**Fred Gordon** (active in 1950s) Born: Cleveland, OH; Studied: University of Michigan. Fred Gordon was raised in Michigan then moved to Northern California after World War II. He worked as a commercial artist for the state of California in the 1950s and has exhibited watercolors on the West Coast. Gordon has also taught painting in California and Oregon.
Biographical information:
*Fred Gordon* (Catalog).

**Henry Gorham** (1872-1936) Born: Vallejo, CA; Studied: Art Students League (New York). Henry Gorham studied art with George Bridgman in New York and then began a long career as a commercial artist being employed by lithograph companies in New York and San Francisco. About 1915, he settled at the Schmidt Lithograph Company in San Francisco where he was an art director. In addition to producing thousands of watercolor illustrations, Gorham also exhibited landscape paintings at local art exhibitions.
Biographical information:
Interview with Pat Jacobsen, 1995.

**Virginia Belle Gould** (1917- ) Born: Sheridan, WY; Studied: University of California (Berkeley); Member: San Francisco Art Association. Virginia Belle Gould received some basic art history from her mother and then went on to study with Worth Ryder and John Haley at the University of California, Berkeley.

By the 1940s, she was exhibiting her stylized, Berkeley School watercolors in San Francisco art exhibitions. Since that time, Gould has lived in several regions of Northern California and continues to produce watercolor paintings. Gould taught art at the University of California, Davis for ten years.
Biographical information:
Interview with Virginia Belle Gould, 1984.

HARDIE GRAMATKY  *Hollywood*  1944  16" x 20"  McClelland Collection

HARDIE GRAMATKY  *Running from the Park*  1930s  15" x 22"  David Tonnemacher

PERCY GRAY  *Poppies and Lupines*  1929  16" x 22"  George Stern Fine Arts

PERCY GRAY  *Oak Tree and Poppies*  1920s  12" x 15"  Joan Irvine Smith Collection

**Elsie H. Grace** (1921- ) Born: Mount Clemens, MI; Studied: Society of Art and Crafts (Detroit); Member: Watercolor West. Elsie Grace has been painting watercolors since she was a teenager growing up in Michigan. After high school she received a scholarship and studied art in Detroit. During the 1940s, she got married and moved to Los Angeles. Grace worked as an artist producing posters and display graphics. She continued her art studies with James Couper Wright and then in the 1950s, began teaching art in the Alhambra area and in later years, in Yucca Valley.
Biographical information:
Interview with Elsie H. Grace, 1996.

**Charles S. Graham** (1852-1911) Born: Rock Island, IL; Member: San Francisco Art Association, Bohemian Club. Charles Graham was a self-taught commercial illustrator and did work as a scenic artist for the theater in New York City. By the 1880s, he was producing illustrations for *Harper's Weekly* and other nationally distributed magazines. Although he traveled regularly, Graham kept a studio in San Francisco during the 1880s and 1890s. He exhibited works in local Bay Area art exhibits and worked as an artist for the California Midwinter Fair.
Biographical information:
*Artists in California, 1786-1940.*

**Hardie Gramatky, N.A.** (1907-1979) Born: Dallas, TX; Studied: Stanford University, Chouinard Art Institute (Los Angeles); Member: National Academy of Design, New York Water Color Club, American Watercolor Society, California Water Color Society. Hardie Gramatky was raised in Southern California. He studied art with F. Tolles Chamberlin, Clarence Hinkle, Pruett Carter and Barse Miller. A dedicated student of watercolor painting, he produced an average of five small watercolors per day. By 1929, he had become a proficient watercolorist and was recognized as one of the true innovators in the development of California Style watercolor painting. These skills helped him to get a job as a senior animator at the Walt Disney Studios.

In the early 1930s, he became active on the board of the California Water Color Society and it was largely through his aggressive moves that the California School of watercolorists was able to take control of the Society and expand it into a nationally recognized organization. In 1937 the Ferargil Gallery became his art agent in New York City and began selling his watercolors. He also exhibited works in other cities in America and established a reputation as one of California's premier watercolorists.

By the 1940s, he was producing commercial art to be used for magazine illustrations and began writing and illustrating a series of children's books. *Hercules, Loopy, Creepers Jeep* and *Sparkey's* were all books he created, but *Little Toot* was the one that would become an all-time best seller. During World War II, he worked in Hollywood producing training films for the United States Air Force and after the war, moved permanently to the East Coast.

Settling in Connecticut he pursued a career as a commercial illustrator producing art for *Fortune, Collier's, Woman's Day, True, American* and *Reader's Digest*.
Biographical information:
Interview with Dorothy Gramatky, 1983.

**Gordon Grant, A.N.A.** (1875-1962) Born: San Francisco, CA; Studied: Lambeth and Heatherley Art School (London); Member: National Academy of Design (Associate), American Watercolor Society Philadelphia Water Color Club. Gordon Grant grew up in California, studied art in London, England, then worked as an illustrator in New York City and San Francisco. He is known for producing watercolors depicting marine subjects and wharf scenes.
Biographical information:
*Who's Who in American Art.*

**Ed Graves** (active in 1950s) Studied: School of Allied Arts (Glendale); Member: American Watercolor Society, California Water Color Society. During the 1940s Ed Graves received instruction in fine art painting and commercial illustration from Stan and Cort Parkhouse in Glendale, California. Throughout the 1950s and 1960s, he exhibited his transparent watercolor paintings and worked as an art director at Twentieth Century-Fox Studios. In addition, he produced freelance commercial illustrations.
Biographical information:
Interview with Frank Ackerman and Noel Quinn, 1984.

**Percy Gray** (1869-1952) Born: San Francisco, CA; Studied: California School of Design (San Francisco), Art Students League (New York); Member: Society of Western Artists, Bohemian Club, Society for Sanity in Art. Percy Gray was born and raised in Northern California. His family was interested in art and music and around 1885, he began studies at the California School of Design. His instructors were Emil Carlsen, Virgil Williams and Raymond Yelland. For several years, he worked as an illustrator for a San Francisco newspaper and then moved to the East Coast to work for the *New York Journal*. While in New York he received additional art instruction from William Merritt Chase at the Art Students League.

In 1906, when San Francisco experienced the earthquake and devastating fire, Gray returned to the Bay Area to report on events. He chose to stay in San Francisco and worked for the *San Francisco Examiner*. He exhibited watercolors in local art exhibitions and sold art through private galleries.

During the first decade of this century, Gray developed a classic representational style of watercolor painting and continued to use this approach throughout his career. He was an expert watercolorist and chose a wide variety of subjects to paint. Most were depictions of California landscape subjects ranging from seascapes and coastal views to inland valley scenes and the Sierra Nevada mountains. On occasion, he produced portraits and on vacations in Southern California and Arizona, he painted watercolors depicting landscape subjects in these regions.

He spent most of his life in Northern California, but moved around a number of times. During various periods, he resided in San Francisco, Alameda, Burlingame, Monterey and San Anselmo. While in Monterey, he was given a major show at the Del Monte Gallery. When modern art began dominating the San Francisco art scene in the 1930s, he found support from the traditionally minded Bohemian Club art exhibitions. In later years, he was a member of the Society for Sanity in Art and participated in their annual shows.

Although he received only modest acclaim from the

Northern California art community during his lifetime, Gray is now considered a major figure in California watercolor painting of the 1920s and his works are included in nearly every important show of California "Plein air" art.
Biographical information:
Alfred C. Harrison, Jr.
North Point Gallery, San Francisco, 1998.

**James Green** (1911-   ) Born: Ware, MA; Studied: Massachusetts School of Art, Otis Art Institute (Los Angeles); Member: California Water Color Society. James Green studied art with Barse Miller and Paul Clemens in the early 1930s. During that period he developed a bold, expressive style of watercolor painting and became an active member of the California Water Color Society. Since the early 1940s, he has been an art instructor at Principia College in Illinois.
Biographical information:
Interview with James Green, 1994.

**Michael Green** (1946-1992) Born: California; Studied: Utah State University, Art Center School (Los Angeles); Member: California Water Color Society, West Coast Watercolor Society. After studying art in Utah and Los Angeles, Michael Green moved to Northern California. He began exhibiting watercolors in the early 1960s and received numerous awards in Bay Area exhibitions through the 1970s. Green also worked as an art instructor, illustrator and gallery director.
Biographical information:
West Coast Watercolor Society (Catalogs).

**Lucille Brown Greene** (1903-1986) Born: Los Angeles, CA; Studied: University of California (Los Angeles); Member: California Water Color Society. Lucille Brown Greene studied to be an artist and educator in the late 1940s. Her art instructors were Stanton MacDonald-Wright, Millard Sheets and Richard Haines. Throughout the 1950s and 1960s, she actively exhibited watercolors in annual art exhibitions on a national level. She also served on the board and jury of the California Water Color Society and taught art at Santa Monica City College.
Biographical information:
*Who's Who in American Art.*

**Herald Gretzner** (1902-1977) Born: Baltimore, MD; Studied: California College of Arts and Crafts (Oakland); Member: American Watercolor Society, California Water Color Society, West Coast Watercolor Society, Society of Western Artists. Harold Gretzner grew up in the eastern United States and attended art school in Washington, D.C. before moving to California in the 1920s. After settling in the Bay Area, he studied fine art in Oakland and lithography in San Francisco.

For over thirty years, he followed a routine. In the predawn morning, providing the weather cooperated, he would wake up and drive toward his workplace in San Francisco. Somewhere along the way, he would stop and paint a watercolor, usually depicting a cityscape or harbor view. He was exclusively a watercolorist and worked only with transparent paints. His style featured a controlled wet-into-wet approach, inspired by his close friend and painting partner, Maurice Logan.

Gretzner was a prolific painter and exhibited from the 1930s to the 1970s. He was a member of the Thirteen Watercolorists, and became a founding member of the West Coast Watercolor Society. On the East Coast, he exhibited in the annual American Watercolor Society shows. Unfortunately a large number of Gretzner's watercolors were destroyed in a fire that swept through Oakland, California.

For most of his life, Gretzner worked as a commercial lithographer in San Francisco. After retiring from this job in the 1960s, he continued painting and taught small groups of advanced students in the Oakland area.
Biographical information:
Interview with Teckla Gretzner, 1983.

**John Grillo** (1917-   ) Born: Lawrence, MA; Studied: Hartford Art School, California School of Fine Arts (San Francisco), Hans Hofmann School of Fine Art. John Grillo studied art in Eastern America and then served in the military during World War II. From 1946 until 1950, he resided in San Francisco where he continued his art studies. During this period, he became known as one of the first artists on the West Coast to aggressively pursue Abstract Expressionist painting. Some of these works were produced using gouache, watercolor and water based poster paints. After 1950, he taught art and pursued an art career on the East Coast.
Biographical information:
*Who's Who in American Art*
*On the Edge of America, California Modernist Art.*

**Daniel Sayre Groesbeck** (1878-1950) Born: San Francisco, CA; Studied: Chouinard Art Institute (Los Angeles); Member: California Water Color Society. Daniel Sayre Groesbeck grew up in Southern California. He became an illustrator for local newspaper publications at the turn of the century and was sent to cover the Russo-Japanese conflict in 1904. His illustrations appeared in the *Illustrated London News* and other important publications.

Upon his return to Los Angeles he began producing sketches and costume studies as pre-production art for epic films by Cecil B. DeMille. Groesbeck's powerful drawings are sited as having an influence on the overall look of the films and in particular, for providing authenticity to the production by supplying extremely accurate depictions of how the costumes should look.

For many years, he sold drawings with watercolor washes added to them. Some were sold through art galleries in Los Angeles and others were sold directly to fellow employees in the motion picture industry. They often were figurative works of Russian peasants, based on the poster-like illustrations he did while on assignment in Russia.

Groesbeck also taught painting and composition classes at the Chouinard Art Institute.
Biographical information:
*Drawings and Illustrations by Southern California Artists* (Catalog).

**Richard Haines** (1906-1984) Born: Marion, IA; Studied: Minneapolis School of Art, Ecole des Beaux Arts (Paris); Member: California Water Color Society. Richard Haines attended art school in Minnesota in the early 1930s and received a scholarship to continue his studies in Europe.

HAROLD GRETZNER *Bus Depot, Oakland* 1950s 22" x 30" Jeff Olsen Collection

JAMES GREEN *Fishermen* 1940s 22" x 30" Goldstein Collection

JOHN HALEY  *Berkeley Train Depot*  1938  16" x 22"  California Art Gallery

JOHN HALEY  *Richmond Ferry Boat*  1930s  16" x 22"  Hilbert Collection

Upon returning to the Minneapolis School of Art, he taught for several years. In the early 1940s, he moved to California and settled in Santa Monica.

In addition to painting, he produced prints, murals, and sculptures. From 1945 to 1954, he taught at the Chouinard Art Institute and from 1954 to 1974, at the Otis Art Institute. Haines was president of the California Water Color Society in 1950.
Biographical information:
Interview with Richard Haines, 1983.

**John Haley** (1905-1991) Born: Minneapolis, MN; Studied: Minneapolis School of Art, Hans Hofmann School of Fine Art; Member: California Water Color Society, San Francisco Art Association. John Haley studied art during the late 1920s with Cameron Booth in Minneapolis and Hans Hofmann in Munich and Capri. He returned to teach in Minnesota for several years and then moved to California where he became an art professor at the University of California, Berkeley.

During the 1930s and 1940s, he was a key artist in the development of the Berkeley School style of watercolor painting. From the mid-1950s he concentrated on working with oil paints and produced large abstract expressionistic works of art. In addition, Haley did lithographs, dioramas, stained glass window designs and fresco murals.
Biographical information:
Interview with John Haley, 1983.

**Clem Hall** (1913-   ) Born: Lowestoft, England; Studied: Academy of Advertising Art (San Francisco), Art Center School (Los Angeles); Member: American Watercolor Society, California Water Color Society. Clem Hall grew up in San Mateo. He was awarded a scholarship to study art in San Francisco and then in the 1930s, moved to Los Angeles where he received additional instruction from Stanley Reckless and Joseph Henninger. He than began producing representational American Scene works that depicted Southern California cityscapes. Hall was president of the California Water Color Society in 1963. Since the 1930s, he has worked as an artist for Columbia, M.G.M., and Paramount studios.
Biographical information:
Interview with Clem Hall, 1985.

**William Haines Hall** (1903-1977) Born: Springfield, MO; Studied: California School of Fine Arts (San Francisco). William Hall started work as a commercial artist in San Francisco during the late 1920s. He was a member of the Thirteen Watercolorists and exhibited watercolors in the Bay Area.
Biographical information:
*Artists in California, 1786-1940*.

**Frank Hamilton** (1930-1999) Born: Kansas City, MO; Studied: Stanford University; Member: California Water Color Society. Frank Hamilton earned a degree in architecture and studied watercolor painting with Eliot O'Hara. From the 1940s through 1970, he exhibited his watercolors in one-man shows in Laguna Beach and New York City.
Biographical information:
Challis Galleries, Laguna Beach (Catalog).

**Leah Rinne Hamilton** (1906-1960) Born: Finland; Studied: University of California (Berkeley); Member: San Francisco Art Association, San Francisco Women Artists. Leah Rinne Hamilton was chairman of the art department at Dominican College in San Rafael from 1930 to 1942. During this period she exhibited her watercolors in San Francisco and Oakland. In 1939, she was included in *The Fourteen Bay Area Watercolorists* show at the San Francisco Museum of Art.
Biographical information:
*Who's Who in American Art*.

**Ejnar Hansen** (1884-1965) Born: Copenhagen, Denmark; Studied: Royal Academy of Art (Copenhagen); Member: California Water Color Society, American Watercolor Society. Ejnar Hansen emigrated from Denmark to the United States in 1914 and after several years in the Midwest, moved to California and settled in Pasadena. He was an active member of the California Water Color Society from the 1930s to the 1950s and was Society president in 1940. He was also an art instructor.
Biographical information:
*Southern California Art*.

**Herman W. Hansen** (1854-1924) Born: Dithmarschen, Germany; Studied: Chicago Art Institute. Herman Hansen studied art in Germany and England before immigrating to the United States in 1877. He produced many realistic watercolor and oil paintings of Western scenes, depicting cowboys, Indians, horses and buffalo, that brought him international acclaim. From the mid-1880s until the late 1890s, he worked as a staff artist at the H.S. Crocker Lithograph Company in San Francisco. After this, he worked full time as a fine artist and exhibited his paintings throughout Europe and America.
Biographical information:
*Artists of the American West*.

**G. Powell Harding** (1892-1974) Born: San Leandro, CA; Studied: University of California (Berkeley), California School of Fine Arts (San Francisco), Columbia University; Member: California Water Color Society. G. Powell Harding painted and exhibited from the mid-1920s to the late 1950s. She participated in the annual California Water Color Society shows from 1944 until 1955 and was active on the board of the Santa Monica City Art Gallery. She also worked with oils and exhibited them in the 1930s.
Biographical information:
*Who's Who in American Art*.

**Henry Gifford Hardy** (1901-1989) Born: Chicago, IL; Studied: Chicago Art Institute, Audubon Tyler School, Harvard University; Member: East Bay Watercolor Society, Society of Western Artists. Henry Gifford Hardy moved to San Francisco in 1937 and set up a law practice specializing in patents, trademarks and copyrights. When not working this job, he produced and exhibited watercolors.
Biographical information:
*Artists in California, 1786-1940*.

**Hazel Harper** (1908-1973) Member: California Water Color Society. Hazel Harper lived in Los Angeles in the 1960s and became a member of the California Water Color Society in

1966 and in 1969 she served as president. She used both transparent and opaque watercolors to produce abstract and non-objective works of art.
Biographical information:
California Water Color Society (Catalogs).

**Herrica Hartmetz** (1925- ) Born: Oakland, CA; Studied: University of Southern California, Chouinard Art Institute (Los Angeles), Pasadena Art Institute (California); Member: California Water Color Society. Herrica Hartmetz began exhibiting watercolors in the 1940s after studying art in the Los Angeles area. She was a resident of Arcadia in the 1950s.
Biographical information:
*Who's Who in American Art.*

**Roger Hayward** (1899-1979) Born: Keene, NH; Studied: Boston Institute of Technology; Member: California Water Color Society. Roger Hayward worked as an architect in Boston before moving to Los Angeles in the late 1920s. He continued working as an architect in California and exhibited watercolors in regional exhibitions. Although he painted a variety of subjects, his watercolors of figurative subjects brought him special attention. He primarily worked with transparent watercolor.
Biographical information:
*Artists in California, 1786-1940.*

**Bessie Ella Hazen** (1862-1946) Born: Waterford, New Brunswick, Canada; Studied: Columbia University, University of California (Los Angeles); Member: California Water Color Society, California Art Club. Bessie Hazen first became active in California art circles about 1914. She exhibited in the California Water Color Society shows from 1922 until 1936 and was active on the board during this period. She served as the Society's president in 1934. She taught at the University of California and the Black Fox Military Institute.
Biographical information:
*Southern California Art*
California Water Color Society (Catalogs).

**Frederick R. Heckman** (active in 1930s) Member: Laguna Beach Art Association. Frederick Heckman was a commercial artist in Southern California during the 1930s. He produced illustrations painted with watercolor and gouache for *Touring Topics* magazine covers and for products that were advertised in the magazine. In addition, he exhibited watercolors in Laguna Beach at the Festival of Arts.
Biographical information:
*Southern California Art*
Laguna Beach Festival of Arts (Catalogs).

**Frederick Heidel** (1915-2000) Born: Corvallis, OR; Studied: University of Oregon, Chicago Art Institute; Member: California Water Color Society. Frederick Heidel was a resident of Long Beach in the 1940s. He taught art at Long Beach State College during that era and exhibited watercolors in the Los Angeles area. Since the early 1950s, he has resided in Oregon.
Biographical information:
*Who's Who in American Art.*

**Z. Vanessa Helder** (1904-1968) Born: Lyndon, WA; Studied: University of Washington, Art Students League (New York); Member: New York Water Color Club, American Watercolor Society, California Water Color Society. Z. Vanessa Helder studied with Robert Brackman, George Picken and Frank Vincent DuMond. She began exhibiting her watercolors with the American Watercolor Society in the 1930s. In the 1940s, she moved to Los Angeles and began exhibiting with the California Water Color Society and teaching at the Los Angeles County Art Institute.
Biographical information:
*Who's Who in American Art.*

**Dale Hennesy** (1926-1981) Studied: School of Allied Arts (Glendale); Member: American Watercolor Society, California Water Color Society. Dale Hennesy studied art in Glendale just after World War II. By the 1950s, he was employed as an artist by the motion picture studios and exhibited watercolors on a national level.
Biographical information:
California Water Color Society (Catalogs).

**Joseph Henninger** (1906-1999) Studied: John Herron Art School (Indiana), National Academy of Design (New York), Ecole des Beaux Arts (Paris); Member: California Water Color Society. Joseph Henninger studied art in Indianapolis, New York and Paris before moving to Southern California in 1933. Since that time, he has painted and exhibited representational watercolors depicting American and European landscape and cityscape subjects. In addition, he has been an influential instructor at Art Center School since the mid-1930s. He also produced illustrations for the aircraft industry and worked as an artist for motion picture studios in Hollywood.
Biographical information:
Interview with Joseph Henninger, 1983.

**Paul Blaine Henrie** (1932- ) Born: Tampa, FL; Member: Laguna Beach Art Association, Carmel Art Association. Blaine McKinley Henrie grew up in Florida and began his art career during his teenage years. After serving in the United States Marine Corps, he traveled to Chicago, New York City and New Orleans working as a mural artist. By the mid-1950s, he had settled in California. He lived in Carmel at first, and then moved to Laguna Beach. After opening a gallery at Main Beach in Laguna, Henrie became well-known for his watercolors depicting local coastline scenes and views of places he had traveled including Tahiti, Mexico and Hawaii. During the 1950s and early 1960s, he signed his art Blaine or Paul Blaine. After 1961, he signed it Paul Blaine Henrie. In addition to producing watercolors, oil paintings and prints, Henrie authored two art instruction books.
Biographical information:
Interview with Paul Blaine Henrie, 1997.

**Caesar A. Hernandez** (1909-1996) Born: Carpenteria, CA; Studied: University of Southern California, Chouinard Art Institute (Los Angeles); Member: California Water Color Society. Caesar Hernandez, a fifth generation Californian, studied art with Edouard Vysekal, Tom Craig, Barse Miller and Loren Barton. In 1935, he moved to Redondo Beach,

FRANK HAMILTON  *Winter on the Farm*  1960s  16" x 20"  E. Gene Crain Collection

FRANK HAMILTON  *Salt Creek Shacks*  1959  18" x 28"  Peregrine Galleries

PAUL BLAINE HENRIE  *Tropical Paradise*  1960  18" x 24"  California Art Gallery

PAUL BLAINE HENRIE  *Young's Beach Camp*  1960  20" x 24"  Claremont Fine Arts

taught art to high school and college students, and began exhibiting his watercolors. He traveled extensively after World War II and painted numerous works based on sketches made during these trips.
Biographical information:
Interview with Caesar Hernandez, 1983.

**Susan Lautman Hertel** (1930-1993) Born: Evanston, IL; Studied: Scripps College (Claremont), Kann Art Institute (Beverly Hills). Susan Hertel grew up near Chicago, then in the late 1940s studied art with Millard Sheets in California. From the early 1950s until the 1980s, she was in charge of project development, mural production, stained glass window production and most other projects that came out of Millard Sheets Designs, Inc. in Claremont. Throughout this period and into the 1990s, when she lived in New Mexico, Hertel produced and exhibited oil, watercolor and gouache paintings that often depicted animals. A book of her poems and art was published by Blackberry Books in Maine.
Biographical information:
Horwitch Lewallen Gallery, Santa Fe, New Mexico, 1995.

**Albert Herter, A.N.A.** (1871-1950) Born: New York City, NY; Studied: Art Students League (New York); Member: National Academy of Design (Associate), American Watercolor Society, New York Water Color Club. Albert Herter studied art in New York and Paris in the 1890s and by 1896, he was teaching at the Chicago Art Institute. He also worked at a textile factory in New York and established homes in Long Island and Santa Barbara. Herter exhibited watercolors throughout his art career and produced several large murals in addition to being a portrait artist.
Biographical information:
*Artists in California, 1786-1940*.

**Henry Melton Hesse** (1908-1985) Born: Greeley, CO; Studied: University of Southern California; Member: California Water Color Society. Henry Melton Hesse moved to Southern California in the 1930s where he studied watercolor painting with Paul Sample and Millard Sheets. He resided in Glendale and produced watercolors depicting landscape and cityscape subjects.
Biographical information:
*Who's Who in American Art*.

**Forrest Hibbits** (1905-1996) Born: Lompoc, CA; Studied: California College of Arts and Crafts (Oakland); Member: California Water Color Society. Forrest Hibbits lived in San Francisco in the 1930s, dividing his time between working as a commercial illustrator and producing fine art paintings. During World War II, he produced posters and training aid illustrations for the United States Air Force. After the war, he taught art at the Santa Barbara Art Institute and painted watercolors of the local area.
Biographical information:
Interview with Forrest Hibbits, 1984.

**Floyd Hildebrand** (1895-1984) Born: California. Floyd Hildebrand spent time in New York before moving to San Francisco in the mid-1920s. He worked as a commercial illustrator in the Bay Area and was an expert watercolor painter. During the later years of his life, Hildebrand lived in Ventura, California.
Biographical information:
*Artists in California, 1786-1940*.

**Lawrence Hinckey** (1900-1987) Born: Fillmore, CA; Studied: Otis Art Institute (Los Angeles); Member: California Water Color Society, Laguna Beach Art Association. Lawrence Hinckley was born in Ventura County and attended art school in Los Angeles. In the 1930s, he opened the Art Barn Art Center in his home town of Fillmore and worked to establish the area as an art community. He was a watercolorist and often painted depictions of local scenery.
Biographical information:
*Who's Who in American Art*.

**Clarence Hinkle** (1880-1960) Born: Auburn, CA; Studied: Art Students League (New York), Pennsylvania Academy of Fine Art, Ecole des Beaux Arts (Paris), Académie Colarossi (Paris), Académie Julian (Paris); Member: California Water Color Society. Clarence Hinkle was raised in Northern California. Just before the turn of the century, he studied art at the Crocker Art Gallery in Sacramento with Arthur Mathews. He continued his studies with John Twachtman in New York and William Merritt Chase in Pennsylvania, and then received a scholarship for six additional years of study in Europe. There, he devoted much of his time to viewing the works of the old masters and became well acquainted with modern art trends.

From 1917 until 1930, he lived in Los Angeles and was an art instructor, first at the Los Angeles School of Art and then at the Chouinard Art Institute. Many of the artists that developed the California Style of watercolor painting attended his classes and were greatly influenced by his teaching and encouragement to experiment with that medium. After 1930, he lived in Laguna Beach and Santa Barbara, devoting all of his time to fine art painting.
Biographical information:
*Plein Air Painters of California*.

**Lucile Hinkle** (1895-1985) Born: Kansas City, MO; Studied: Stanford University; Member: California Water Color Society. Lucile Hinkle studied art in Northern California and in the early 1920s moved to Fullerton. By 1924, she was exhibiting watercolors depicting Southern California coastal views and landscapes. She taught art in Fullerton schools and continued to paint watercolors through the 1950s.
Biographical information:
Interview with Lucile Hinkle, 1978.

**Jane Hofstetter** (1936- ) Born: Oakland, CA; Studied: University of California (Berkeley), Chouinard Art Institute (Los Angeles); Member: National Watercolor Society, Society of Western Artists. Jane Hofstetter worked as a fashion designer in Los Angeles and received watercolor instruction from Millard Sheets, Richard Yip and Jade Fon. Since the 1960s, she has resided in Northern California, exhibited her watercolors nationally and taught private art classes for advanced watercolor students.
Biographical information:
Interview with Jane Hofstetter, 1992.

**Robert Holdeman** (1912-1994) Born: Fremont, NE; Studied: Chouinard Art Institute (Los Angeles); Member: California Water Color Society. Robert Holdeman grew up in Long Beach, California. After studying art, he worked at the Walt Disney Studios doing cartoon animation and as a commercial artist. In the early 1950s, he moved to the San Francisco area where he continued exhibiting watercolors and taught art at the California College of Arts and Crafts and California School of Fine Arts. Holdeman served on the board of directors for the California Water Color Society in 1951 and 1952.
Biographical information:
*Artists in California, 1786-1940.*

**Winfield Scott Hoskins** (1905-1962) Born: Los Angeles, CA; Member: American Watercolor Society, Audubon Artists, California Water Color Society. Winfield Hoskins began exhibiting watercolors while working as an illustrator in Los Angeles during the 1930s. In the late 1940s he moved to New York, continued exhibiting watercolors on a national level, and produced illustrations for books and magazines.
Biographical information:
*Who's Who in American Art*
American Watercolor Society (Catalogs).

**Thelma Speed Houston** (1914-   ) Born: Bronx, NY; Studied: Pratt Institute (New York); Member: Laguna Beach Art Association. Thelma Speed Houston was a textile designer for A. Sulka and Company of New York and Paris, and a colorist for St. Andrews Textile Company of New York. By the 1940s, she had moved to San Diego County, and was producing expressionist watercolors based on downtown San Diego cityscape subjects. She also spent time on Maui in the Hawaiian Islands and traveled to other parts of the world on painting excursions. In addition, she has taught watercolor painting.
Biographical information:
*Thelma Speed Houston* (Catalog).

**Charles Howard** (1899-1978) Born: Montclair, NJ; Studied: University of California (Berkeley), Harvard University, Columbia University; Member: San Francisco Art Association. Charles Howard grew up in Northern California and studied to be a journalist. In the 1920s, while in New York City, he began painting and developed a surrealist style. He often used gouache, watercolor, ink and tempera paints.

Although he spent much of his time in New York City and abroad, Howard often visited his two brothers, John Langley Howard and Robert B. Howard, who were successful artists living in San Francisco. Together they exhibited in Bay Area art shows and for a period in the 1940s, Charles Howard taught at the California School of Fine Arts.
Biographical information:
*The Art of California.*

**John Langley Howard** (1902-1999) Born: Montclair, NJ; Studied: University of California (Berkeley), California College of Arts and Crafts (Oakland), Art Students League (New York); Member: San Francisco Art Association, Carmel Art Association. John Langley Howard settled in Northern California in 1926, first in Monterey, and then in San Francisco Some of his Regionalist works of the 1930s and 1940s were painted with watercolors or opaque water-based paints and were exhibited in Bay Area art shows.
Biographical information:
*Scenes of California Life* (Catalog).

**James Hueter** (1925-   ) Born: San Francisco, CA; Studied: Pomona College (California), Claremont Graduate School (California); Member: California Water Color Society. James Hueter studied with Henry Lee McFee and Millard Sheets, and was exhibiting watercolors in the early 1950s with the California Water Color Society and in the Los Angeles County Museum annual shows. Since that time, he has worked primarily with wood and oils, and has been an art instructor at Mount San Antonio College, Pomona College and Claremont Graduate School.
Biographical information:
*Who's Who in American Art.*

**Ray Huffine** (1905-1967) Born: Missouri; Member: California Water Color Society. Ray Huffine settled in Los Angeles around 1927 and by the early 1930s was working at the Walt Disney Studios. He was an expert painter and produced watercolor backgrounds for many Disney classics including *Pinocchio, Fantasia, Bambi, The Three Caballeros, Make Mine Music, Cinderella, Peter Pan* and *Lady and the Tramp*. In addition, he exhibited California Scene watercolors in the annual California Water Color Society shows during the 1930s.
Biographical information:
*The Disney Films*
*Artists in California, 1786-1940.*

**Virginia McCallister Huffman** (1911-   ) Born: Los Angeles, CA; Studied: Chouinard Art Institute (Los Angeles); Member: California Water Color Society. Virginia McCallister Huffman has been a lifelong resident of Southern California; living in Sherman Oaks and Laguna Beach. From 1932 through the 1960s, she produced watercolors for use as illustrations and exhibition art.
Biographical information:
Interview with Virginia Huffman, 1995.

**Louis Hughes** (1893-1973) Born: Oklahoma. Louis Hughes was a commercial artist in Northern California during the 1930s and 1940s and a resident of San Francisco. He and his cousin, Willard Cox, took painting excursions with Maurice Logan and Louis Siegriest and in the 1930s, exhibited with the Thirteen Watercolorists.
Biographical information:
*Artists in California, 1786-1940*
David Howard Fine Arts, Mill Valley, 1985.

**Ralph Hulett** (1915-1974) Born: Kankakee, IL; Studied: Chouinard Art Institute (Los Angeles); Member: American Watercolor Society, California Water Color Society. Ralph Hulett came to California as a teenager and attended high school in Glendale. From a young age, his artistic talents were obvious and upon graduation, he was awarded a four year scholarship to study at the Chouinard Art Institute. His instructors were Millard Sheets, Phil Dike, Phil Paradise and

RALPH HULETT  *Winter Near Bishop*  1952  22" x 30"  Private Collection

RALPH HULETT  *Out of the Tunnel*  1940s  22" x 30"  E. Gene Crain Collection

JOAN IRVING  *Swinging Signs*  1954  13" x 19"  Courtesy Joan Irving Brandt

JOAN IRVING  *Hari Kari House*  1954  15" x 22"  E. Gene Crain Collection

Herb Jepson. While still at college, he was hired by the Walt Disney Studios to work on *Snow White and the Seven Dwarfs*.

After graduation in 1938, he went to work full-time at Disney. He did watercolor backgrounds for *Pinocchio, Fantasia, Dumbo, Bambi, Saludos Amigos* and *The Three Caballeros*. By the 1940s, he had earned enough seniority to receive screen credits for his work on *Make Mine Music, Song of the South, Melody Time, Cinderella, Peter Pan, Lady and the Tramp, Sleeping Beauty, 101 Dalmations* and *The Jungle Book*.

Hulett was also a prolific fine art watercolorist with an amazing command of the medium. By 1937, he was an exhibiting member of the California Water Color Society and sold his works through local art galleries. In the 1940s, he was also exhibiting in New York City in the American Watercolor Society's annual shows. Most of the subjects he chose to depict were scenes of California and Mexico, but he also did work while traveling in Japan, Europe and Central America.

Other projects he worked on included a series of oil paintings depicting old areas of Los Angeles and the Bunker Hill region in particular. He produced watercolor illustrations that appeared in *Ford Times, Westways* and other magazine publications. In the 1950s, he designed a very popular series of cards for the Designers' Showcase Company and did commercial work for Swiss-Air, Capital Records and KNBC. During the 1960s, he also received acclaim for animated films he produced. Hulett was also the author of an art instruction book for the Walter Foster Company.
Biographical information:
Interview with Shirley Hulett Sullivan, 1983.

**La Verne Hutchings** (1918- ) Born: Idaho Falls, ID; Studied: Brigham Young University (Utah), Idaho State College, Chouinard Art Institute (Los Angeles), Art Students League (New York); Member: California Water Color Society, Watercolor West. La Verne Hutchings grew up in Idaho Falls, Idaho. He attended college in Utah and Idaho, then served in the United States Armed Forces in Manila during World War II. After the war, he continued his art education in Los Angeles and New York. He studied watercolor painting with John Pike and Sergei Bongart. Since the 1950s, he has lived in California and actively exhibited watercolors on the West Coast and in the Midwest. Hutchings has also authored several books on watercolor painting and has taught watercolor workshops throughout the west.
Biographical information:
Interview with La Verne Hutchings, 1998.

**Mabel Hutchinson** (1903-1999) Born: Blackfoot, ID; Studied: University of Utah (Logan); Member: California Water Color Society. Mabel Hutchinson moved to Riverside in 1927 and took watercolor painting instruction from Rex Brandt during the 1930s. She exhibited her works with the California Water Color Society from 1939 to 1959. Most of her paintings were representational views of farm areas around Riverside and beach scenes in Orange County. After the 1940s, she lived in South Orange County and concentrated on sculpture and wood crafts.
Biographical information:
Interview with Mabel Hutchinson, 1983.

**William Rich Hutton** (1826-1901) Born: Washington, D.C. William Rich Hutton came to California in 1847 and worked on a survey crew in Los Angeles and San Luis Obispo until 1853. His drawings and watercolors of Los Angeles and the region are among the earliest pictorial views known.
Biographical information:
*Artists in California, 1786-1940.*

**Alex Ignatiev** (1913-1995) Born: Russia; Studied: Chouinard Art Institute (Los Angeles); Member: Valley Artist Club. Alex Ignatiev grew up in San Francisco and in the 1930s received a scholarship to study with Millard Sheets, Phil Paradise and Lawrence Murphy. His watercolor paintings are American Scene works done with transparent and opaque paints. In addition, he produced murals and animated film art for a number of Hollywood studios including Walt Disney, Warner Brothers and Hanna-Barbera.
Biographical information:
Interview with Alex Ignatiev, 1984.

**Joan Irving** (1916-1995) Born: Riverside, CA; Studied: Art Center School (Los Angeles); Member: American Watercolor Society, California Water Color Society. Joan Irving spent her childhood in Southern California. She attended Riverside City College, studying art with Richard Allman and then took additional instruction from Barse Miller and Edward Kaminski in Los Angeles. She began to exhibit her watercolors professionally in the late 1930s and after that time, was included in exhibitions in the United States and Europe.

Beginning in 1946, Irving taught painting with her husband, Rex Brandt, in Corona del Mar, California. She had been an instructor at the Chouinard Art Institute and the Coronado School of Fine Arts. She also produced sculptures, murals, greeting cards and commercial illustrations for national magazines. In later years, she traveled to Mexico and Europe on painting excursions and often spent time working at her second studio in the state of Washington.
Biographical information:
Interview with Joan Irving, 1983.

**Robert Irwin** (1928- ) Born: Long Beach, CA; Studied: Otis Art Institute (Los Angeles), Jepson Art Institute (Los Angeles), Chouinard Art Institute (Los Angeles). In the 1940s and 1950s Robert Irwin produced and exhibited abstract watercolors in annual art shows. Since then he has taken a completely different direction and is currently recognized as an important American conceptual artist.
Biographical information:
*Chouinard, A Vision Betrayed.*

**Miyoko Ito** (1918-1983) Born: Berkeley, California; Studied: University of California (Berkeley), Smith College (Massachusetts), Chicago Art Institute; Member: San Francisco Art Association. Miyoko Ito received art instruction from John Haley and Erle Loran. In the late 1930s and early 1940s, she produced Berkeley School style watercolors and was associated with that group of artists. After being interned at a camp for Japanese Americans during World War II, she continued her art education and settled in Chicago.
Biographical information:
*Views From Asian California, 1920-1965.*

**John Ivey** (1842-1910) Born: England. John Ivey immigrated to Los Angeles and in 1887 became a Professor of Art at the University of Southern California. After the turn of the century, he lived in Northern California and sent his watercolors to the East Coast for exhibition and sale.
Biographical information:
*Artists in California, 1786-1940.*

**Everett Gee Jackson** (1900-1995) Born: Mexia, TX; Studied: Texas A & M, San Diego State College, University of Southern California; Member: San Diego Fine Art Society. Everett Gee Jackson moved to San Diego in 1930 and taught at San Diego State College for over 30 years. He actively painted with watercolors during the 1930s and exhibited with the California Group show. His style was abstract, done mainly with transparent watercolors. After the 1940s, he worked primarily with oils on canvas and illustrated several well-known children's books.
Biographical information:
Interview with Everett Gee Jackson, 1983.

**Gordena Parker Jackson** (1900-1993) Born: Pleasanton, California; Studied: California College of Art and Crafts (Oakland); Member: Laguna Beach Art Association, Santa Cruz Art League. Gordena Parker Jackson studied art in Oakland, California during the early 1920s. By 1932, she was exhibiting watercolors in annual exhibitions in California and after 1942 exhibited nationally.
Biographical information:
*Who's Who in American Art.*

**Robert L. Jackson** (1919- ) Born: Pasadena, CA; Studied: Chouinard Art Institute (Los Angeles); Member: California Water Color Society. Robert Jackson grew up in South Pasadena and received a scholarship to study at the Chouinard Art Institute. He took watercolor instruction from Millard Sheets and Phil Paradise. In the late 1930s, he began work as a sketch artist at Paramount Studios, working on many of the classic Cecil B. DeMille productions. In the 1950s and 1960s, he produced architectural renderings. Since the 1930s, Jackson has painted watercolors that he has exhibited in annual art shows.
Biographical information:
Interview with Robert Jackson, 1996.

**Neil Jacobe** (1924- ) Born: Hawarden, IA; Studied: Jepson Art Institute (Los Angeles); Member: Long Beach Art Association. Neil Jacobe grew up in Iowa, came to California in 1942, and immediately joined the United States Army. After World War II, he studied art in Los Angeles with Rico Lebrun, F. Tolles Chamberlin and Elmer Plummer. Since the late 1940s, he has worked as a commercial illustrator and exhibited his watercolors in Southern California.
Biographical information:
Interview with Neil Jacobe, 1995.

**George James** (1932- ) Born: Detroit, MI; Studied: Chouinard Art Institute (Los Angeles), Long Beach State College; Member: California Water Color Society. George James grew up in Southern California. During his teenage years he attended the Brandt-Dike Summer School of Painting in Corona del Mar and studied watercolor painting with Rex Brandt, Phil Dike and George Post.

During the 1950s, he developed a geometric, abstractionist style of watercolor painting. Most of his works of this era were inspired by beach-city subjects in the Newport and Balboa area of Orange County. They were exhibited with the California Water Color Society and sold through local art galleries.

James has taught art since the 1960s and became an Associate Professor at California State University, Fullerton. In more recent years he has produced photorealist watercolors and is actively exhibiting.
Biographical information:
Interview with George James, 1983.

**James Jarvaise** (1927- ) Born: Indianapolis, IN; Studied: Carnegie Institute (Pennsylvania), Ecole D'Art (France), University of Southern California. James Jarvaise studied in France with Fernand Lèger before moving to Southern California. By the early 1950s, he was exhibiting abstract works of art, some of which were watercolors, and has shown at galleries and museums all over the world. He has been an art instructor at the University of Southern California, Pennsylvania State University, University of Madrid, Occidental College and California Institute of the Arts.
Biographical information:
*Who's Who in American Art.*

**William Jekel** (1927-2000) Born: Pueblo, CO; Studied: Art Center School (Los Angeles), University of California (Los Angeles); Member: Nevada Watercolor Society. William Jekel grew up in Los Angeles and studied art there prior to entering the United States Navy in 1944. He was employed, before and after his naval service, as a scenic artist at M.G.M. Studios. During those years, he frequently joined George Gibson, Emil Kosa, Jr., Duncan Spencer, John Coakley and other film studio artists on location painting trips. He later formed his own scenery production company to supply backdrops for the film and emerging television industries. Jekel's early works depict cityscape scenes of the Los Angeles region, painted in the classic California Style of the late 1930s era. Since the 1960s, his works reveal more carefully rendered watercolors, and often depict rural ranch scenes, landscape views and coastline subjects in California and desert landscapes of Nevada. He was an expert watercolorist and produced most of his paintings while on location.
Biographical information:
Interview with William Jekel, 1995.

**Robert Jensen** (1922- ) Born: San Francisco, CA; Studied: California College of Arts and Crafts (Oakland); Member: Society of Western Artists. Robert Jensen lived in the San Francisco area all of his life. After high school he attended art classes in Oakland and became interested in painting with watercolors while studying with Louis Myljarack. He took further instruction from George Post and Alexander Nepote.

After the 1950s, Jensen worked as an art instructor in the San Francisco Bay area and exhibited his transparent watercolor paintings in local art galleries and with the Society of Western Artists.
Biographical information:
Interview with Robert Jensen, 1983.

GEORGE JAMES  *Untitled*  1950s  12" x 22"  Courtesy George James

NEIL JACOBE  *Nu-Pike, Long Beach*  1950  22" x 30"  Courtesy Ken Cody

WILLIAM JEKEL  *San Pedro Street*  1940s  15" x 22"  Courtesy William Jekel

WILLIAM JEKEL  *Fruit Vendor*  1940s  15" x 22"  Courtesy William Jekel

**Addison Johnson** (1892-1986) Studied: Art Students League (New York), Otis Art Institute (Los Angeles); Member: Fine Arts Guild of Riverside. Addison Johnson studied art with Frank Vincent DuMond in 1917 and 1918. In the early 1920s, he moved to Santa Monica. He worked as an illustrator, often using watercolors, and exhibited fine art works in local exhibitions. After the early 1950s, he lived in Riverside and continued to produce watercolors and oil paintings. In addition, he taught art at the Riverside Art Center.
Biographical information:
Appleby International Arts, Ocean City, 1997.

**Doris Miller Johnson** (1909- ) Born: Oakland, CA; Studied: California College of Arts and Crafts (Oakland), University of California (Berkeley); Member: San Francisco Art Association. Doris Miller Johnson is a native Californian and was raised and educated in the San Francisco area. During the 1930s, she studied art in Oakland and then took further instruction from John Haley.

Her watercolor paintings were exhibited in museum and gallery shows in the San Francisco area and are examples of the Berkeley School of watercolor painting. Johnson was active on the board of directors of the San Francisco Art Association in the 1950s and taught art in Oakland at that time. Since 1960, she has traveled extensively, painting foreign landscape and cityscape subjects.
Biographical information:
Interview with Doris Miller Johnson, 1984.

**Reginald Johnson** (1905-1984) Born: New York City, NY; Studied: Chouinard Art Institute (Los Angeles); Member: California Water Color Society. Reginald Johnson moved to Los Angeles when he was fifteen and studied art with F. Tolles Chamberlin in the 1920s. By the 1930s he was showing American Scene paintings with the California Water Color Society. He also worked as a freelance illustrator.
Biographical information:
Interview with Reginald Johnson, 1984.

**Stan Johnson** (1907- ) Born: Los Angeles, CA; Member: California Water Color Society. After high school, Stan Johnson studied architecture and did architectural renderings on a freelance basis. In the early 1930s, he studied with Millard Sheets and began exhibiting with the California Water Color Society. In the 1940s, he worked in the film industry as a set designer and art director.
Biographical information:
Interview with Stan Johnson, 1983.

**Ynez Johnston** (1920- ) Born: Berkeley, CA; Studied: University of California (Berkeley); Member: California Water Color Society. Ynez Johnston grew up in Northern California. She studied art with John Haley, Worth Ryder and Margaret Peterson. After receiving a Master's degree from the University of California, Berkeley, she began to teach in the University's art department. During this period, she was primarily interested in etching and other forms of printmaking. In 1951, she moved to Los Angeles and began producing drawings that were similar to her etching style, but with the addition of watercolor or tempera paint. She has exhibited nationally and has art works in the collections of the Whitney Museum of American Art, Museum of Modern Art, Metropolitan Museum of Art and Philadelphia Museum of Art. In 1952, she was awarded a Guggenheim grant. In addition to a successful art career, she has taught at the Colorado Springs Fine Art Center and the Chouinard Art Institute.
Biographical information:
Interview with Ynez Johnston, 1998.

**Dorothy Jordan** (1912- ) Born: Ontario, Canada; Studied: Art Students League (New York); Member: California Water Color Society. Dorothy Jordan studied art in New York with George Bridgman in the late 1930s. She moved to Los Angeles in the 1940s and became an active member of the California Water Color Society. Since 1961, she has signed her paintings with the name Jean Jourdain.
Biographical information:
Interview with Dorothy Jordan, 1983.

**Christian A. Jorgensen** (1860-1935) Born: Oslo, Norway; Studied: California School of Design (San Francisco); Member: Bohemian Club. Chris Jorgensen came to San Francisco from Norway in 1870. He studied with Virgil Williams and by 1881, was teaching art at the California School of Design. In addition, he worked as a draftsman at a local architectural firm. Toward the turn of the century, he began painting in Yosemite and by 1900, was able to build a small lodge with a studio across from Yosemite Falls.

His many watercolors are accurate, realistically painted views of this beautiful region. Another series of watercolors he produced, depicts California missions. These works received favorable press when exhibited in Washington, D.C. in 1906. Other subjects he painted included coastal views near his home in Carmel and scenes of Mexico, Eastern America, and Canada from his travels to those areas in the early 1900s. Jorgensen was an expert watercolor artist and considered to be one of early California's leading artists in this medium.
Biographical information:
The North Point Gallery, San Francisco, 1997.

**William Lees Judson** (1842-1928) Born: Manchester, England; Member: California Art Club. William Lees Judson came to California in 1893 at the age of fifty-one. Prior to this, he lived in England and Canada and had studied art in New York and Paris. In Canada, he directed the Department of Art at Dellmuth College. In 1890, he moved to Chicago and produced art for the Colombian Exposition of 1893.

After the death of his wife, Judson moved to California and in 1895, the University of Southern California hired him to establish an art department. By the early 1900s, he persuaded the university to build the College of Fine Arts and over the following 20 years, he built the school into one of the foremost art schools in California.

Judson was an accomplished portrait artist, but after moving to California, he primarily painted landscape subjects using oils and watercolors. His works were realistic in style and looked like traditional English landscape watercolors. Although many of his watercolors were destroyed in a 1910 studio fire, the ones that remain have established him as one of Southern California's premier pioneer watercolor artists.
Biographical information:
*U.S.C. Trojan Family Magazine*, 1997.

**Paul Julian** (1914-1995) Born: Illinois; Studied: Chouinard Art Institute (Los Angeles); Member: California Water Color Society. Paul Julian studied art with Millard Sheets and Lawrence Murphy in the 1930s. He resided in Santa Monica, worked in the motion picture business, and exhibited his watercolors from the 1930s to the 1950s in Southern California.
Biographical information:
*Artists in California, 1786-1940.*

**Karl Kasten** (1916- ) Born: San Francisco, CA; Studied: California School of Fine Arts (San Francisco), University of California (Berkeley), Hans Hofmann School of Art; Member: San Francisco Art Association. Karl Kasten was raised in the San Francisco area and attended the California School of Fine Arts. While attending the University of California, Berkeley in the 1930s, he was known as one of the Berkeley School watercolor artists.

After serving in World War II, he studied with Hans Hofmann in Massachusetts and then returned to Berkeley. Since then, he has produced abstract expressionist paintings; primarily using oil on canvas.

Kasten has taught art at San Francisco State College and the University of California, Berkeley. He designed a unique, light-weight etching press and has received international recognition for his etchings and lithographs.
Biographical information:
Interview with Karl Kasten, 1983.

**Arthur L. Kaye** (1915- ) Born: New York City, NY; Studied: Art Center School (Los Angeles), Chouinard Art Institute (Los Angeles); Member: California Water Color Society, Watercolor West. Arthur Kaye moved from New York to Los Angeles at the age of ten. Following graduation from high school, he worked at an animation studio, then as a freelance commercial artist, and later as a layout artist for the *Los Angeles Times*. Kaye is best known for his abstract paintings done with watercolor and acrylics. He was twice president of the California Water Color Society (1967, 1985) and has lectured on art.
Biographical information:
Interview with Arthur Kaye, 1995.

**Elizabeth Emerson Keith** (1838-1882) Born: Thomaston, ME. Elizabeth Emerson Keith received an education in art before moving to California in 1860. In 1864, she became the wife of artist William Keith and is credited with giving him instruction in watercolor and encouraging him to pursue a career in fine art painting. Her watercolors of still life and animal subjects were exhibited in San Francisco in the 1870s.
Biographical information:
*Artists in California, 1786-1940.*

**William Keith** (1838-1911) Born: Aberdeen, Scotland; Studied: In Germany with Flamm, Arhenbach, and Carl Marr; Member: San Francisco Art Association, Bohemian Club. William Keith, often referred to as the "Dean of California Artists," painted with watercolors throughout his career. Often the trees and hills near his home in Berkeley were depicted in these watercolors. Although his international reputation was built primarily on his tonally dark California landscape works (painted with oils on canvas) his watercolors have been singled out as superb examples of turn-of-the-century California art.
Biographical information:
*Artists in California, 1786-1940*
*Art in California.*

**Richmond Kelsey** (1905-1987) Born: San Diego, CA; Studied: Otis Art Institute (Los Angeles), Art Center School (Los Angeles); Member: American Watercolor Society, California Water Color Society. Richmond Kelsey began painting and exhibiting watercolors while studying art in Los Angeles during the 1930s. After serving in World War II, he settled in Southern California and worked in the animated film business, producing watercolor backgrounds for Walt Disney Studios' feature films and cartoons. In addition to his animation work and fine art watercolor painting, Kelsey also illustrated eight children's stories for the Golden Book series and wrote and illustrated a book called *Good Enough Gismo*.
Biographical information:
Interview with Elmer Plummer, 1984
*Who's Who in American Art.*

**Robert H. Kennicott** (1892-1983) Born: Luverne, MN; Member: California Water Color Society. Robert Kennicott lived in Los Angeles and between 1935 and 1950, exhibited in the annual California Water Color Society exhibitions.
Biographical information:
*Who's Who in American Art.*

**Ada Howe Kent** (1858-1942) Born: Rochester, NY; Studied: Art Students League (New York); Member: New York Water Color Club, American Watercolor Society. Ada Howe Kent studied art with George de Forest Brush and Abbott H. Thayer in New York, then continued studies in Paris with Whistler. During the 1920s and 1930s, Kent lived in Carmel and sent watercolors to the East Coast for annual exhibitions.
Biographical information:
*Who's Who in American Art*
New York Water Color Club (Catalogs).

**Lenard Kester, N.A.** (1917-1997) Born: New York City, NY; Member: National Academy of Design, American Watercolor Society, California Water Color Society. Lenard Kester lived his first twenty-one years in New York near the East River. After high school he worked for the Max Fleisher Cartoon Studio in New York and Florida. In 1939, on vacation in California, he decided to settle in Los Angeles and took a job at the Walt Disney Studios.

In the mid-1940s, he quit his Disney job to pursue a full-time fine art career. The watercolors he began to produce and exhibit at this time often depicted moody cityscape subjects and innovative, abstract interpretations of California coastline subjects.

In 1949, he was awarded a Louis Comfort Tiffany Foundation Fellowship which enabled him to paint a pictorial record of the Pacific Northwest. Other projects he pursued included large murals and stained glass window designs. Throughout his career, he also painted with oils.
Biographical information:
Interview with Lenard Kester, 1983.

CHRISTIAN A. JORGENSEN  *Yosemite*  1918  15" x 10"  Claremont Fine Arts

DONG KINGMAN  *San Francisco*  1944  20" x 27"  David & Sally Martin Collection

DONG KINGMAN  *Mott Street*  1953  18" x 22"  Philip H. Greene Collection

**Atsushi Kikuchi** (active in 1940s) Born: Seattle, WA; Studied: California College of Arts and Crafts (Oakland). Atsushi Kikuchi was born just after the turn of the century and spent his childhood in Japan. After moving to the San Francisco area, he received a scholarship to study art and moved to Los Angeles to pursue an art career. During World War II, he was confined in Japanese internment camps for a period of time and then was inducted into the United States Army. After the war, he moved to Chicago. Kikuchi produced watercolors before and after the war.
Biographical information:
*Beyond Words.*

**Charles Kinghan, N.A.** (1895-1984) Born: Anthony, KS; Studied: Chicago Art Institute, Chicago Academy of Fine Art; Member: National Academy of Design, American Watercolor Society. Charles Kinghan studied art in Chicago, then pursued a long successful career as an East Coast commercial artist. He exhibited watercolors nationally and taught art. Kinghan eventually retired on the West Coast, first in Laguna Beach and later near Carmel.
Biographical information:
*American Artist* (Magazine)
*Who's Who in American Art.*

**Dong Kingman, N.A.** (1911-2000) Born: Oakland, CA; Studied: Ling Nan School (Hong Kong); Member: National Academy of Design, American Watercolor Society, California Water Color Society. Dong Kingman was born in California of Chinese parents. While still a child, he returned with them to China. There, he received art instruction from traditional Chinese watercolorists and Sze-To-Wai, a Paris-educated artist who was very knowledgeable about modern art trends. In 1929, Kingman moved back to San Francisco and started producing watercolor paintings depicting Bay Area cityscape subjects.

During the Depression, he did watercolors for the P.W.A. Art Relief Project in San Francisco and his works were included in the *Frontiers of American Art* show. By the mid-1930s, when California watercolors were beginning to receive national attention, Kingman was recognized as one of the Bay Area's finest watercolorists. The San Francisco Museum of Art acquired a number of his works and exhibited them in numerous watercolor shows.

In 1942, he was awarded a Guggenheim Fellowship which enabled him to travel around the United States painting watercolors of American scene subjects. When Kingman got to New York City, he found it to his liking and produced a number of works depicting cityscape subjects. He went into the service during World War II and ended up producing art for the war effort in Washington, D.C. After the war, he decided to live in New York City and spend less time in San Francisco.

Kingman's early works featured loose washes, often done using a wet-into-wet technique, with some dry brush calligraphy for definition. His post war works became increasingly complex in subject matter and usually had a geometric, abstractionist look. Between 1945 and 1965, he painted a large number of outstanding cityscape watercolors of New York City and San Francisco. The best of these works have exceptional compositions, interesting subject matter and an exciting sense of drama. They are among the finest examples of American watercolor produced during that era.

In addition to painting and exhibiting fine art, his works have been reproduced as covers for *Fortune* and as article illustrations inside the magazine. *Life, Time, Westways* and numerous other magazines also reproduced his works. As an art instructor, he has taught at the Rhode Island School of Design, Columbia University, Hunter College, Famous Artists School, and has been the featured teacher at dozens of significant watercolor workshops throughout the world.

Kingman's watercolors are in major museums throughout America and the Orient. There have been three books written about his life and work, and a film documenting his approach to watercolor painting was released in 1954.
Biographical information:
Interview with Dong Kingman, 1994
*The Watercolors of Dong Kingman.*

**David Klein** (active in 1930s) Member: California Water Color Society. David Klein was a resident of Los Angeles in the 1930s. He exhibited watercolors of regional subjects and was a commercial illustrator.
Biographical information:
California Water Color Society (Catalogs).

**Earl Klein** (1915- ) Born: Cleveland, OH; Studied: Chouinard Art Institute (Los Angeles); Member: California Water Color Society. Earl Klein grew up in Cleveland and studied watercolor painting with George Fisher in Detroit. He then traveled to Florida where he worked at the Max Fleisher Studios on cartoon shorts. In the early 1940s, he moved to Los Angeles, studied with Pruett Carter, and began exhibiting his watercolor paintings.

For twenty years, Klein was involved with the motion picture industry in Hollywood. First as an animation artist for the Warner Brothers Studios, and later as operator of his own film production business. He has also produced freelance commercial illustrations for magazines and taught art in California and Mexico.
Biographical information:
Interview with Earl Klein, 1983.

**Herbert Klynn** (1917-1999) Born: Cleveland, OH; Studied: Ohio State University, Cleveland School of Art; Member: California Water Color Society. Herbert Klynn studied painting with Henry Keller from 1937 to 1939, and then operated a freelance commercial art business in Ohio. He came to Los Angeles during World War II, working as an animator for United States Government training films. He worked on animated cartoons at U.P.A. Pictures after the war, and in the late 1950s, started his own animated film company; Format Film, Inc. Throughout this entire period, he painted watercolors and exhibited with the California Water Color Society.
Biographical information:
Interview with Herbert Klynn, 1983.

**Joseph Knowles** (1907-1980) born: Kendall, MT; Studied: Santa Barbara School of the Arts; Member: California Water Color Society. Joseph Knowles grew up in San Diego. When he was twenty years old, he moved to Santa Barbara and studied art with Frank Morley Fletcher. He then traveled to Italy,

France and England where he continued his art education.

In the 1930s, he returned to Santa Barbara, established himself as a fine art painter and designer, and began exhibiting his watercolor paintings. For many years, he taught art at the University of California, Santa Barbara and served as president and co-director of the fine arts department at the Brooks Institute in Santa Barbara. He was also an accomplished oil painter, printmaker, designer and muralist, and did several large stained glass windows for public and private buildings.
Biographical information:
Studio 2 Gallery, Santa Barbara, 1985.

**Gerd Koch** (1929- ) Born: Detroit, MI; Studied: Wayne University; Member: California Water Color Society. Gerd Koch became a member of the California Water Color Society in the mid-1950s. He paints abstract, non-objective works and has taught art at Ventura College since 1959.
Biographical information:
*Who's Who in American Art*
California Water Color Society (Catalogs).

**Irene Koch** (1929- ) Born: Detroit, MI; Studied: Wayne University; Member: California Water Color Society. Irene Koch, a Ventura County resident, exhibited her abstract, non-objective watercolors in shows throughout the 1950s and 1960s. She has taught art in Los Angeles and Ojai.
Biographical information:
*Who's Who in American Art*
California Water Color Society (Catalogs).

**Josephine Kopenhaver** (1908-1991) Born: Seattle, WA; Studied: University of California (Los Angeles), Chouinard Art Institute (Los Angeles); Member: California Water Color Society, Audubon Association. Josephine Kopenhaver studied with Millard Sheets, and from 1938 to 1954, painted and exhibited watercolors depicting scenes from Southern California and Mexico. She taught art at Los Angeles City College.
Biographical information:
*Who's Who in American Art.*

**Emil Kosa, Jr., N.A.** (1903-1968) Born: Paris, France; Studied: Academy of Fine Arts (Prague), Ecole des Beaux Arts (Paris), Chouinard Art Institute (Los Angeles); Member: National Academy of Design, American Watercolor Society, California Water Color Society, Philadelphia Water Color Club, New York Water Color Club. Emil Kosa, Jr. received art instruction and music lessons at a very early age. When he was in his late teens, he had to decide between being a professional musician or artist. He chose art, but his family and instructors believed he could have been a famous musician had he chosen that occupation.

In the 1920s, he moved to California, but returned to France several times to continue his art education. He received traditional painting instruction from Pierre Laurens and studied non-objective painting with Frank Kupka. After settling in California in 1928, he worked as a mural artist and operated a business with his father that produced decorative art for churches and auditoriums. When that line of work was slow, he took on portrait commissions and sold fine art paintings through local galleries.

In the early 1930s, Kosa became friends with Millard Sheets and with Sheet's encouragement, began aggressively pursuing a national reputation as a California watercolor artist. He sent up to sixty watercolors every year to museum shows all over America and was among the first California Style watercolorist whose work brought attention to the West Coast watercolor style. He was an active member of the California Water Color Society and served as president in 1945. Kosa was one of the first of the California watercolorists to be accepted into annual shows in New York City at the National Academy of Design and in the American Watercolor Society shows.

To financially support his family, Kosa worked as a scenic artist in the special effects division at Twentieth Century-Fox Studios for thirty-five years. He produced art for matt shots and was known as a top artist in this field. The motion picture industry acknowledged his contributions and awarded him an Oscar for his special effects work for *Cleopatra*.

A compulsive painter, Kosa would often paint for three or four hours after dinner each night and spend most of his weekends outdoors, painting with watercolors or oils. Alexander Cowie was his Los Angeles agent and the Macbeth Gallery sold his work in New York City. The Cowie Gallery, located in the Biltmore Hotel, had several one-man shows every year and included his work in all of their group showings.

Through his studio connections, he also produced a large number of commissioned portraits for movie stars, businessmen and politicians. In the 1950s, he was known as the premier portrait painter in Southern California. His official portrait of Earl Warren from this era, is in the collection of the National Portrait Gallery in Washington, D.C.

Kosa is best known for his representational watercolors and oils, but also won awards for pencil drawings and pastels depicting figurative subjects and prints. During the 1940s and through the mid-1960s, he occasionally revisited his interest in non-objective art and produced a body of work which expresses his love for music and experimental art concepts.
Biographical information:
Interviews with Elizabeth Kosa, George Gibson, and Marian Kosa Saund, 1988.

**Peter Krasnow** (1886-1979) Born: Ukraine, Russia; Member: Painters and Sculptors Club. Peter Krasnow emigrated from Russia to America just after the turn of the century and settled in Los Angeles in the early 1920s. While he produced a number of watercolor paintings from the 1930s, to the 1950s, he was not affiliated with the California School of watercolor artists. His works were often colorful and very modern in concept. Usually, they were exhibited along with his sculptural works in West Coast galleries and museums.
Biographical information:
*Southern California Art.*

**Roger Kuntz** (1926-1975) Born: San Antonio, TX; Studied: Pomona College (California), Claremont Graduate School (California). Roger Kuntz was a student of Henry Lee McFee and began exhibiting while still a student. Although he is primarily remembered for his large oil paintings, Kuntz did spontaneous watercolors while on location, that were used as reference for larger works.
Biographical information:
*Who's Who in American Art.*

EMIL KOSA, JR.  *Los Angeles*  1940s  22" x 30"  McClelland Collection

EMIL KOSA, JR.  *Back from the Ride*  1954  18" x 24"  E. Gene Crain Collection

WAYNE LA COM  *Scotties Castle*  1950s  15" x 22"  Courtesy Wayne La Com

ROBERT LANDRY  *Wiamanalo, Oahu*  1960s  11" x 15"  California Art Gallery

**Oswald Kurman** (1900-1991) Born: Tallinn, Estonia; Studied: Tartu University, California School of Fine Arts (San Francisco); Member: San Francisco Art Association. Oswald Kurman studied art in Europe before moving to San Francisco in 1924. He worked as a commercial illustrator in the Bay Area for several years before finding employment in the metal scrap business. In the 1930s, he resumed his art education and began exhibiting in annual museum art shows. Most of Kurman's watercolor and gouache paintings were done between 1930 and 1950 and often depicted cityscapes.
Biographical information:
Interview with Harold R. Wilson, Jr, 1995.

**Dorothy Browdy Kushner** (1909-2000) Born: Kansas City, MO; Studied: Kansas City Art Institute, Columbia University, Art Students League (New York); Member: California Water Color Society. Dorothy Kushner studied with Thomas Hart Benton and Reginald Marsh, and then taught art in New York from 1940 to 1947. She moved to Southern California in 1947 and joined the California Water Color Society. She continued to paint and exhibit her watercolors into the 1970s.
Biographical information:
Interview with Dorothy Kushner, 1983.

**John Kwok** (1920-1983) Born: Shanghai, China; Studied: Chouinard Art Institute (Los Angeles); Member: California Water Color Society. John Kwok and his family moved to Northern California from China when he was very young. He received a scholarship to study at the Chouinard Art Institute, and returned to live in Los Angeles after serving in World War II. He primarily painted with opaque watercolors, producing large abstract works based on still life subjects. He also worked as a fashion designer and a commercial artist.
Biographical information:
Interview with Mrs. Kwok, 1984.

**Diana La Com** (1931- ) Born: Los Angeles, CA; Studied: Chouinard Art Institute (Los Angeles). Diana La Com was awarded a scholarship to the Chouinard Art Institute where she studied with Ed Reep and Richard Haines. She and her husband, Wayne La Com, have spent extended periods of time in Hawaii, where she has found inspirational subject matter and wide acceptance through gallery exhibitions.
Biographical information:
Interview with Diana La Com, 1989.

**Wayne La Com** (1922- ) Born: Glendale, CA; Studied: Art Center School (Los Angeles), Chouinard Art Institute (Los Angeles), Jepson Art Institute (Los Angeles); Member: California Water Color Society. Wayne La Com grew up in Southern California and attended art schools in Los Angeles where he studied watercolor painting with Hardie Gramatky, Watson Cross, Rico Lebrun and Stanton MacDonald-Wright. During World War II, he worked with Hardie Gramatky producing illustration art for the war effort and after the war, spent a brief period in New York producing commercial art. By the late 1940s, he was back in Southern California and was receiving notoriety for the watercolors he produced. In 1965, he was elected president of the California Water Color Society.

La Com also taught art for thirty years, worked as a graphic designer, and operated an art gallery in Encino. When California Style watercolors were receiving attention in the 1960s, he was among the most prominent of the post World War II group. His watercolors often depict coastline subjects in California. In addition, he has produced a body of work painted on location in Hawaii, where he and his wife Diane have spent a great deal of time.
Biographical information:
Interview with Wayne La Com, 1984.

**Irene Lagorio** (1921-1994) Born: Oakland, CA; Studied: California College of Arts and Crafts (Oakland), University of California (Berkeley), Columbia University; Member: California Water Color Society, San Francisco Art Association. Irene Lagorio exhibited watercolors in Northern and Southern California in the 1950s. In addition, she worked as an art teacher and gave numerous lectures on art.
Biographical information:
*Who's Who in American Art.*

**Robert Landry** (1921-1991) Born: Washington, D.C.; Studied: Abbott Art School, Art Instruction, Inc.; Member: San Diego Watercolor Society, Watercolor West. Robert Landry attended high school on the East Coast then went into the service during World War II. After the war, he studied art in Washington, D.C. and Minneapolis on the G.I. Bill. This led to work as a commercial illustrator for the United States Air Force Graphic Arts Division at the Pentagon, and as an art director for the Federal Aviation Agency and Convair Astronautics.

After the late 1940s, he began a serious painting career and started exhibiting fine art watercolors. His paintings often depicted regional subjects with buildings, boats or coastline structures. Creating a "mood" was important to him and gives his works a narrative quality. His watercolors were primarily sold through art galleries in San Diego and Dallas. Landry also became a well known instructor at watercolor workshops near his home in San Diego and in traveling workshops held in Oregon, Arizona and Hawaii.
Biographical information:
Interview with Phyllis Landry, 1996.

**Art Landy** (1904-1977) Born: Newark, NJ; Studied: Fawcett School of Art (New Jersey), Otis Art Institute (Los Angeles); Member: California Water Color Society, California Art Club. Art Landy was born Arthur Charles Landmesser and grew up on the East Coast. He studied art with George Biddle, Alexander Brook and F. Tolles Chamberlin. By the late 1930s, he was painting watercolors and was employed in the animation art business. He produced background watercolors for the Walt Disney Studios and became a key background artist at Walter Lantz Productions (where *Woody Woodpecker* was created). For exhibitions, he primarily painted landscape and cityscape depictions of Southern California subjects. In the late 1940s, he and Milford Zornes often painted together and occasionally took painting excursions to Mexico. Landy also produced prints and taught watercolor.
Biographical information:
Interview with Milford Zornes, 1992.
*Who's Who in American Art.*

**Frank Lane** (1917- ) Studied: Columbia University, University of California (Los Angeles); Member: California Water Color Society. Frank Lane moved to Los Angeles in the late 1940s and studied with Stanton MacDonald-Wright. Many of his abstract works are based on still life and landscape subjects. He has been an art teacher since the 1940s.
Biographical information:
Interview with Frank Lane, 1984.

**Mildred Lapson** (1923- ) Born: New York City, NY; Studied: Boston Museum School of Art, Art Students League (New York), Jepson Art Institute (Los Angeles); Member: Los Angeles Art Association. Mildred Lapson began exhibiting watercolors with the Connecticut Watercolor Society in the mid-1940s and then in 1949, moved to California. Since the 1950s, she has exhibited works nationally and taught art at Pasadena City College.
Biographical Information:
Interview with Mildred Lapson 1985.

**Lorenzo P. Latimer** (1857-1941) Born: Goldhill, CA; Studied: California School of Design (San Francisco); Member: San Francisco Art Association. Lorenzo Latimer was born at the height of the California Gold Rush and was among the state's first native born watercolor artists. After studying art in San Francisco from 1879 to 1881, he began selling his art and supplementing his income by teaching art classes in the Bay Area.

Throughout his sixty year career, Latimer worked in a conservative watercolor style and often chose to depict landscape subjects. He loved nature and traveled to remote areas in Northern California and throughout the Sierra Nevada mountains to sketch and paint watercolors on location. Latimer was an expert watercolor artist and is considered an important figure in California art at the turn of the century.
Biographical information:
The North Point Gallery, San Francisco, 1995.

**Paul Lauritz** (1889-1975) Born: Larvik, Norway; Studied: Larvik Art School; Member: Royal Society of Arts (England). Paul Lauritz was raised in a small resort village in Norway. While still very young, he took watercolor painting lessons from a visiting English artist, followed by his formal art education. He then immigrated to Canada, traveled across the Northwest Territory, and spent several years in Alaska where he became friends with Sydney Lawrence.

In the 1920s, he settled in California and established an art career producing watercolors and oil paintings. He taught at the Chouinard Art Institute and the Otis Art Institute.
Biographical information:
*Plein Air Painters of California.*

**Dillon Lauritzen** (1904-1952) Born: Salt Lake City, UT; Member: California Water Color Society. Dillon Lauritzen moved to California in 1917 and settled in Los Angeles. He became an illustrator and by the 1930s, was employed by the Automobile Club. He later became an art director for their publications *Touring Topics* and *Westways*. Lauritzen also exhibited fine art watercolors in annual art shows.
Biographical information:
*Westways,* 1949.

**Harry Law** (active in 1920s) Member: California Water Color Society. Harry Law produced representational watercolors painted in a traditional English style. The subjects often depict the California landscape. He lived in Northern California before the mid-1920s. Throughout the 1930s and 1940s he lived in Los Angeles and produced watercolors depicting Southern California scenes.
Biographical information:
*Who's Who in American Art*
California Water Color Society (Catalogs).

**James A. Lawrence** (1910- ) Born: San Francisco, CA; Studied: Art Center School (Los Angeles), Chouinard Art Institute (Los Angeles); Member: California Water Color Society. James Lawrence studied art with Barse Miller, Phil Paradise and Rico Lebrun in Los Angeles during the 1930s. He established a commercial art business in San Francisco where he specialized in illustration and photography. He also exhibited as a member of the Thirteen Watercolorists group.
Biographical information:
*Who's Who in American Art.*

**Jack Laycox** (1921-1984) Born: Auburn, CA; Studied: University of California (Berkeley), San Francisco State College; Member: Society of Western Artists. Jack Laycox grew up in Northern California and after receiving a Bachelor of Arts degree, took a job producing technical illustrations for the Atomic Energy Commission. During the 1950s and 1960s, he did commercial illustrations for the Donald Art Company. Throughout his career, Laycox has produced fine art watercolor paintings and lectured on art. He has exhibited in American Watercolor Society annuals and been active in regional Northern California art clubs and shows.
Biographical information:
*Who's Who in American Art.*

**Rico Lebrun** (1900-1964) Born: Naples, Italy; Studied: Beaux Arts Academy (Italy). Rico Lebrun moved to America in the 1920s. First to New York City and then to the Los Angeles area in 1938. Throughout his life he produced gouache and watercolor works often mixed with heavy drawing. During the post World War II era, Lebrun was a key figure in the promotion and teaching of modern art concepts in Southern California. His art has received international acclaim and his influence on students at the Chouinard Art Institute, Jepson Art Institute, and later at the University of California, Santa Barbara, is still evident in art being produced today.
Biographical information:
*Who's Who in American Art.*

**Chee Chin S. Cheung Lee** (1896-1966) Born: Hoy Ping, China; Studied: California School of Fine Arts (San Francisco); Member: California Water Color Society. Chee Chin Lee came to San Francisco when he was eighteen years old. After studying with Spencer Macky and Gottardo Piazzoni, he began exhibiting watercolors in Northern and Southern California.
Biographical information:
*Views from Asian California*
California Water Color Society (Catalogs).

JAKE LEE *San Francisco's China Town* 1948 22" x 15" Courtesy Roger Genser

NAT LEVY  *Monday Breeze*  1940s  22" x 30"  Buck Collection

NAT LEVY  *White Barns*  1940s  18" x 24"  Jeff Olsen Collection

**Jake Lee** (1915-1991) Born: Monterey, CA; Studied: Otis Art Institute (Los Angeles), San Jose State College (California); Member: California Water Color Society. Jake Lee began painting at an early age, depicting views of the Chinese communities in California and fishing docks near his home in Monterey. He studied art at San Jose State College and after taking a job as a commercial artist for a San Francisco newspaper, became friends with artist Dong Kingman. They spent a great deal of time painting on location in the city and Lee credits Kingman as being an influential instructor and artistic inspiration to him.

By 1944, Lee was settled in Los Angeles and was exhibiting with the California Water Color Society. He worked as a commercial illustrator producing magazine covers, product advertisements, posters and children's book illustrations. Most of these were done with watercolors or gouache on illustration board. For over forty years, he enjoyed a successful career in this field and still found plenty of time to paint and exhibit fine art watercolors. He was also an influential art instructor in Southern California.
Biographical information:
Interview with Jake Lee, 1984.

**John Leeper** (1909-1985) Born: Dandridge, TN; Studied: Phoenix College (Arizona), Otis Art Institute (Los Angeles); Member: California Water Color Society. John Leeper grew up in Phoenix, Arizona and studied art there while in high school and college. From 1931 to 1933, he continued his art education in Los Angeles, then returned to Phoenix. While in Arizona, he produced watercolors, oil paintings and murals depicting regional subjects. In 1942, he moved to Los Angeles and began working on films at Paramount Studios. He was a sketch artist and specialized in designing graphic art to accompany opening credits of films. Leeper worked on a number of classic black and white "Film Noir" movies of that era and received special attention for his "Growing Shadow" art work used in the opening sequence of *Double Indemnity*.

After settling in Los Angeles, he began exhibiting in the California Water Color Society annual exhibitions and established gallery representation in Los Angeles and Laguna Beach. He worked with both transparent and opaque watercolors and alternated between producing art featuring figurative subjects and doing radical abstractions based on landscape scenes. He would often start a painting with a vague reference or idea from memory and then abandon all references to details of the original subject. He would let the work evolve in whatever direction it developed. These paintings ended up looking like non-objective works, as no subject matter was discernible.
Biographical information:
Interview with John Leeper, 1983.

**Frank Lenfest** (1909-1968) Born: Oakland, CA; Studied: University of California (Berkeley), California College of Arts and Crafts (Oakland). Frank Lenfest grew up in Northern California and studied art in Berkeley and Oakland. His primary interest was commercial illustration and cartooning. He produced advertising illustrations using gouache and watercolor for advertising agencies in San Francisco and Seattle. He also produced cartoons that were published in *The Saturday Evening Post* and other magazines. During World War II, he served in the United States Army and produced art work for military publications. He also did a number of portraits for his Army friends. After the war, he continued his freelance commercial business in San Francisco.
Biographical information:
Interview with Mrs. Frank Lenfest, 1998.

**David Levine** (1910- ) Born: South Pasadena, CA; Studied: University of Southern California, Art Center School (Los Angeles); Member: California Water Color Society. David Levine exhibited his watercolors with the California Water Color Society from the early 1930s until the mid-1940s. He often chose to depict American scene subjects with people, cars and other cityscape subjects. His works were included in several major exhibitions of California watercolor artists.
Biographical information:
*Who's Who in American Art*
Tobey C. Moss Gallery, Los Angeles, 1996.

**Hilda Levy** (active in 1940s) Born: Pinsk, Russia; Studied: University of California (Berkeley), Jepson Art Institute (Los Angeles), University of California (Los Angeles); Member: California Water Color Society. Hilda Levy exhibited in the San Francisco area in the 1930s and by the 1950s, settled in Pasadena. She exhibited modern, non-objective works in Southern California in the 1950s and 1960s and served on the board for the California Water Color Society.
Biographical information:
*Who's Who in American Art*
California Water Color Society (Catalogs).

**Nat Levy** (1896-1984) Born: San Francisco, CA; Studied: Mark Hopkins Institute of Art (San Francisco), California School of Fine Arts (San Francisco); Member: Society of Western Artists. Nat Levy was born and raised in San Francisco and after attending high school, studied art with Maynard Dixon, Harold Von Schmidt, Armin Hansen and Frank Van Sloan. By the 1920s, he was an expert watercolor artist and exhibited his works professionally from that time on.

His paintings were included in the Thirteen Watercolorists exhibitions. In addition to being one of the original members of that group, he was an early member of the Society of Western Artists and was the Society's president in 1955. Throughout the years, he taught watercolor painting and produced illustrations, poster designs and prints. He also traveled and painted in New England, Europe and the Far East.
Biographical information:
Interview with Nat Levy, 1982.

**Harry Emerson Lewis** (1892-1958) Born: Hutchinson, KS; Studied: Northwestern University, Sorbonne (Paris), Chicago Art Institute; Member: Palette and Chisel Club, San Francisco Art Association, Oakland Art Association, Society for Sanity in Art. Emerson Lewis moved to California in the 1920s and by the 1930s, was settled in the San Francisco area. He was an expert illustrator, working primarily with watercolors and gouache. In addition, he was active in local art circles and exhibited works in art association shows. After World War II, he became a resident of Laguna Beach and later, Santa Ana.
Biographical information:
*Artists in California, 1786-1940*.

**Tom E. Lewis** (1909-1979) Born: Los Angeles, CA; Studied: University of Southern California; Member: California Water Color Society, San Francisco Art Association. Tom E. Lewis was raised in Pasadena, and became interested in watercolor painting while studying architecture. During the late 1920s, he developed a unique style of painting with watercolors and in 1931, became a member of the California Water Color Society.

Throughout the 1930s, he lived in Laguna Beach and was an active member of the art colony there. He also exhibited his watercolors regularly in Northern California museum shows, receiving several major awards and favorable reviews. After 1950, Lewis lived in the San Francisco area and continued to produce fine art paintings.
Biographical information:
California Water Color Society (Catalogs)
*Tom E. Lewis* (Catalog).

**Orson Alf Linn** (1893-1952) Born: Stockholm, WI. Orson Linn was a commercial illustrator in San Francisco during the 1930s and 1940s. He produced art for the W.P.A. art project during the Depression and exhibited watercolors as a member of the Thirteen Watercolorists group.
Biographical information:
*Artists in California, 1786-1940*
Interview with Hubert Buel, 1983.

**Phillip H. Little** (1887-1960) Born: Worchester, MA. Phillip Little was a commercial illustrator in San Francisco beginning around 1914. He produced watercolors and exhibited with the Thirteen Watercolorists group.
Biographical information:
*Artists in California, 1786-1940*.

**Maurice Logan, N.A.** (1886-1977) Born: San Francisco, CA; Studied: Mark Hopkins Institute of Art (San Francisco), California College of Arts and Crafts (Oakland), Chicago Art Institute; Member: National Academy of Design, American Watercolor Society, California Water Color Society. Maurice Logan was raised in Northern California. He began to receive attention as a professional artist about 1915 and by the mid-1920s, was one of San Francisco's best known commercial illustrators and poster designers. During this era, he produced colorful expressionist oil paintings and exhibited them as a member of a group known as the Society of Six. In the 1930s, he began exhibiting his transparent watercolor paintings and helped to form the Thirteen Watercolorists group.

For many years, he was an influential art instructor at the California College of Arts and Crafts in Oakland. Logan was also on the board of directors of the Society of Western Artists, the West Coast Watercolor Society, and other local art clubs. He also juried art exhibitions at the Oakland Art Museum and was a member of the Bohemian Club, where he showed his paintings on a regular basis.
Biographical information:
Interview with Richard Logan, 1983.

**Arthur Lonergan** (1906-1989) Born: New York City, NY; Studied: Columbia University School of Architecture, Ecole des Beaux Arts (Paris); Member: American Watercolor Society, California Water Color Society. Arthur Lonergan grew up on the East Coast and was introduced to watercolor painting while studying architecture at Columbia University. He received additional art instruction in Paris, then settled in the Los Angeles area in 1935.

Lonergan made a living producing architectural renderings for clients all over the United States and taught classes in the history of architecture and interior design. He also worked for many years as an art director on motion pictures produced by Paramount, Universal and M.G.M. Studios. Throughout his life, he painted and exhibited watercolors on a national level.
Biographical information:
Interview with Arthur Lonergan, 1983.

**Stanley Long** (1892-1972) Born: Oakland, CA; Studied: California School of Fine Arts (San Francisco), Académie Julian (Paris); Member: Society of Western Artists. Stanley Long grew up on a horse ranch in Napa County. After studying art in San Francisco, he received a scholarship to further his education in Paris. When he returned to Northern California, he began producing watercolors of Western life and taught art for nearly twenty years.
Biographical information:
*The Cowboy in Art*.

**René Lopez** (active ca. 1930s) Studied: Otis Art Institute (Los Angeles); Member: California Water Color Society. After attending the Otis Art Institute in the early 1930s, René Lopez began exhibiting his watercolors of local Los Angeles scenes with the California Water Color Society. He was given a one-man show at the Los Angeles Museum of Art in 1935.
Biographical information:
California Water Color Society (Catalogs).

**Erle Loran** (1905-   ) Born: Minneapolis, MN; Studied: Minneapolis School of Art; Member: San Francisco Art Association, California Water Color Society. Erle Loran attended the University of Minnesota in the early 1920s and then continued his education with Cameron Booth. He was awarded the Chaloner Foundation Prize in 1926 and spent the following four years in France studying art, painting and writing. When he returned to America, he settled in Northern California and became a professor of art at the University of California, Berkeley. It was during this period that he began to exhibit his watercolor paintings and helped to develop what became known as the "Berkeley School" style of watercolor painting.

In addition to his fine art painting and teaching, he wrote *Cezanne's Composition*, in print for over forty years and still considered the most thorough study of the formal aspects of that artist's work. He has also written articles for numerous national art magazines.
Biographical information:
Interview with Erle Loran, 1983.

**Janice Penney Lovoos** (1903-   ) Born: Dubuque, IA; Studied: Chouinard Art Institute (Los Angeles); Member: California Water Color Society. Janice Lovoos studied art at the Chouinard Art Institute in the 1920s with F. Tolles Chamberlin and Karl Godwin. Throughout the 1930s, she regularly exhibited her transparent watercolors with the

MAURICE LOGAN  *Fisherman's Wharf*  1950s  18" x 12"  Studio 2 Antiques

DAN LUTZ  *Train Depot*  1940s  15" x 22"  Claremont Fine Arts

DAN LUTZ  *Soft Ball*  1940s  22" x 28"  Mike and Sue Verbal Collection

California Water Color Society; mostly still still-lifes and landscapes. She also produced murals, book illustrations and textile designs. Since World War II, she has concentrated on writing art books and has regularly contributed articles about West Coast artists to *American Artists* magazine and other national publications.
Biographical information:
Interview with Janice Lovoos, 1984.

**Dan Lutz** (1906-1978) Born: Decatur, IL; Studied: Chicago Art Institute; Member: American Watercolor Society, California Water Color Society, Philadelphia Water Color Club. Dan Lutz grew up in Illinois. He attended the Chicago Art Institute for four years and in 1931, received the James Nelson Raymond Traveling Fellowship which enabled him to study and paint in Europe. After returning to the United States, he settled in Southern California.

Throughout the 1930s and 1940s, he primarily produced watercolors featuring regional subjects. After 1950, he concentrated on abstract works painted with oils on canvas.

He taught art at the University of Southern California in the 1930s and at the Chouinard Art Institute in the 1940s. In the 1950s and 1960s, he lectured occasionally, while continuing to paint.
Biographical information:
Interview with Dorothy Lutz Fleurat, 1983.

**Jack Macartney** (1893-1976) Born: San Francisco, CA; Member: Laguna Beach Art Association, Artists of the Southwest. Jack Macartney studied watercolor painting with Eliot O'Hara and Arthur Beaumont. Most of his works are representational depictions of Southwestern landscape subjects, harbor scenes of the San Pedro area, and seascapes of the coast near his home in Laguna Beach. Macartney also taught art at the Businessman's Art Institute in Los Angeles.
Biographical information:
*Six Decades* (Catalog).

**Stanton MacDonald-Wright** (1890-1973) Born: Charlottesville, VA; Studied: Art Students League (Los Angeles), Sorbonne (Paris), Académie Julian (Paris), Ecole des Beaux Arts (Paris); Member: California Water Color Society. When Stanton MacDonald-Wright was ten years old, his family moved to Southern California and settled in Santa Monica. After studying art in Los Angeles, he continued his education in France.

In Paris, he and Morgan Russell developed an abstract painting style known as Synchronism that brought them international attention. After exhibiting all over Europe, MacDonald-Wright traveled to New York City for a brief period before returning to the Los Angeles area in 1918. While he is best known for his large, colorful oil paintings, he also produced many highly imaginative watercolors.

During the 1920s, he taught at the Art Students League in Los Angeles. In the 1930s, he was a regional advisor for the W.P.A. Art Program. After World War II, he became a professor at the University of California, Los Angeles, and was a major influence on many post-war artists who preferred to paint in abstract styles.
Biographical information:
*Southern California Artists (1890-1940)*.

**Louis Macouillard** (1913-1987) Born: San Francisco, CA; Studied: California College of Arts and Crafts (Oakland), Art Students League (New York). Louis Macouillard's paintings from the 1930s through the 1950s depict local cityscape scenes of the Bay Area. He exhibited them with the Thirteen Watercolorists group at local art galleries and in annual museum shows. During World War II, he was stationed in the South Pacific and produced many watercolors, some of which appeared in *Life* magazine. After the war, he continued to paint representational transparent watercolor paintings of cityscape scenes and landscape subjects in the Sonoma County area.
Biographical information:
Interview with Louis Macouillard, 1983.

**Robert Majors** (1913-1960) Born: Ottumwa, IA; Studied: Chouinard Art Institute (Los Angeles); Member: California Water Color Society. Robert Majors grew up in Ontario and studied art with Millard Sheets, Phil Dike and Stanton MacDonald-Wright in the early 1930s. By 1936, he was living in Honolulu, where he did commercial illustration and painted watercolors depicting local Hawaiian scenes. He returned to Southern California a few years later and produced inspirational sketches for the animated film *Fantasia* at the Walt Disney Studios. After serving in the United States Army Motion Picture Unit during World War II, Majors went back to Honolulu. Throughout his career, he exhibited watercolors in California and Hawaii.
Biographical information:
*Who's Who in American Art*
Interview with Maurice Noble, 1997.

**Grace Elizabeth Mallon** (1911-1997) Born: Elizabeth, NJ; Studied: Otis Art Institute (Los Angeles), Chouinard Art Institute (Los Angeles); Member: American Watercolor Society, California Water Color Society. Grace Elizabeth Mallon studied with Millard Sheets and Phil Paradise and began exhibiting her watercolors in the mid-1930s. She lived in Hollywood and worked in the art departments at Universal Studios (1941-1946), Fairbanks Film Productions (1946-1950) and Churchill-Wexler Film Productions (1951-1956). She also illustrated several books.
Biographical information:
*Who's Who in American Art*.

**Albert Marshall** (1891-1970) Member: California Art Club. Albert Marshall lived in Northern California before moving to the Los Angeles area in the 1920s. He produced representational watercolors of California landscape subjects, often focusing on famous landmarks.
Biographical information:
*California Art*
*Artists in California, 1786-1940*.

**Fletcher Martin**, N.A. (1904-1979) Born: Palisade, CO; Member: National Academy of Design, California Water Color Society. After working as a lumberjack, boxer, and sailor, Fletcher Martin got a job in 1926 with a printing firm in Los Angeles and began a self-taught art education. His watercolors, oil paintings, murals and lithographs often depict regional subject matter; featuring people as the central

themes. He taught at the Art Center School, Mills College, Otis Art Institute and Claremont College, and was an artist war correspondent during World War II.
Biographical information:
*Southern California Art.*

**Sandy Martin** (1897-1974) Born: Atlanta, GA; Studied: University of Washington, Chouinard Art Institute (Los Angeles); Member: San Clemente Art Club. Sandy Martin studied art in Washington State and eventually worked as an illustrator in Tacoma until the early 1930s. He then moved to the Los Angeles area where he received watercolor painting instruction from Millard Sheets, Phil Dike and Rex Brandt. In addition, he studied illustration art with Pruett Carter. During the 1930s and 1940s, he worked as a freelance commercial artist producing illustrations for advertisement agencies. By the early 1950s, he was living in San Clemente and exhibiting works in regional art shows and at the Royal Hawaiian Art Gallery in Honolulu. As a service to local police departments, he produced drawings of wanted criminals. Martin primarily worked with watercolors when painting illustrations and fine art works. The Sandy Martin Memorial Art Gallery, a city owned art center in San Clemente, was given his name in honor of his contributions to art in that region.
Biographical information:
San Clemente Art Club (Catalogs).

**Marciano Martinez** (1939-    ) Born: Claremont, CA; Studied: Otis Art Institute (Los Angeles), California College of Arts and Crafts (Oakland), University of San Carlos (Guatemala), Claremont Graduate School (California). Marciano Martinez grew up in Claremont and received a scholarship to study at the Otis Art Institute while still in high school. In the late 1950s, he studied with George Post, then took additional instruction from Phil Dike, Robert E. Wood, Rex Brandt, Millard Sheets and Milford Zornes. He prefers to paint on location using transparent watercolors and has primarily worked in a representational style. Martinez has exhibited in Southern California galleries and taught art at Cal Poly Pomona and Fullerton College.
Biographical information:
Interview with Marciano Martinez, 1996.

**Roy M. Mason, N.A.** (1886-1972) Born: Gilbert Mills, NY; Member: National Academy of Design, American Watercolor Society, Philadelphia Water Color Club. Roy Mason grew up on the East Coast and received basic art instruction from his father. While he was developing his watercolor painting style, his close friend Chauncey Ryder provided professional criticism, but for the most part, Mason was a self-taught watercolorist.

By 1916, he was settled in Batavia, New York and producing watercolors for exhibition and sale. Most of the time he would paint small watercolor sketches while out on location, making notes if there were people or animals included in the work. From these sketches he would work up larger watercolors in his studio. Although he is best known for his depictions of hunting and fishing scenes, he has also done a number of works with landscape and coastal subjects.

At times during his art career, Mason produced commercial illustrations for magazines including *Collier's*, *True* and *Reader's Digest*. His studio was in New York for most of his career, but he began spending time in California starting in the 1930s. Gradually, he stayed longer each year until most of the last twenty years of his life were spent on the West Coast.
Biographical information:
*Watercolor Methods*
Interview with Eileen Whitaker, 1995.

**Arthur Mathews** (1860-1945) Born: Markesan, WI; Studied: Académie Julian (Paris); Member: Philadelphia Art Club. Arthur Mathews came to San Francisco with his family in 1867. After working as a designer and commercial illustrator, he traveled to France to study art. He returned to San Francisco where he became an influential art instructor at the California School of Design. He and his wife, Lucia, were leaders of the California Decorative Style and received national recognition for their contributions to the American Arts and Crafts Movement. Throughout his career, Mathews produced watercolor and gouache paintings.
Biographical information:
*Who's Who in American Art*
*California Design, 1910.*

**Lucia K. Mathews** (1870-1955) Born: San Francisco, CA; Studied: Mills College (Oakland), Mark Hopkins Institute of Art (San Francisco); Member: San Francisco Art Association. Lucia Mathews grew up in California and after studying in Paris, settled in San Francisco with her husband Arthur Mathews. Together they painted and produced all types of decorative furniture, murals, frames and other artistic objects. In addition, they published the *Philopolis*, a magazine devoted to the Arts and Crafts Movement. She produced watercolors throughout her career.
Biographical information:
*California Design, 1910.*

**Paul Mays** (1887-1961) Born: Cheswick, PA; Studied: Oberlin College, Hawthorne School, Art Students League (New York), Académie Colarossi (Paris), Académie de la Grande Chaumiére (Paris); Member: Carmel Art Association. Paul Mays grew up in northeast America and came to San Francisco in 1915. Although he maintained a residence in Northern California for the remainder of his life, he spent a great deal of time traveling and painting in other parts of the world. Mays was included in the 1937 California Group traveling exhibition and produced a number of works using water based media throughout his career.
Biographical information:
Trotter Galleries, Carmel, 1994.

**Douglas McClellan** (1921-  ) Born: Pasadena, CA; Studied: Art Center School (Los Angeles), Colorado Springs Fine Art Center (Colorado); Member: California Water Color Society. Douglas McClellan studied art in Colorado with Boardman Robinson and Jean Charlot. He exhibited watercolors in California in the 1950s and 1960s. In addition, he has been an art instructor and administrator in Southern California since 1950.
Biographical information:
*Who's Who in American Art.*

LOUIS MACOUILLARD  *San Francisco*  1949  18" x 24"  Mettler Collection

LOUIS MACOUILLARD  *California and Montgomery*  1930s  20" x 24"  Papillion Gallery

ROY MASON  *Old Friends*  1950s  21" x 30"  Braarud Fine Art

ROY MASON  *Red Heads*  1940s  18" x 24"  Michael A. Latragna Fine Art

**Francis McComas** (1875-1938) Born: Fingal, Tasmania; Studied: Sydney Technical College (Australia); Member: American Watercolor Society, Philadelphia Water Color Club. Francis McComas studied art in Australia before sailing to San Francisco, via Samoa and Hawaii. In 1898, he spent a brief period in Monterey, studied art with Arthur Mathews in San Francisco, and then went to Paris where he continued his art education at the Académie Julian. Upon his return to the West Coast in 1901, he began traveling throughout the Southwest painting depictions of desert landscapes which often included monumental rock formations and Indian dwelling places.

In 1912, he returned to California, got married and settled in Monterey. McComas was a well traveled man, having visited many parts of the world including Greece, Mexico, Tahiti, Alaska and greater North America. He was socially connected and early in his career, established art connections on the East Coast and in Europe. When he began seriously exhibiting his works in the early 1920s, these connections proved valuable.

Although he produced many oil paintings and murals, McComas received most of his national acclaim for his bold and directly painted watercolors. On the East Coast, he received awards and notoriety from his many watercolors exhibited in annual shows of the Philadelphia Water Color Club and American Watercolor Society. On the West Coast, he was a prominent exhibitor at the Del Monte Gallery and was honored with a special two-man show with his former art instructor Arthur Mathews at the Panama-Pacific International Exposition in San Francisco. Most importantly, his works were included in the Armory show, the exhibition that is credited with changing the coarse of American art.

For twenty-six years, McComas was a key figure in the development of California watercolor painting and was an inspiration to younger artists who were considering pursuing watercolors as their primary painting medium. He was a popular, well-liked person and a respected artist in the Monterey community where he spent much of his life.
Biographical information:
Interview with Margaret Bruton, 1980
*Yesterday's Artists on the Monterey Peninsula* (Catalog).

**Betty McCoon** (active in 1960s) Born: Fresno, CA; Studied: Monterey Peninsula College, San Francisco Art Institute; Member: West Coast Watercolor Society. Betty McCoon began painting in the late 1950s and received art instruction from Peter Blos. She has remained in Central California and become known for her watercolors, oils and works done in a variety of art mediums. Her works have been exhibited nationally and she has occasionally given art instruction.
Biographical information:
Interview with Betty McCoon, 1996.

**James McCray** (1912-1993) Born: Niles, CA; Studied: University of California (Berkeley); Member: San Francisco Art Association. James McCray studied with Worth Ryder and John Haley, and then went on to teach at the University of California, Berkeley, and the California School of Fine Arts.

In the 1940s and early 1950s, he produced non-objective, geometric, abstractionist works with hard edge designs with bright primary colors. For a period in the late 1950s, he concentrated on still life and figurative subjects. By the 1960s, he was painting non-objective works which had geometric shapes weaving in and out of expressionistic fields of color. Throughout his career, McCray worked with watercolor, tempera and gouache.
Biographical information:
Interview with James McCray, 1984.

**William T. McDermitt** (1884-1961) Born: Percy, IL; Studied: Pomona College (California), Art Students League (New York), Pratt Art Institute (New York); Member: California Water Color Society. William T. McDermitt studied art in California in 1908 and then traveled to the East Coast, Washington State, and finally settled in Pomona, California in 1931. He exhibited his watercolors locally and taught at the Businessman's Art Association.
Biographical information:
Interview with Melissa Webster, 1988.

**Dixie McElroy** (1909-1972) Born: Hartley, Iowa; Studied: Chouinard Art Institute; Member: California Water Color Society. Dixie McElroy grew up in Iowa and Colorado and moved to California in 1932. She studied art in Los Angeles and received instruction in watercolor painting from Dong Kingman and Rex Brandt. She was employed as a commercial artist, but found plenty of time to produce fine art watercolors which she exhibited in art galleries and in annual watercolor exhibitions.
Biographical information:
Jay Crawford.

**Robert McIntosh** (1916- ) Born: Vallejo, CA; Studied: California School of Fine Arts (San Francisco), Art Center School (Los Angeles). Robert McIntosh grew up in Stockton and briefly studied art in San Francisco. He was then awarded a three year scholarship to Art Center School where he received instruction from Stanley Reckless. While working at the Walt Disney Studios in the 1930s, he produced art for several animated films including *Pinocchio*, *Fantasia* and *Bambi*. During World War II, he served in the United States Army-Air Force producing art work for training films. After the war, he produced watercolor background paintings for animated productions. For ten years, he worked on the cartoon shorts of *Mr. Magoo* at U.P.A. From the 1940s through the 1970s, he painted and exhibited watercolors. Most were colorful works done in a geometric, abstractionist style.
Biographical information:
Interview with Robert McIntosh, 1998.

**David McKay** (1905-1992) Born: Montana; Studied: Chicago Academy of Fine Arts, Fornish Art School (Seattle); Member: California Water Color Society, West Coast Watercolor Society. David McKay studied art in Chicago and Seattle and eventually became a commercial artist in Seattle during the 1930s. In 1944, he moved to the San Francisco area and began working as an artist at the *San Francisco Chronicle*. Throughout his career, McKay produced abstract watercolors for exhibition in annual art shows.
Biographical information:
Interview with Mrs. David McKay, 1996.

**Marcelle McKusik** (active ca. 1950s) Born: Minnesota; Studied: University of Minnesota, Walker Art Center (Minneapolis), Chouinard Art Institute (Los Angeles). Marcelle McKusik grew up in Minnesota and then moved to La Jolla, California. By the early 1950s, she moved to El Centro. McKusik has produced watercolors depicting this area and worked as a portrait painter.
Biographical information:
*Widening Horizons*, 1949.

**Richard McLean** (1934- ) Born: Hoquiam, WA; Studied: California College of Arts and Crafts (Oakland), Mills College (Oakland). Richard McLean grew up in Idaho, and then moved to the Bay Area in the 1950s to study art in Oakland. After earning a Master's degree, he began teaching art at San Francisco State College. In the 1960s, he started exhibiting photo realist paintings. Some were painted with oils on canvas, others were transparent watercolors on paper. By the early 1970s, he received international recognition and was selling his works through the O.K. Harris Gallery in New York City. McLean's works are part of important museum collections including the Guggenheim Museum and the Whitney Museum of American Art.
Biographical information:
*Who's Who in American Art.*

**Elizabeth Baskerville McNaughton** (1906-1991) Born: Los Angeles, CA; Studied: Chouinard Art Institute (Los Angeles), Pennsylvania Academy of Fine Arts; Member: National Society of Arts and Letters. Elizabeth Baskerville McNaughton grew up in a family with a love for art and music. Upon graduating from Manual Arts High School in Los Angeles, she attended Chouinard Art Institute where she studied under Clarence Hinkle and F. Tolles Chamberlin.

Married to an Air Force Lieutenant, McNaughton lived all over the United States and in Japan. She exhibited her work throughout the 1930s, 1940s and 1950s; and again in the 1970s and 1980s. McNaughton came back to California and settled in Pebble Beach in 1964, where she continued to paint until the year before her death. She is known best for her work in watercolors, oils and pastels.
Biographical information:
Stary-Sheets Fine Art Galleries, Laguna Beach, 1995.

**Henry Meier** (1916-1977) Born: Ashtabula, OH; Member: San Diego Watercolor Society. During the 1940s Henry Meier lived in Michigan and spent summers painting watercolors in California. By 1951, he was living in Carlsbad and exhibiting locally. For several years, he taught at Mira Costa College.
Biographical information:
Interview with Mrs. Henry Meier, 1995.

**Fred Meiers** (1916-1992) Born: El Paso, TX; Studied: San Diego State College, Claremont Graduate School (California); Member: California Water Color Society. Fred Meiers came to California with his parents when he was nine years old. He grew up in San Diego, attended college there, and went on to study watercolor painting with Millard Sheets in Claremont. During the 1930s he painted many watercolors of regional subjects and exhibited locally. During World War II, he served in the United States Navy. He was stationed in the South Pacific and whenever possible he produced art depicting island subjects. After the war he taught painting at Long Beach City College and continued producing art in watercolor and oils. By 1957, he became interested in designing fabric and stoneware. He and his wife ran an import business bringing these products and Mexican folk art into California.
Biographical information:
Interview with Susanna Meiers
and Mayde Herberg, 1998.

**Robert Hiram Meltzer** (1921-1987) Born: New Rochelle, New York; Studied: Southern Methodist University, University of Hawaii, Art Students League (New York); Member: American Watercolor Society, Society of Western Artists. Robert Hiram Meltzer studied art with Ernest Fiene and Jean Charlot. He served as a combat artist-journalist in Korea during the early 1950s and spent time in Hawaii in the later 1950s. He was an expert watercolorist; primarily using transparent paints. Meltzer lived in Beaumont, California in the early 1960s and exhibited in important watercolor shows throughout America. He was also an art instructor and heavy-weight-lifting champion.
Biographical information:
San Juan Fine Arts.

**Daniel Marcus Mendelowitz** (1905-1980) Born: Linton, ND; Studied: Stanford University, California School of Fine Arts (San Francisco), Art Students League (New York); Member: California Water Color Society. Daniel Mendelowitz grew up in California and began exhibiting watercolors in the 1930s. He was an art instructor at San Jose State College from 1927 to 1934 and at Stanford University from 1934 to 1970.
Biographical information:
*Artists in California, 1786-1940.*

**Knud Merrild** (1894-1954) Born: Denmark; Member: California Water Color Society. Knud Merrild came to Los Angeles about 1923 and worked as a house painter. During the 1940s, he began creating non-objective art using a technique he called "Flux Painting" (that involved pouring and dripping paint into wet areas of a paper or canvas surface). Some of these paintings were exhibited in California Water Color Society shows.
Biographical information:
*Southern California Art.*

**Ben Messick** (1901-1981) Born: Strafford, MO; Studied: Chouinard Art Institute (Los Angeles); Member: California Art Club. Ben Messick was born in the Ozarks and spent his childhood there. When he was sixteen, he joined the armed forces and was sent to the European battle front. After recuperating from his wartime experiences, he moved to Los Angeles and studied with F. Tolles Chamberlin, Clarence Hinkle and Pruett Carter.

By the mid-1930s, he had developed his own style of painting and became known as one of the West Coast's key Regionalist artists. While Messick was an extremely competent watercolorist, these works were not exhibited frequently and

OTHELLO MICHETTI  *Closed for Winter*  1940s  22" x 30"  Dr. & Mrs. Larry Ho Collection

BEN MESSICK  *Circus Barker*  1940s  14" x 16"  Buck Collection

BARSE MILLER  *Balboa Inlet*  1942  18" x 24"  Philip H. Greene Collection

BARSE MILLER  *Auburn, California*  1945  15" x 22"  David & Sally Martin Collection

did not receive the attention given to his oils on canvas. During the 1940s and early 1950s, he taught life drawing at the Chouinard Art Institute and the San Diego School of Arts and Crafts. He was also an instructor at the Messick-Hay Studio in Long Beach. In addition, he produced and exhibited lithographic prints.
Biographical information:
Interview with Velma Messick, 1983.

**Othello Michetti** (1895-1981) Born: Allano, Abruzzi, Italy; Studied: Art Students League (New York), Academy of Art (New York), Mark Hopkins Institute of Art (San Francisco); Member: Society of Western Artists. Othello Michetti came to America with his family when he was ten and settled in New York. He studied art with Frank Vincent DuMond and George Bridgman at the Art Students League and went on to attend the Academy of Art. When he was twenty-one, he moved to San Francisco where he continued his art education and began painting regularly with watercolors.

Michetti actively exhibited his watercolors on the West Coast for over fifty years and was a director of the Society of Western Artists from the time of its formation. Between 1921 and the early 1970s, he was the art director of a major San Francisco commercial lithographic firm. He was considered an authority on color design for commercial uses, gave lectures on the subject, and wrote a trade booklet, *Color Harmony*, which explained his theories.
Biographical information:
Interview with Louise Michetti, 1983.

**Harold Miles** (1887-1963) Born: Des Moines, IA; Studied: Académie Colarossi (Paris), Cumming Art School; Member: California Water Color Society. Harold Miles studied art in midwestern America and France before settling in Los Angeles. By 1927, he was employed as an artist in the motion picture industry and was exhibiting watercolors in art association shows. In the 1930s and 1940s, he emerged as a key artist in Hollywood, producing pre-production art for most of the major movie studios. The Walt Disney Studios brought him in on several of their animated feature films including *Fantasia* and *Bambi*. Often these studio works were painted with watercolors or gouache. In addition, he painted and exhibited fine art watercolors.
Biographical information:
*Who Was Who in American Art*
Interview with Jessie Payzant, 1988.

**Barse Miller, N.A.** (1904-1973) Born: New York City, NY; Studied: National Academy of Design (New York), Pennsylvania Academy of Fine Arts; Member: National Academy of Design, American Watercolor Society, California Water Color Society, Philadelphia Water Color Club. Barse Miller began formal art instruction at the National Academy of Design while still in elementary school. There he received instruction from Henry Snell. A few years later, he continued his education with Hugh Breckenridge at the Pennsylvania Academy of Fine Arts. Both of these teachers were award winning watercolorists. At eighteen years of age he was awarded the Cresson Traveling Scholarship which enabled him to study and paint in Europe for two years. In 1924, he moved to Los Angeles and settled.

The next year he began exhibiting with the California Art Club and by 1928, was an active member of the California Water Color Society, serving as its president in 1936, 1937, and 1938. His watercolors from this era were quite different than most works being produced on the West Coast. They often included cityscape subjects with people, automobiles and industrial objects. As the new era of California watercolorists, led by Millard Sheets and Phil Dike, emerged in the early 1930s, they welcomed Miller into the movement and revered him as one of the leading figures.

Throughout the 1930s and 1940s, his watercolors became increasingly popular. His ability to manipulate wet-into-wet washes had a huge impact on many of his students and fellow artists. His many years of formal art instruction gave him a superior knowledge of color and design and when the California Group was being scrutinized in the 1930s, his work helped greatly to give the overall movement credibility.

During World War II, he went into the United States Army and became head of the Combat Art Section in the South Pacific. He produced a number of outstanding watercolors and was awarded for his artistic contributions that visually documented the war in that region. After the war, he received a Guggenheim Fellowship and eventually settled in New York State. His watercolors after this period became increasingly modern, as he sought to relate to a changing art world.

During his period in California, Miller taught at the Chouinard Art Institute and, for ten years, at the Art Center School. As a teacher of watercolor painting, he was extremely influential and helped many of the most successful California watercolorists to understand the possibilities of this unique medium. In later years, he also made special visits to the West Coast to teach at the Brandt-Dike Summer School of Painting and other watercolor workshops. In addition to watercolor painting, he also exhibited oil paintings and produced a number of murals.
Biographical information:
Interview with Betty Miller, 1984
Interview with Rex Brandt, 1983
*A Century and a Half of American Art.*

**Arthur Millier** (1893-1975) Born: Somerset, England; Studied: California School of Fine Arts (San Francisco); Member: California Water Color Society. Arthur Millier came to California when he was fifteen years old and graduated from Los Angeles High School. After serving in World War I, he studied art in San Francisco and then moved to the Los Angeles area. He produced watercolors and etchings throughout his life, but is best known as the premier Southern California art critic from 1926 until the early 1960s. His columns appeared in the *Los Angeles Times* and the *Christian Science Monitor*. Through these and other nationally published articles, Millier helped to bring many of California's finest watercolor artists to the attention of the American public.
Biographical information:
*Who's Who on the Pacific Coast.*

**Theodore Modra** (1873-1930) Born: Poland; Studied: Académie Colarossi (Paris), with Robert Henri (New York); Member: California Water Color Society. Theodore Modra spent most of his life working as an artist in the eastern

United States. In 1915, he moved to Los Angeles and exhibited his watercolors annually until 1930. He was involved with the organization of art exhibitions at the Pacific Southwest Exposition in Los Angeles and at the Pomona Fair. He was also president of the California Water Color Society in 1927 and 1928.
Biographical information:
*Southern California Art.*

**Thomas Moran, N.A.** (1837-1926) Born: England; Studied: with James Hamilton (Philadelphia); Member: National Academy of Design, American Watercolor Society. Thomas Moran grew up in Philadelphia and began producing art while in his teens. By the late 1870s, he was established as one of America's premier landscape painters, known especially for his depictions of Yellowstone and Grand Canyon National Parks. Although his large oil paintings brought the most attention, Moran's watercolors are also considered an important contribution to American art.

His first watercolors depicting California landscape subjects were produced in 1872 when he and his wife visited Yosemite. Numerous others were done on subsequent painting excursions. After the turn of the century, Moran spent extended periods of time in Pasadena and Santa Barbara.
Biographical information:
*California Design, 1910*
*Thomas Moran.*

**Mary DeNeale Morgan** (1868-1948) Born: San Francisco, CA; Studied: California School of Design (San Francisco); Member: California Water Color Society, San Francisco Art Association, Carmel Art Association. Mary DeNeale Morgan grew up in the Bay Area and studied art with Virgil Williams, Emil Carlsen and William Keith. Between 1900 and 1924, she was known for producing opaque watercolors of landscape subjects. She was a resident of Carmel and became known for painting depictions of local coastal views. Her works were included in the majority of important exhibitions of pre-1930s California art and she received a number of awards.

Morgan worked with oil paints on canvas after 1924, but still continued to produce watercolors and oleo tempera works for inclusion in watercolor exhibitions. She was a prominent figure in the development of the art community on the Monterey Peninsula and one of the key artists who sold works at the Del Monte Art Gallery.
Biographical information:
*Plein Air Painters of California.*

**Joseph Emil Morhardt** (1906-1988) Born: Pasadena, CA; Studied: Pomona College (California). J.E. "Aim" Morhardt is a native Californian and spent most of his youth in the Los Angeles area. During the 1920s, he attended college and earned a Master's degree in music and received his secondary teaching credentials. In 1938, he received art instruction from Ben Norris and from that time on, he painted representational, transparent watercolors. He lived in Bishop until the end of his life, where he painted the majestic scenery found near his home.
Biographical information:
Interview with Aim Morhardt, 1984.

**Julon Moser** (1900-1997) Born: Schenectady, NY; Studied: Chouinard Art Institute (Los Angeles), University of California, Scripps College (California); Member: California Water Color Society, Women Painters of the West. Julon Moser moved to Los Angeles in 1925 and studied with Millard Sheets and Nicolai Fechin. In the 1930s she began exhibiting her watercolors with the California Water Color Society. During World War II, she was the Director of an art department for the United States Navy Rehabilitation Center at Port Hueneme. She served as president of the Women Painters of the West in the late 1950s and exhibited for many years in Southern California art galleries.
Biographical information:
Interview with Julon Moser, 1984.

**Joseph Mugnaini** (1912-1992) Born: Tuscany, Italy; Studied: Otis Art Institute (Los Angeles). Joseph Mugnaini came to California in 1926 and settled in Los Angeles. During the Depression, he studied art with Ejnar Hansen and Ralph Holmes while working as a poster artist and commercial illustrator. After serving in the Army during World War II, he began teaching at the Otis Art Institute. In addition to producing watercolors, oil paintings and lithographs, Mugnaini illustrated numerous books for Heritage Press and Limited Editions.
Biographical information:
*American Artist* (Magazine).

**Lawrence Murphy** (1871-1947) Studied: Académie Julian (Paris); Member: Group of Independent Artists. Lawrence Murphy grew up in Denver, Colorado. About 1913, he studied art in France and then took further instruction in New York City with George Bridgman and Frank Vincent DuMond. By late 1915, he had become a resident of Los Angeles, where he remained the rest of his life. Murphy was a prolific artist, but rarely exhibited his work. He is best remembered as a key art instructor at the Chouinard Art Institute, where he taught life drawing and painting. His emphasis on composition and drawing skills gave some of California's finest California Style watercolorists a solid, foundational art education.
Biographical information:
*Chouinard, A Vision Betrayed.*

**Darwin Musselman** (1916- ) Born: Selma, CA; Studied: Art Center School (Los Angeles), University of California (Berkeley), Member: American Watercolor Society, California Water Color Society. Darwin Musselman was born in California and grew up in the central part of the state. He attended college in Fresno and later went to the Art Center School in Los Angeles on a scholarship. There, he studied with Barse Miller and Fletcher Martin. He received additional art instruction at the University of California, Berkeley, and with Lyonel Feininger and Yasuo Kuniyoshi.

For the past forty years, Musselman has taught art at the California College of Arts and Crafts and at Fresno State College. He has traveled throughout Europe and the United States since the 1950s using sketches made on these trips as subjects for his watercolor and oil paintings.
Biographical information:
Interview with Darwin Musselman, 1983.

ALEXANDER NEPOTE  *Mystic Tower*  1940  15" x 22"  Courtesy Hanne-Lore Nepote

ALEXANDER NEPOTE  *Untitled*  1955  15" x 22"  Courtesy Hanne-Lore Nepote

BEN NORRIS  *Arming the B17E*  1942  15" x 22"  Claremont Fine Arts

BEN NORRIS  *Hula Dancers, U.S.O. Show*  1942  15" x 22"  Marty & Ronnie Lomeli Collection

**Alexander Nepote** (1913-1986) Born: Valley Home, CA; Studied: California College of Arts and Crafts (Oakland), Mills College (Oakland); Member: California Water Color Society, San Francisco Art Association. Alexander Nepote grew up in Central California. In the 1930s, he received a scholarship to study art at the California College of Arts and Crafts and then went on to earn a Master's of Fine Arts degree from Mills College. During World War II, he worked at the Kaiser Shipyards in Richmond. In 1945, he became a Professor and Dean of the faculty at the California College of Arts and Crafts. From 1950 to 1977 he was an Art Professor at California State University, San Francisco.

His early works are lush watercolors, painted wet-into-wet, that often depict regional farm scenes and cityscapes. By the 1940s, he was producing abstract works with floating shapes, lost and found edges, and complex geometric compositions. During the 1950s, he painted non-objective works and radical abstractions based on landscapes. After the 1960s, he painted many works inspired by rock formation shapes and textures. They were produced using waterbased paints in combination with innovative paper collage techniques.

Nepote was a prominent watercolor artist in Northern California and exhibited in most of the annual watercolor exhibitions at the San Francisco Museum of Art and Oakland Art Museum between 1935 and 1960. He was an active member of the California Water Color Society and was the first artist to receive a purchase prize for a non-objective art work. He was a founding member of a group of artists known as "Layerists" and exhibited his multi media works in their shows.
Biographical information:
Interview with Alexander Nepote, 1984.

**Hanne-Lore Sutro Nepote** (1923-   ) Born: Freiburg, Germany; Studied: University of California (Berkeley). Hanne-Lore Sutro immigrated to the United States in 1939 and settled near San Francisco. She studied art in the 1940s with John Haley, Erle Loran and Margaret Peterson O'Hagen. For ten years, in the late 1940s and early 1950s, she painted opaque watercolors that depicted houses and cityscapes. She and her artist-husband, Alexander Nepote, took many trips to the Mother Lode area of California where she painted views of the old mining camps.
Biographical information:
Interview with Hanne-Lore Sutro Nepote, 1984.

**Ethel Pearce Nerger** (1901-1985) Born: Norfolk, VA; Studied: California School of Fine Arts (San Francisco). Ethel Pearce Nerger was raised in Virginia and Washington State. In the late 1930s, she studied art with Spencer Macky and Otis Oldfield, then later received instruction from David Park. She produced Abstract Impressionist works and exhibited them in the Bay Area until the late 1960s.
Biographical information:
Art Exchange Gallery, San Francisco.

**Maurice Noble** (1910-   ) Born: Spooner, MN; Studied: Chouinard Art Institute (Los Angeles). Maurice Noble spent his teenage years living in Pomona and by the early 1930s, was studying art in Los Angeles with Lawrence Murphy, Millard Sheets, Phil Dike and Clarence Hinkle. He then began a job at the Walt Disney Studios producing development sketches and watercolor backgrounds for animated films. During the 1930s, he made many important contributions to classic Disney films, including the *Silly Symphonies* series, *The Old Mill, Snow White and the Seven Dwarfs, Fantasia, Dumbo* and *Bambi*. During World War II, he was in the United States Army Photographic Signal Corps working under Frank Capra and Ted Geisel (Dr. Seuss) producing cartoon booklets and animated films for the Army. Since the 1940s, Noble has produced art works for many memorable Chuck Jones animated film productions including episodes of; *Bugs Bunny*, the *Road Runner,* and *Daffy Duck*. Although he produced a large number of watercolors for animated films and occasionally did landscape paintings on location, Noble has not pursued exhibiting art work in art shows.
Biographical information:
Interview with Maurice Noble, 1997.

**Ben Norris** (1910-   ) Born: Redlands, CA; Studied: Pomona College (California), Harvard University, Sorbonne (Paris); Member: California Water Color Society, Philadelphia Water Color Club. Ben Norris grew up in Southern California and graduated from Pomona College. He was awarded a scholarship to attend Harvard University studying art history and watercolor painting. This was followed by art classes in Spain, Italy and at the Sorbonne in France. When he returned to Southern California in 1934, he began regularly painting watercolors out on location with friend Tom Craig. In addition, he took art classes from Stanton MacDonald-Wright. For about a year he painted California Style watercolors of Los Angeles regional scenes and produced animation art at the Harmon-Ising Studios.

In 1936, he moved to Honolulu, Hawaii and began a 30 year career as an art instructor. He immediately began producing watercolors depicting regional Hawaiian scenes and within the year was given the first of many one-man shows at the Honolulu Academy of Arts. These works were also widely exhibited in California and a number of them were reproduced in *Paradise of the Pacific* magazine.

During World War II, he worked in an army camouflage shop in Honolulu. Because of a friendship with a General, he was able to go out on the airstrip and paint watercolors of wartime activity. Several of these works appeared in *Life* magazine. He also produced a series of watercolors which depict the impact of the increased military presence in downtown Honolulu.

After the war, Norris became chairman of the art department at the University of Hawaii, a time consuming job which left him less time to produce fine art. In the mid-1950s, when he returned to painting regularly, the works became increasingly abstract. They were often painted with opaque watercolors and featured bold patterns and solid shapes. In 1976, he moved to the East Coast and has since painted watercolors and exhibited in New York City.

While living in Hawaii, he also was an art supervisor on many architectural projects and painted murals in the Royal Hawaiian Hotel and First National Bank in Honolulu.
Biographical information:
Interview with Ben Norris, 1997
Claremont Fine Arts Gallery, Claremont, 1997
*Who's Who in American Art.*

**Crandall Norton** (1920- ) Born: Springfield, MA; Studied: Art Center School (Los Angeles); Member: American Watercolor Society, California Watercolor Society. Crandall Norton has lived in Southern California since 1927. He grew up in Pasadena and during World War II, did illustrations for handbooks produced by Douglas Aircraft and the California Institute of Technology. He studied art with James Couper Wright and Milford Zornes. In the 1950s, he was exhibiting watercolors on a national level. From the beginning, he produced classic California Style watercolors with bold composition and clean transparent colors. His natural flair for handling large wet-into-wet washes also brought him much attention. Norton has received many awards for his watercolors and in 1968, presented a one-man show that toured 19 states. In addition, he has taught at the Laguna Beach School of Art, was Assistant Director for Gallery One-Eight-Five in Pasadena and produced a number of architectural renderings.
Biographical information:
Interview with Crandall Norton, 1990.

**Gordon Nunes** (1914-1991) Born: Porterville, CA; Studied: University of California (Los Angeles); Member: California Water Color Society. Gordon Nunes worked as a Professor of Art at the University of California, Los Angeles and exhibited his watercolors of still life subjects in regional art exhibitions.
Biographical information:
*Who's Who in American Art.*

**Vernon Nye** (1915- ) Born: Batavia, NY; Studied: Mechanics Institute (New York); Member: American Watercolor Society, Society of Western Artists. Vernon Nye was raised in New York State and studied art with Eliot O'Hara, Roy Mason, Ted Kautzky and Harry Anderson. After a successful career working as a book illustrator for the Review and Herald Publishing Association in Washington, D.C., he moved to Northern California. He became chairman of the art department at Pacific Union College and began teaching watercolor classes on the Mendocino Coast.

He has primarily worked with transparent watercolors and occasionally adds opaque colors. In many works, he feels the need for the image to tell a story, so figures are often included. Fisherman, campers, farmers or beach walkers often become subjects included in his watercolor landscapes.

In more recent years, he has taught art on college campuses in Riverside, California and College Place, Washington. As an instructor for watercolor workshops, he has traveled to Japan, Europe and Hawaii. His watercolors have been exhibited on the West Coast in Society of Western Artists exhibitions, on the East Coast in American Watercolor Society annual exhibitions and in galleries in Northern and Southern California.

Nye has contributed greatly to California watercolor painting and was one of the key artists to emerge on the West Coast during the Post World War II era.
Biographical information:
Interview with Vernon Nye, 1983.

**N. Eric Oback** (1920-1979) Born: Sweden; Studied: California College of Arts and Crafts (Oakland); Member: American Watercolor Society, Society of Western Artists. N. Eric Oback moved to Northern California from Sweden in 1946 and began to professionally exhibit his watercolor paintings in the early 1950s. From the 1950s until 1979, he lived in San Jose and was an art instructor at San Jose State College.
Biographical information:
Interview with Mrs. N. Eric Oback, 1984.

**Chiura Obata** (1885-1975) Born: Sendal, Japan; Studied: Bijitsuin Art Institute (Japan); Member: California Water Color Society. Chiura Obata moved to San Francisco in 1903. He worked as an illustrator through the 1920s, and from 1932-1954, taught at the University of California, Berkeley. During World War II, he was forced to live in a Japanese internment camp. Obata painted and exhibited watercolors throughout his life. Those depicting scenes of the 1906 San Francisco earthquake and of the Japanese camps have received special attention.
Biographical information:
*Artists in California, 1786-1940.*

**Helen G. Oehler** (1893-1979) Born: Ottawa, IL; Studied: Chicago Art Institute; Member: New York Water Color Club, American Watercolor Society, Audubon Artists. Helen Oehler studied art in Chicago and then received private instruction in watercolor painting from George Elmer Browne in Gloucester, Massachusetts. In the early 1950s, she moved to California and resided in Mill Valley and Carmel. She was active on the board of directors for several national art organizations and exhibited watercolors on the West Coast and in New York City.
Biographical information:
*Who's Who in American Art*
New York Water Color Club (Catalogs).

**Eliot O'Hara, N.A.** (1890-1969) Born: Waltham, MA; Studied: Norwich University; Member: National Academy of Design, American Watercolor Society, Philadelphia Water Color Club. Although Eliot O'Hara was never a permanent resident of California, he held art instruction classes in Laguna Beach and other West Coast locations throughout the 1940s and 1950s. He was one of America's premier transparent watercolorists and had an influence on many California watercolor artists through his personal teaching, instructional books and movies. His studio and residence was in Goose Rocks Beach, Maine.
Biographical information:
Interview with Margaret Sheppard, 1983.

**Miné Okubo** (1912- ) Born: Riverside, CA; Studied: Riverside City College (California), University of California (Berkeley); Member: San Francisco Art Association. Miné Okubo grew up in Riverside and received her art education at the University of California, Berkeley studying with John Haley. While still attending college, she began exhibiting her bold, colorful opaque watercolor paintings in the annual San Francisco Art Museum exhibitions and in other Bay Area art shows.

After graduation, she received a fellowship to study and travel in Europe and returned to the West Coast as World War II broke out. In 1942, she was put in a relocation camp for Japanese Americans in Topaz, Utah. She became a staff

**VERNON NYE** *Stream Fishing* 1950s 15" x 22" Courtesy Vernon Nye

**VERNON NYE** *Beach Camp* 1960s 15" x 22" Courtesy Vernon Nye

JOSEPH O'MALLEY  *Hollywood Diner*  1948  15" x 20"  McClelland Collection

JOSEPH O'MALLEY  *Tubes Under Moore Hill*  1946  15" x 20"  McClelland Collection

artist for the camp magazine *Trek* and produced large numbers of charcoal drawings documenting life in the camp. After her release, she moved to New York and wrote and illustrated *Citizen 13660*, a book about her camp experiences.
Biographical information:
Interview with Miné Okubo, 1983.

**Nathan Oliveira** (1928- ) Born: Oakland, CA; Studied: Mills College (Oakland), California College of Arts and Crafts (Oakland). Nathan Oliveira grew up in Northern California and studied art in Oakland after graduating from high school. His primary interest became figure painting and by 1959 he was receiving national acclaim and exhibiting in New York City. He primarily painted with oils on canvas but also produced many figurative studies with watercolor and gouache on paper. Oliveira has also taught art throughout his career. His works are in numerous American museums.
Biographical information:
*Who's Who in American Art*
*Bay Area Figurative Art.*

**Joseph M. O'Malley** (1903- ) Born: Fostoria, OH; Studied: Carnegie School of Fine Arts (Pittsburgh), Chicago Art Institute; Member: American Watercolor Society, California Water Color Society. Joseph O'Malley grew up in Ohio. He moved to Chicago in the 1930s, where he continued his education at the Chicago Art Institute and painted street scenes, usually in the South Side of the city.

He came to Hollywood in the early 1940s and began producing cityscapes of the Los Angeles area, which he exhibited with the California Water Color Society.

O'Malley worked as a pre-production artist for M.G.M., Columbia, Universal and the Walt Disney Studios. In addition, he produced illustrations for magazines and children's books on a freelance basis.
Biographical information:
Interview with Joseph O'Malley, 1982.

**Don O'Neill** (1924- ) Born: Buffalo, NY; Studied: Catholic University of America, School of Architecture; Member: American Watercolor Society, West Coast Water Color Society. Don O'Neill served in the United States Air Force flying B-24s during World War II. After the war, he went to college on the G.I. Bill. He studied to be an architect and as part of the curriculum, received instruction in watercolor painting. After founding his own architectural design business in Riverside, he produced watercolors as renderings for proposed projects. In his free time, he studied watercolor painting with Milford Zornes. After a few years of serious study, he decided to close his architectural business and paint fine art watercolors on a full time basis.

He first established a regional reputation for the watercolors he produced depicting local street scenes and landscape subjects. After opening an art gallery and exhibiting nationally, he received widespread notoriety. O'Neill paints exclusively with transparent watercolors and is known for producing works with bold pattern and powerful compositions. He has also taught watercolor workshops throughout California and operated an art gallery featuring shows of his work.
Biographical information:
Interview with Don O'Neill, 1995.

**Ruth Powers Ortlieb** (1893-1982) Born: Riverside, CA; Studied: San Diego State College, Claremont College (California); Member: San Diego Moderns. Ruth Powers Ortlieb grew up in San Diego and began exhibiting in the late 1920s. She was a student of Millard Sheets and an active member of the San Diego art community.
Biographical information:
Interview with Robert Ortlieb, 1990.

**John O'Shea** (1876-1956) Born: Ballintaylor, Ireland; Studied: Art Students League (New York), Adelphi Academy; Member: American Watercolor Society. John O'Shea immigrated to America with his family as a teenager. He eventually moved to California; first to the Los Angeles area and then finally settling on the Monterey Peninsula. Although he produced a large number of watercolors and exhibited them nationally, he is primarily known for his oil paintings.
Biographical information:
*Artists in California, 1786-1940.*

**Don Osterloh** (1921- ) Born: Prescott, AZ; Studied: San Francisco School of Fine Arts, California College of Arts and Crafts (Oakland); Member: Society of Western Artists. After serving in World War II, Don Osterloh began painting landscape and seascape views of the San Francisco Bay region done in a bold wet-into-wet style. He often paints with transparent watercolors while working on location. He has exhibited on a national level and his watercolors have been reproduced as fine art prints and have been featured in magazines and other publications.
Biographical information:
Interview with Don Osterloh, 1983.

**Alfred Owles** (1894-1978) Born: Nottingham, England; Studied: Nottingham Academy of Fine Art (England). Alfred Owles immigrated to America as a teenager, served in World War I, and then settled in the San Francisco area. He became a well-known commercial illustrator and received national acclaim for his watercolors depicting aviation subjects. Owles also produced works depicting landscape and cityscape scenes, painted with opaque watercolors. He exhibited these in Bay Area annual art shows.
Biographical information:
Interview with Hubert Buel
*Artists in California, 1786-1940.*

**Horace S. Page** (1913-1997) Born: Parowan, UT; Studied: California College of Arts and Crafts (Oakland); Member: American Watercolor Society, Society of Western Artists. Horace Page grew up in Utah and moved to the San Francisco area with his family during the 1920s. At that time, he received art instruction from Hamilton Wolf and Maurice Logan. He also began to produce watercolor paintings during this period. After serving in World War II, he continued his art education at the American University in England, then returned to settle in the San Francisco area.

Throughout the 1950s and 1960s, he painted on location with a small group of artists including Maurice Logan and Harold Gretzner. They were all living in the Oakland area and usually chose to paint depictions of local cityscape subjects or dock scenes near the estuary.

Page primarily exhibited his watercolors in Northern California and on the East Coast in annual American Watercolor Society shows. In addition, his works were selected to travel around the United States in art association traveling shows.
Biographical information:
Interview with Horace S. Page, 1983.

**Alton Painter** (1895-1948) Born: Reno, NV. Alton Painter was a commercial illustrator in the San Francisco area during the 1920s and 1930s. He exhibited watercolors with the Thirteen Watercolorists group.
Biographical information:
*Artists in California, 1786-1940.*

**William Pajaud** (1925- ) Born: New Orleans, LA; Studied: Xavier University (New Orleans), Chouinard Art Institute (Los Angeles); Member: California Water Color Society. William Pajaud grew up in New Orleans where his father was a jazz musician. While attending college, he exhibited watercolors in the South at art exhibitions of black artists. He came to California via Chicago in 1948 and has lived in Los Angeles ever since; exhibiting his work in annual art shows and gallery exhibitions. Primarily a watercolorist, he has often drawn his subject matter from Negro Spirituals and Old Testament subjects.
Biographical information:
Interview with William Pajaud, 1995.

**Abraham Palansky** (1890- ) Born: Lodz, Poland; Studied: Chicago Art Institute; Member: California Water Color Society. Abraham Palansky exhibited his art work in Chicago during the early 1940s. He moved to Los Angeles in the mid-1940s and was an active member of the California Water Color Society for about a decade. He exhibited in galleries and museums throughout California.
Biographical Information:
*Who's Who in American Art.*

**Phil Paradise, N.A.** (1905-1997) Born: Ontario, OR; Studied: Chouinard Art Institute (Los Angeles); Member: National Academy of Design, American Watercolor Society, California Water Color Society. Phil Paradise spent his childhood in Bakersfield. After graduating from high school, he studied art with F. Tolles Chamberlin, Rico Lebrun and Leon Kroll.

He worked in a regional style in the late 1920s and 1930s. These works received a great deal of attention and were part of many important watercolor shows including the California Group exhibitions. By the late 1930s, he was actively selling his paintings in galleries in both New York and Los Angeles.

After the mid-1940s, his paintings changed in both style and subject matter. He traveled and lived in Mexico, Central America and Caribbean countries drawing most of his subject matter from these areas.

Paradise taught at the Chouinard Art Institute and at Scripps College. He also worked as an artist in the motion picture industry and did some commercial illustration. In 1939, Paradise served as president of the California Water Color Society. During the 1940s, he set up a print workshop in the central California town of Cambria and began producing limited edition serigraph prints. In addition, he created metal sculpture, pottery and ceramic murals which he sold out of his studio-home in Cambria.
Biographical information:
Interview with Phil Paradise, 1988.

**David Park** (1911-1960) Born: Boston, MA; Studied: Otis Art Institute (Los Angeles); Member: San Francisco Art Association. David Park, one of California's most prominent post World War II artists, settled in Berkeley in the fall of 1941. Although his most celebrated works are large oil paintings of abstract figurative subjects, he also produced a number of watercolor and gouache paintings on paper. Like his oils, they are bold and colorful. Park was also an influential art instructor at the California School of Fine Arts and the University of California, Berkeley.
Biographical information:
*David Park* (Catalog).

**Douglass Parshall, N.A.** (1899-1990) Born: New York City, NY; Studied: Arts Students League (New York); Member: National Academy of Design, American Watercolor Society, California Water Color Society. Douglass Parshall grew up in New York and began receiving art instruction from his father at an early age. He continued his education at the Art Students League, and in 1917, moved west with his family to settle in Santa Barbara. In the late 1920s and early 1930s, he traveled with his family to China, North Africa, Italy, France and Mexico. He painted extensively on these travels and had a chance to view a wide variety of art.

In addition to painting watercolors, Parshall produced oil paintings, limited edition lithographic prints and portraits. Occasionally, he instructed small groups of advanced art students and in 1947, was president of the California Water Color Society.
Biographical information:
Interview with Walter Silva, 1983.

**Richard Langtry Partington** (1868-1929) Born: Stockport, England; Member: San Francisco Art Association, Bohemian Club. Richard Langtry Partington moved with his family to Oakland, California from England in 1889. He and his father opened the Partington Art School in San Francisco and ran it until it was destroyed by the 1906 Earthquake and fire. He exhibited watercolors in the San Francisco area until 1916 and then moved to Philadelphia. Partington also produced art for the *San Francisco Examiner* newspaper around the turn of the twentieth century.
Biographical information:
*Artists in California, 1786-1940.*

**James Patrick** (1911-1944) Born: Cranbrook, British Columbia; Studied: Chouinard Art Institute (Los Angeles); Member: California Water Color Society. James Patrick grew up in Southern California and attended high school in Hollywood. In the late 1920s, he received a three-year scholarship to study at the Chouinard Art Institute.

During the 1930s and 1940s, he was an important figure in the development of the California Style. His paintings were exhibited with the California Water Color Society and in 1942, he served as the Society's president.

PHIL PARADISE  *Evening on the Home Front*  1942  17" x 23"  David & Sally Martin Collection

PHIL PARADISE  *Delivery at Headquarters*  1942  12" x 18"  David & Sally Martin Collection

CHARLES PAYZANT  *Wilshire Blvd.*  1930s  19" x 24"  McClelland Collection

CHARLES PAYZANT  *Loading the Circus*  1930s  14" x 20"  Michael Johnson Collection

Patrick also taught figure drawing and landscape painting at the Chouinard Art Institute. He often took groups of students to various locations in the Los Angeles area and taught them to do spontaneous watercolor paintings of local city scenes. In addition, he worked on several large mural projects with Millard Sheets and did pre-production art for the motion picture industry.
Biographical information:
California Water Color Society (Catalogs)
Claremont Fine Arts Gallery, Claremont, 1994.

**Edgar Payne** (1882-1947) Born: Washburn, MO; Studied: Chicago Art Institute; Member: California Art Club, Laguna Beach Art Association. Edgar Payne, one of California's premier early twentieth century landscape painters, settled in Southern California around 1920. He is well-known for his oil paintings of the Sierra Mountains, landscape subjects near Laguna Beach and depictions of boats on the Brittany coast. Throughout his career, Payne also produced gouache paintings and watercolor sketches of landscape subjects, especially scenes in the Sierra Mountains.
Biographical information:
*Southern California Art.*

**Elsie Palmer Payne** (1884-1971) Born: San Antonio, TX; Studied: Chicago Fine Art Academy, Best's Art School; Member: California Water Color Society, Laguna Beach Art Association. In about 1918, Elsie Palmer Payne moved to Laguna Beach and eventually settled in Los Angeles. She and her husband, Edgar, were founding members of the Laguna Beach Art Association and Elsie was a co-founder of the Women Painters of the West. She exhibited her transparent watercolor and gouache paintings nationally and ran the Elsie Palmer Art School in Beverly Hills.
Biographical information:
DeRu's Fine Art, Bellflower, 1994.

**Charles Payzant** (1898-1980) Born: Halifax, Canada; Studied: Victoria School of Art (Halifax, Canada), Chouinard Art Institute (Los Angeles), Otis Art Institute (Los Angeles); Member: American Watercolor Society, California Water Color Society. St. George Charles Payzant, as his birth certificate reads, was born and raised in Nova Scotia, Canada. After serving with the 193rd Nova Scotia Highlanders and the Royal Flying Corps in World War I, he received art instruction in England and Canada. In the early 1920s, he moved to Los Angeles and continued his art education at the Otis Art Institute and Chouinard Art Institute.

By the mid-1920s, he was a freelance commercial artist, producing illustrations in watercolor and line art. Payzant also began producing fine art watercolors painted on location around Los Angeles. His background in illustration was apparent in many of these works and gave them a quality unlike what most of the California watercolorists were producing. They were very early examples of what would later become known as the California Style of watercolor painting.

In 1930, he began exhibiting these works in the California Water Color Society shows and as the younger artists were developing their style, he was refining his already developed approach and was winning a number of awards. He painted on location and often chose to depict city street scenes with people, cars and buildings. His approach to watercolor painting was direct and confident. One of his close friends and painting partners during this period was Hardie Gramatky.

The freelance art business in Los Angeles during the Depression was not very lucrative. In 1934, he took a job painting watercolor backgrounds for the Walt Disney Studios. He produced art for many cartoon shorts and did elaborate backgrounds for *Snow White and the Seven Dwarfs, Pinocchio, Fantasia, Dumbo, Make Mine Music, Bambi* and *The Three Caballeros.* The skills he developed while painting with watercolor on a daily basis, greatly improved his ability to produce fine art watercolors when painting for pleasure.

After the World War II era, he left Disney to again pursue a freelance commercial art business. He began working with his wife, Terry Shannon Payzant, on a series of over fifty children's books; she wrote the text and he did the illustrations. In addition, he became the director of the *Dick and Jane* series of school readers which contained over 6,000 pictures. Payzant also continued to paint California Style watercolors well into the 1970s.
Biographical information:
Interview with Terry Shannon Payzant, 1983.

**Channing Peake** (1910-1989) Born: Marshall, CO; Studied: Art Students League (New York), California College of Arts and Crafts (Oakland), Santa Barbara School of Art. Channing Peake studied with Rico Lebrun in the 1930s and then worked with Diego Rivera in Mexico. He eventually settled in Santa Barbara. He exhibited opaque watercolor paintings in museum and gallery shows, produced a mural with Howard Warshaw for the Santa Barbara Library, and was a founding member of the Santa Barbara Museum of Art.
Biographical information:
*Artists in California, 1786-1940.*

**Bob Peck** (1924- ) Born: Chicago, IL; Studied: Chicago Academy of Fine Arts. Bob Peck served as a staff artist in the United States Navy and eventually went to work at Northrop Aviation in Long Beach. During the 1950s and 1960s, he produced watercolor illustrations for the aviation industry and fine art watercolors for exhibitions at the Challis Gallery in Laguna Beach. After the 1960s, he spent extended periods of time in the Middle East and eventually moved there.
Biographical information:
Challis Galleries, Laguna Beach (Catalog)
Interview with Sue Decker, 1998.

**Fred Penney** (1900-1988) Born: Fullerton, NE; Studied: Chicago Art Institute, Art Students League (New York), Chouinard Art Institute (Los Angeles); Member: California Water Color Society. Fred Penney moved to Los Angeles in the 1930s and studied art with F. Tolles Chamberlin, Clarence Hinkle and Pruett Carter. When he arrived in California, he was already well-known as an illustrator for his fine depictions of clowns and circus subjects. He exhibited his works with the California Water Color Society for about ten years and then moved to the Palm Springs area where he concentrated on painting desert scenes.
Biographical information:
Interview with Janice Penny Lovoos
*Who's Who in American Art.*

**Albert Sheldon Pennoyer** (1888-1957) Born: Oakland, CA; Studied: Pennsylvania Academy of the Fine Arts, University of California (Berkeley), Ecole des Beaux Arts (Paris), Académie Julian (Paris), Académie de la Grande Chaumiére (Paris); Member: American Watercolor Society, San Francisco Art Association. Albert Pennoyer grew up in Northern California and studied art in Philadelphia, Berkeley and Paris. He exhibited watercolors nationally and drew his subject matter from a wide variety of landscape subjects in the United States, Europe, and South America.
Biographical information:
*Artists in California, 1786-1940.*

**Robert Perine** (1922-  ) Born: Los Angeles, CA; Studied: Chouinard Art Institute (Los Angeles), University of Southern California; Member: California Water Color Society, West Coast Watercolor Society. Robert Perine is a native Southern Californian and attended art school in Los Angeles during the 1940s. He studied with Rex Brandt, Phil Dike, Tom Craig, Richard Haines and Francis de Erdely. He quickly became an excellent watercolorist and before graduation was exhibiting in art exhibitions. Through the 1950s and 1960s, he divided his time between commercial illustration and fine art watercolor painting.

During this period, his watercolors were classic California Style paintings. He produced them on location with transparent paints and usually chose to depict regional scenes of the city and coastline. He exhibited nationally and sold his work at art galleries in Southern California. His commercial illustrations appeared on magazine covers, record album jackets and other commercial products. He designed posters, brochures, book cover designs, and directed a visually interesting and historically important promotional campaign for Fender Musical Instruments.

Perine was one of the key California Style watercolorists to emerge during the post war era. He was an active member of the California Water Color Society and taught art at the Chouinard Art Institute, University of Alabama, and Mira Costa College. In addition to working as a fine artist and teacher, he has authored two books: *California Romantics,* a history of the California Water Color Society and *Chouinard - A Vision Betrayed,* a history of the Chouinard Art Institute.
Biographical information:
Interview with Robert Perine, 1984.

**James March Phillips** (1913-  ) Born: Fresno, California; Studied: Turner Art Center (San Francisco). James March Phillips studied art in San Francisco. His instructors were Alfred Owles and Louis Rogers, both well-known illustrators. During the 1940s and 1950s, Phillips produced watercolor and gouache paintings depicting California landscape and seascape subjects. His works were sold at art galleries in Northern California.
Biographical information:
Promotional brochure.

**Rollin Pickford, Jr.** (1912-  ) Born: Fresno, CA; Studied: Fresno State College, Stanford University; Member: California Water Color Society. Rollin Pickford, Jr. grew up in Central California. He attended Fresno State College in the 1930s and then continued his education at Stanford University. During this time, he took instruction in watercolor painting from Alexander Nepote.

Beginning in the 1940s, his works were focused on very stylized depictions of the farmlands near his home and studio in Fresno. A number of his watercolor paintings were reproduced on the cover of *Ford Times* magazine and that gave his work additional national exposure.

Pickford also worked as a commercial illustrator and from 1948 until 1962, he taught art at Fresno State College.
Biographical information:
Interview with Rollin Pickford, Jr., 1984.

**Lucy Valentine Pierce** (1887-1974) Born: San Francisco, CA; Studied: California College of Arts and Crafts (Oakland), Boston Museum School of Art. Lucy Pierce began studying art at the turn of the century with private instruction from Xavier Martinez. After completing additional studies in Oakland and Boston, she taught at the California College of Arts and Crafts.

While teaching, Pierce maintained a studio in the New Montgomery block in San Francisco and produced New Vogue designs for handmade furniture. In 1920, she acquired the historical Abrego adobe building in Monterey and used it as a studio-home where she produced watercolors, large oil paintings and fine art prints. For about twenty years, she exhibited in numerous museum shows on the West Coast with a small group of local artist including Armin Hansen, Clayton Price and August Gay.
Biographical information:
California College of Arts and Crafts (Catalog).
Interview with Helen and Margaret Bruton 1980.

**William H.C. Pierce** (1858-1940) Born: Hamilton, NY; Studied: Lowell School of Design, Massachusetts Institute of Technology; Member: San Diego Art Guild. William Pierce studied art in Massachusetts and continued his art education in Paris. By 1893, he was living in California and settled in San Diego in 1899. In addition to exhibiting watercolors, Pierce was an art teacher.
Biographical information:
*Artists in California, 1786-1940.*

**Elmer Plummer** (1910-1987) Born: Redlands, CA; Studied: Chouinard Art Institute (Los Angeles); Member: California Water Color Society. Elmer Plummer grew up in Redlands, California. As a child, he was friends with Phil Dike, Lee Blair and Preston Blair, but when he was a teenager, he was sent to military school in the San Diego area. He studied watercolor painting in high school and received further instruction from Millard Sheets when he attended the Chouinard Art Institute during the late 1920s.

Plummer soon became close friends with Walt Disney and worked at the Disney Studios. He produced art and developed many of the gag and comic ideas for cartoon shorts featuring Goofy. Some of the feature films he contributed to include *Fantasia, Dumbo* and *The Three Caballeros.*

During the 1930s, he produced many outstanding California Style regionalist watercolors. He often chose to depict city scenes with cars, buildings and people. They were sold at Los Angeles art galleries and exhibited in West Coast art shows.

ELMER PLUMMER  *Early Morning Traffic*  1936  14" x 18"  Courtesy Mrs. Elmer Plummer

ELMER PLUMMER  *The Dead Palm*  1936  15" x 22"  Courtesy Mrs. Elmer Plummer

JULIE POLOUSKY  *Woven Fences*  1940s  16" x 20"  Buck Collection

JULIE POLOUSKY  *Backyard View*  1940s  16" x 20"  Buck Collection

After World War II, Plummer continued working on special projects for Walt Disney and taught art at the Chouinard Art Institute. He occasionally painted, but rarely exhibited his art after the mid-1940s.
Biographical information:
Interview with Elmer Plummer, 1984.

**Leo Politi** (1908-1996) Born: Fresno, CA; Studied: Art Institute of Milan (Italy); Member: California Water Color Society, California Art Club. Leo Politi began producing watercolors of city scenes in Los Angeles during the 1930s. Bunker Hill and the surrounding residential streets were of special interest to him. Some of these paintings were exhibited in art shows, while others were used to illustrate the books which he wrote. His books, particularly those written for children, brought Politi national recognition.
Biographical information:
*Who's Who in American Art.*

**Pauline Polk** (1896- ) Born: New York City, NY; Studied: With George Grosz and Millard Sheets; Member: California Water Color Society. Pauline Polk grew up on the East Coast and after traveling to Europe, settled in Southern California in the mid-1930s. For several years, she worked on mosaics for Millard Sheets at his Claremont studio, and actively exhibited watercolors in the annual California Water Color Society shows. Her abstract works, inspired by still life subjects, received special notice and several awards.
Biographical information:
California Water Color Society (Catalogs).

**George Polkinghorn** (1898-1967) Born: Leadville, CO; Studied: University of California (Berkeley), Stanford University, Otis Art Institute (Los Angeles); Member: California Water Color Society, California Art Club. George Polkinghorn moved to Los Angeles in the mid-1920s and studied art with Edouard Vysekal and E. Roscoe Shrader at the Otis Art Institute. He exhibited his watercolors with the California Water Color Society from the late 1920s to the 1950s.
Biographical information:
*Southern California Art.*

**Theodore Polos** (1902-1976) Born: Mytelene, Greece; Studied: California College of Arts and Crafts (Oakland); Member: San Francisco Art Association. Theodore Polos studied with Xavier Martinez and Constance Macky. He taught at the California College of Arts and Crafts and the Academy of Advertising Art in San Francisco and exhibited his watercolors at the annual Oakland Museum and San Francisco Museum of Art shows.
Biographical information:
*Who's Who in American Art.*

**Julie Polousky** (1908-1976) Born: Philadelphia, PA; Studied: Art Students League (New York); Member: California Water Color Society. Julie Polousky grew up on the East Coast. After studying art in New York State, she took additional instruction from Loren Barton and Vanessa Helder in Los Angeles. Her husband was a career serviceman in the Marines. He was stationed in a number of different locations and traveling gave her an opportunity to paint a wide variety of subjects.

While in San Diego, she painted the dock workers and cityscapes of Southern California. In Hawaii, she produced watercolors of floral still life subjects and views of Pearl Harbor. She was on the military base at the time of the attack on Pearl Harbor in December 1941 and produced several watercolors depicting the event.

After World War II, Polousky lived in Vallejo and Long Beach. She primarily exhibited her works with the California Water Color Society in the 1940s and 1950s.
Biographical information:
Interview with Anthony Polousky, 1983.

**Elsie Lower Pomeroy** (1882-1971) Born: New Castle, PA; Studied: Corcoran School of Art (Washington, D.C.); Member: California Water Color Society, San Francisco Art Association, Washington Water Color Club. Elsie Lower Pomeroy studied art in California with Phil Dike, Millard Sheets and Eliot O'Hara. She exhibited with the California Water Color Society from 1931 to the late 1940s. She taught art in the Mill Valley area north of San Francisco and was active in local art circles. In addition to painting and exhibiting, she produced botanical illustrations for the United States Department of Agriculture publications.
Biographical information:
*Who's Who in American Art.*

**Tino Pontrelli** (1922-1995) Born: Los Angeles, CA; Studied: Frank Wiggins Trade School. Tino Pontrelli grew up in California and began drawing and painting as a youth. He took instruction in watercolor from Rex Brandt, Noel Quinn, Robert E. Wood and Milford Zornes. In addition to exhibiting watercolors, Pontrelli produced illustrations for magazine covers and taught painting on the West Coast.
Biographical information:
Anderson Art Gallery, Sunset Beach, 1995.

**Fritz Poock** (1877-1945) Born: Halberstadt, Germany; Member: California Art Club. After studying art in Spain and Germany, Fritz Poock moved to Los Angeles in the 1930s. He worked as a technical illustrator, did murals for the W.P.A. Project and exhibited watercolor paintings.
Biographical information:
*Scenes of California Life.*

**Al Porter** (1923- ) Born: Brooklyn, NY; Studied: Ecole des Beaux Arts (Paris), Chouinard Art Institute (Los Angeles), Otis Art Institute (Los Angeles), University of California (Los Angeles); Member: California Water Color Society. Al Porter came to California as a teenager and after serving in the United States Air Force, studied art in Paris. Upon returning to Los Angeles, he received instruction from Loren Barton and chose watercolor as his primary painting medium. In addition to exhibiting his works nationally, Porter has worked as a supervisor for high school art programs and as an art instructor at Cal State University, Fullerton. In 1982, Davis Publications published his book *Expressive Watercolor Techniques.*
Biographical information:
Interview with Al Porter, 1995.

**George Post** (1906-1997) Born: Oakland, CA; Studied: California School of Fine Arts (San Francisco), Académie Frochot (Paris); Member: American Watercolor Society, California Water Color Society. George Post was born and raised in Oakland, spent several years in Gold Hill, Nevada, then returned to California to live in San Francisco. In 1921, he received a scholarship to study at the California School of Fine Arts. His teachers were Gottardo Piazzoni, Otis Oldfield, Ray Boynton, Spencer Macky and Constance Macky.

By 1930, he was married and working as a commercial artist, while privately painting watercolors of San Francisco cityscape subjects. Although he received little instruction in watercolor at art school, he became very interested in this medium while viewing a show of outstanding watercolors by Stanley Wood in 1929. After that he became a committed watercolorist, producing works on a daily basis.

When California became known as the center of a new movement in watercolor painting, Post had already produced a large body of work and was prepared to do exhibitions at museum and gallery shows. He presented one-man shows at the San Francisco Art Center, San Francisco Museum of Art, Oakland Art Gallery, Sacramento College Art Gallery, California Palace of the Legion of Honor, Sacramento Art Center and in a number of private galleries. His watercolors done for the P.W.P.A. Art Project were exhibited at the M.H. de Young Memorial Museum and a mural he painted in Sonora received positive reviews in the newspaper. As a member of the California Group, his works traveled in shows throughout America.

During World War II, he helped with the war effort by working as a cargo storage planner for military ships. He would draw detailed charts showing where food, ammunition, and other supplies would be stored on board. These ships went to aid soldiers fighting in the South Pacific. While working on the docks, he also painted watercolors of the ships and harbor.

Post's watercolors, particularly the geometric abstractionist works done after the war, were well received in art circles throughout California. His style was modern enough to be exhibited in the progressive art shows and representational enough to be included in more conservative ones. His goals were to capture the essence of design and feeling offered by the subject, rather than to produce a realistic picture of the scene. Although many of his watercolors look deceptively simple, they are masterfully composed, spontaneously painted, and have a creative use of shadow and light to establish a definite mood.

In addition to his painting career, Post also taught art for many years. At first, he was opposed to the idea because he did not want to do anything except paint. But in 1947, he was offered a job teaching at the California College of Arts and Crafts that only required him to teach two days per week. He took the job with the understanding that he would be painting on location with his students. In the summers, he taught at the Brandt-Dike Summer School of Painting. When they closed the school, he taught summers for the T.H. Hewett Watercolor Workshops at various locations around the world. In 1991, a book titled *George Post*, which documents his life and art, was published by Hillcrest Press, Inc.
Biographical information:
Interview with George Post, 1983.

**Kenneth Potter** (1926- ) Born: Bakersfield, CA; Studied: San Francisco Academy of Art, Académie Frochot (Paris), Institute Statale dei Belle Arte (Florence); Member: Society of Western Artists. Ken Potter is a third generation Californian. He grew up in Northern California during the Depression and began drawing regularly at an early age. While living in Sacramento, he received art instruction through a W.P.A. sponsored program. As a teenager, he visited the 1939 World's Fair art exhibit in San Francisco where he viewed works by many of the world's greatest artists. He was particularly excited about modern works, especially the French modernists.

When America entered World War II, Potter was well prepared. He had been in an Explorer Sea Scout program as a youth and in the R.O.T.C. as a teenager. As a United States Marine, he moved right into a position providing security for admirals and chiefs of staff. He later saw action as a combat machine gunner. He manned 20 and 40 mm anti-aircraft weapons on battleships engaged in daily combat off the coast of Japan. He spent his free moments sketching portraits of his fellow shipmates; marines and sailors. Many of these sketches were sent home to their loved ones.

After the war, he visited New York and Chicago before returning to San Francisco. Upon his return, he studied art on the G.I. Bill with Carl Beetz, Hamilton Wolf and Richard Stevens. Both Wolf and Stevens taught geometric abstractionist ideas in art. In addition, his interest in the watercolor medium was heightened after attending presentations by Millard Sheets and Dong Kingman.

Potter was painting expert watercolors by this time but felt he wanted additional instruction. He traveled to France and Italy and studied painting with famed Cubist Jean Metzinger. He attended less formal classes with Fernand Léger and Albert Gleizes. In Italy, he received instruction in fresco painting and printmaking.

By the early 1950s, he presented one-man shows in Paris, San Francisco and Rio de Janeiro and contributed works to groups shows in New York and California. For a brief time, he lived in New York and Brazil and eventually returned to San Francisco. He settled into a flat in North Beach, which was the West Coast center for artists, poets, jazz musicians and philosophers, and began to paint. He painted watercolors daily, visiting the waterfront and Embarcadero where he produced depictions of ships, cranes and industrial objects. When they decided to tear down the old produce district, he did a series of paintings which are masterful works of art and serve as valuable historical documents.

He has primarily worked with transparent watercolors and is known for his ability to manipulate large areas of flowing paint into bold compositions with expert design. His art often shows the influence of cubism and divisionist modern art ideas, but true to all innovative artists, his personal style dominates his work.

In addition to his career as a watercolor painter, Potter has produced murals in California and France. He was an art director for advertising agencies in New York, Rio de Janeiro and San Francisco, created set designs for theater productions and worked as a fine art printmaker. Since the 1960s, he has become an instructor of watercolor painting, presenting workshops in California and other parts of the world.
Biographical information:
Interview with Ken Potter, 1990.

**GEORGE POST** *From San Francisco North* 1950s 18" x 24" Stary-Sheets Fine Arts

**GEORGE POST** *Ship Interior* 1950s 16" x 20" Stary-Sheets Fine Arts

KEN POTTER  *Draw Bridge*  1960s  22" x 30"  Courtesy Ken Potter

KEN POTTER  *Shipping Strike*  1950s  22" x 30"  Courtesy Ken Potter

**Marshall Potter** (1920-  ) Born: Coeur d'Alene, ID; Studied: California College of Arts and Crafts (Oakland), University of California (Berkeley); Member: West Coast Watercolor Society. Marshall Potter was born in Idaho and moved to Northern California with his family when he was eight years old. After serving in the United States Army in World War II, he returned to the Bay Area and studied art, including classes with Reginald Marsh at Mills College.

Since the 1940s, he has painted with watercolors, exhibiting with the Thirteen Watercolorists group for many years. Most of his works depict cityscapes and landscapes of the Bay Area, often including buildings, factories and other structures.

Potter was employed as a commercial illustrator and art director for more than thirty years.
Biographical information:
Interview with Marshall Potter, 1983.

**Raymon Price** (1915-  ) Studied: Chouinard Art Institute (Los Angeles); Member: Pasadena Society of Artists. Throughout the 1940s and 1950s, Raymon Price lived in Pasadena and worked as a commercial artist. His illustrations appeared in *Touring Topics, Sunset,* and other west coast magazine publications. He also produced transparent watercolors depicting Southern California scenes which were exhibited in local art shows and galleries.
Biographical information:
Paulsen Galleries, Pasadena, 1988.

**Wilfred Provan** (1923-  ) Born: Philadelphia, PA; Studied: School of Allied Arts (Glendale); Member: Society of Western Artists. Wilfred Provan grew up in California and studied watercolor painting with Charles Payzant and Arthur Beaumont in Glendale. Since the late 1940s, he has lived in San Francisco and has divided his time between working as a commercial artist and producing fine art watercolor paintings.
Biographical information:
Interview with Wilfred Provan, 1984.

**Hanson Puthuff** (1875-1972) Born: Waverly, MO; Studied: Chicago Academy of Fine Arts, University Art School (Denver); Member: California Water Color Society, California Art Club. Hanson Puthuff settled in Southern California around 1903 and for many years worked as a commercial artist. By the mid-1920s, he was pursuing a career as an easel painter and was a founding member of the California Water Color Society. Although he produced some watercolors, he is primarily known for his large scale oil paintings depicting the California landscape.
Biographical information:
*Southern California Artists (1890-1940).*

**Noel Quinn** (1915-1993) Born: Pawtucket, RI; Studied: Rhode Island School of Design, Ecole des Beaux Arts (Paris), Parsons School of Fine Arts (Paris); Member: American Watercolor Society, California Water Color Society, Society of Motion Picture Illustrators. Noel Quinn was born on Christmas day and grew up in Rhode Island. After studies at the Rhode Island School of Design, he received a fellowship to do post graduate studies in France and Italy. He studied with Andre L'Hote, known as a key teacher in the Cubist movement, and with Andre Cassandre, a famous poster artist. He eventually went to work as an art director for the Paris division of the J. Walter Thompson Advertising Agency.

When World War II started, he moved to the Los Angeles area and began working in the motion picture industry. He produced pre-production art for many studios including Paramount, M.G.M. and Twentieth Century-Fox. In addition, he became a watercolor painting instructor at the Otis Art Institute and worked as a freelance commercial illustrator.

Throughout his career, Quinn painted and exhibited fine art watercolors. The style he worked in featured bold patterns, bright colors, and were usually geometric abstractions, based on cubist ideas. He sold work through galleries in Paris, New York and Los Angeles and exhibited nationally in annual art shows. In 1959, he toured the Pacific and Japan doing commissioned art works for the United States Air Force. In the years following, he produced a series of educational films on watercolor painting. He was president of the California Water Color Society in 1962 and president of the Society of Motion Picture Illustrators from 1963-1965.
Biographical information:
Interview with Noel Quinn, 1983.

**G.D. Arul Raj** (1925-1972) Born: Kodiakanal, India; Studied: Government School of Arts and Crafts (India); Member: Laguna Beach Art Association. G.D. Arul Raj attended art school in Madras, South India, where he learned the watercolor medium. After World War II, he moved to California and settled in Laguna Beach where he painted, exhibited, and sold watercolors depicting scenes of both India and California. A book discussing his painting techniques was released in the 1960s by the Walter Foster Company. He also sold watercolors painted by his brother J.D. Paul Raj, and other artist-relatives who lived in India.
Biographical information:
Interview with Nandinee and Prathiba Raj, 1997.

**Henry Raleigh** (1880-1944) Born: Portland, OR; Studied: Mark Hopkins Institute of Art (San Francisco); Member: Society of Illustrators. Henry Raliegh grew up in Portland, Oregon and San Francisco. After attending art school he began producing art for the *San Francisco Bulletin*. This eventually led to a higher paying job working as an artist for the *San Francisco Examiner*, a publication owned by William Randolph Hearst. By 1916, he was transferred to New York City where he continued working on various Hearst publishing projects. Raleigh was a prolific illustrator and developed a unique style which combined expert pencil drawings with watercolor and ink washes.
Biographical information:
*The Illustrator in America, 1880-1980.*

**Jo Rebert** (1915-  ) Born: Detroit, MI; Studied: Detroit Society of Arts and Crafts, Institute of Musical Arts (Detroit); Member: California Water Color Society, West Coast Watercolor Society. Jo Rebert studied art in Detroit and then in Columbus, Ohio with Joseph Canzani. She moved to California where she became an instructor at the Pasadena School of Fine Art and the Glendale Fine Arts Gallery. It was during this period that she began to exhibit her watercolors.
Biographical information:
*Arts of Southern California XVII-Watercolor* (Catalog).

**Edward Reep** (1918- ) Born: Brooklyn, NY; Studied: Art Center School (Los Angeles); Member: American Watercolor Society, California Water Color Society. Edward Reep grew up in Southern California. He became interested in watercolor painting while studying with Stanley Reckless and received further instruction from Barse Miller. During World War II, he became a combat artist for the United States Army and was sent to Italy. With the war going on all around him, Reep managed to paint depictions of what was happening. These watercolor and gouache works became property of the War Department at the Pentagon. Additional war-time works produced after 1945 are in various museums including the National Museum of American Art in Washington, D.C.

As a result of his outstanding contributions to war art, Reep was awarded a Guggenheim Fellowship to help finance his pursuit of art. From 1947 to 1950, he painted, exhibited and taught art at the Art Center School. In the 1950s, he worked with one of his former teachers, Emil Bisttram, at the Bisttram School of Art. He also began a nineteen year job as an art instructor for the Chouinard Art Institute during this era.

Although he has never restricted himself to any one medium, Reep has often painted with watercolors throughout his career. His works from the late 1930s are classic California Style regional watercolors. By the 1950s, he was working in the more modern abstract style for which he received several important awards and some national exposure. Since that time, he has continued to develop his personal style of art. He was hired as chairman of the art department and honored as Artist in Residence at East Carolina University and has authored two books: *The Content of Watercolor* and *A Combat Artist in World War II*.
Biographical information:
Interview with Ed Reep, 1983.

**Lawrence Rehag** (1913-1989) Born: San Antonio, TX; Studied: California College of Arts and Crafts (Oakland). Lawrence Rehag studied art in the 1930s and then became a commercial artist in San Francisco. He produced watercolors and exhibited with the Thirteen Watercolorists group.
Biographical information:
Carlson Gallery, Carmel, 1996.

**Marques S. Reitzel** (1896-1964) Born: Fulton, IN; Studied: Chicago Art Institute, Ohio State University; Member: Society of Western Artists. Marques Reitzel studied art in the 1920s with George Bellows, Leon Kroll, Leopold Seyffert and James R. Hopkins. From 1927 to 1938, he was chairman of the art department at Rockford College in Illinois, and from 1938 to 1956, was head of the art department at San Jose State College. In addition to teaching and exhibiting his fine art works, Reitzel wrote articles on watercolor painting.
Biographical information:
*American Artist*, 1964.

**William Rice** (1873-1963) Born: Manheim, PA; Studied: Pennsylvania School of Industrial Art, Drexel Institute; Member: San Francisco Art Association. William Rice grew up in Pennsylvania and studied art with Howard Pyle. in 1901, he moved to Northern California where he began teaching art and working as an administrator in the public school system. Although he was an expert watercolorist and produced many fine works, he is best known for his outstanding contributions to fine art color printmaking.
Biographical information:
*Artists in California 1786-1940*.

**John Hubbard Rich** (1876-1954) Born: Boston, MA; Studied: Art Students League (New York), School of the Boston Museum; Member: California Water Color Society, Salmagundi Club, Laguna Beach Art Association. John Hubbard Rich began working as an illustrator for the *Minneapolis Times* while still in his teens. At the turn of the century, he continued his art studies on the East Coast, and in Europe. In 1914, he moved to Los Angeles and helped establish the School for Illustrating and Painting. He also taught at the University of Southern California and for twenty-eight years was a key instructor at the Otis Art Institute. Rich was an expert watercolorist, figure painter and portrait artist.
Biographical information:
*Artists in California, 1786-1940*.

**Henry Richter** (1870-1960) Born: Plumenau, Austria; Studied: Chicago Art Institute, Royal Academy of Munich; Member: California Water Color Society, Laguna Beach Art Association. Henry Richter moved from Europe to Chicago when he was in his early twenties. After a succession of jobs he found work as a portrait painter and attended the Chicago Art Institute at night. He went to Germany for further art education and then moved to Southern California about 1920. He taught art and painted with watercolors and oils, usually choosing to depict landscapes. He exhibited with the California Water Color Society from 1924 to 1934.
Biographical information:
*Southern California Art*.

**Art Riley** (1911-1998) Born: Boston, MA; Studied: Art Center School (Los Angeles); Member: California Water Color Society, American Watercolor Society. Art Riley settled in the Los Angeles area in the early 1930s. He studied watercolor painting with Barse Miller and then began working at the Walt Disney Studios. For nearly thirty years, he produced art work for animated feature films including background watercolors for *Cinderella*, *Pinocchio*, *Snow White and the Seven Dwarfs* and other classic Disney productions. When Disneyland was created in the 1950s, he painted watercolor illustrations showing what the park would look like.

For many years, Riley also produced fine art watercolors that he exhibited nationally. They often depicted regional scenes near his home in Burbank and his second home on the Monterey Peninsula.
Biographical information:
Interview with Art Riley, 1983.

**Larry Rink** (active in 1950s) Born: Anaheim, CA; Studied: Art Center School (Los Angeles), University of California (Los Angeles); Member: California Water Color Society. Larry Rink was raised in San Pedro, attended art school in Los Angeles, and then became a resident of Laguna Beach. He has worked as a commercial illustrator and exhibited watercolors in regional exhibitions.
Biographical information:
*Orange County Illustrated*, 1950 .

ED REEP  *Grand Central Market*  1946  24" x 30"  Courtesy Ed Reep

ED REEP  *The Grinder*  1930s  15" x 22"  Courtesy Ed Reep

JOHN HUBBARD RICH *Self Portrait* 1934 24" x 18" De Ru's Fine Arts

**William Frederick Ritschel, N.A.** (1864-1949) Born: Nuremburg, Germany; Studied: Royal Academy (Munich); Member: National Academy of Design, American Watercolor Society, California Water Color Society. William Ritschel settled in Carmel, California in 1911. Although he is primarily known for his oil paintings of local marine subjects, he also produced watercolors which were internationally exhibited. Ritschel was a founding member of the California Water Color Society and a prominent figure in the Monterey Peninsula art colony.
Biographical information:
*Artists in California, 1786-1940.*

**Paul Rivas** (1930-  ) Born: Mexico City, Mexico; Studied: University of California (Los Angeles), University of California (Berkeley), California College of Arts and Crafts (Oakland); Member: California Water Color Society. Paul Rivas began exhibiting watercolors in the mid-1950s with the California Water Color Society and other West Coast annual exhibitions. He has been an art instructor at the Otis Art Institute and operated the Paul Rivas Gallery in Los Angeles.
Biographical information:
*Who's Who in American Art.*

**Antony Rizzo** (1919-  ) Born: Rochester, NY; Studied: Chouinard Art Institute (Los Angeles); Member: California Water Color Society. Antony Rizzo studied art with Dan Lutz and Richard Haines. He then divided his time between painting fine art watercolor and working as a background artist for animated cartoon features at the Walt Disney Studios. He actively exhibited his paintings with the California Water Color Society in the 1940s and 1950s. Most of these works were done on location with transparent paints and depict cityscape subjects.
Biographical information:
Interview with Antony Rizzo, 1983.

**Marie MacDonnell Roberts** (1915-  ) Born: Lawrence, MA; Studied: Massachusetts College of Art, California College of Arts and Crafts (Oakland); Member: American Watercolor Society. Marie MacDonnell Roberts grew up in Massachusetts and attended the Massachusetts College of Art in the 1930s. After graduation, she worked as a commercial illustrator, specializing in fashion figures and greeting card designs. In 1956, she moved to Northern California and began exhibiting her fine art watercolor paintings.

Roberts has taught art, been active in several major art organizations, and is the author of *The Artist's Design: Structure in Realist Painting.*
Biographical information:
Interview with Marie MacDonnell Roberts, 1983.

**Irene Bowen Robinson** (1891-1973) Born: South Bend, WA; Studied: University of Chicago, Broadmoor Art Academy (Colorado); Member: California Water Color Society. Irene Robinson exhibited her watercolors with the California Water Color Society from the mid-1920s to the early 1950s. She also worked as a book illustrator in the 1940s.
Biographical information:
*Who's Who in American Art.*

**Cleveland Rockwell** (1837-1907) Born: Youngstown, OH; Studied: Polytechnic School (New York), New York University. In the mid-1850s Cleveland Rockwell studied mapmaking and watercolor painting. He was hired by the United States Geological Survey Department and in 1858 was sent to the West Coast. For several years, he was stationed in the San Francisco area and during this time, painted watercolors of beach scenes, harbor views and fishermen. As the survey crew moved up the coast to Northern California and Oregon, he continued producing watercolors depicting coastal views of those regions.
Biographical information:
*Who Was Who in American Art.*

**Richards Ruben** (1924-  ) Born: Los Angeles, CA; Studied: Chouinard Art Institute (Los Angeles); Member: California Water Color Society. Richards Ruben began exhibiting his watercolors in the 1950s and was among the first artists to exhibit radically abstract and non-objective works in California Water Color Society exhibitions. In the following years, he exhibited nationally and gave art instruction at Chouinard Art Institute and Pomona College.
Biographical information:
*Who's Who in American Art.*

**Herbert Ryman** (1910-1989) Born: Illinois; Member: Society of Western Artists. Herbert Ryman studied art in Chicago during the 1930s before moving to Southern California. After settling near Los Angeles, he began a career as a commercial illustrator, teacher and fine art watercolorist. He became a specialist in pre-production artwork for the motion picture industry working on select projects for M.G.M. Studios, Twentieth Century-Fox Studios, and Walt Disney Studios. While at Disney in the 1940s, he worked as an art director on several classic animated films including *Fantasia* and *Dumbo*, and as art supervisor on *Saludos Amigos*. He was also in charge of layout for *The Three Caballeros*.

From 1939 to 1945, he taught set design class at the Chouinard Art Institute. In the 1950s, he was credited with designing the structures to be built on Main Street in Disneyland. Throughout his career, Ryman exhibited fine art watercolors in regional California art exhibitions and in one-man shows at local art galleries.
Biographical information:
Society of Western Artists (Catalog)
Walt Disney Studios, 1995.

**John Saccaro** (1913-1981) Born: San Francisco, CA; Studied: California School of Fine Arts (San Francisco); Member: San Francisco Art Association. John Saccaro exhibited his regionalist style watercolors in the 1930s and 1940s. During this era he was part of the W.P.A. art program and contributed to murals at the Treasure Island World's Fair in 1939. In the 1950s, he was influenced by David Park and Elmer Bischoff and began producing non-objective works.
Biographical information:
*Art in the San Francisco Bay Area (1945-1980).*

**Norman St. Clair** (1863-1912) Born: England; Member: California Art Club. Norman Saint Clair was a successful architect and watercolor artist. Around 1900, he went to

Laguna Beach and began producing watercolors depicting local landscape subjects. In 1902, he presented an exhibition at the Yoch Hotel, giving him the honor of being considered Laguna's pioneer artist.
Biographical information:
*Six Decades* (Catalog).

**George Samerjan** (1915-  ) Born: Boston, MA; Studied: Otis Art Institute (Los Angeles), Chouinard Art Institute (Los Angeles); Member: California Water Color Society. George Samerjan studied with Barse Miller and Stanley Reckless in the 1930s. Throughout the 1940s, he exhibited watercolors in many of America's most prestigious exhibitions including the National Academy of Design, Denver Art Museum and Grand Central Art Galleries, and in local California exhibitions. He taught art at Occidental College.
Biographical information:
*Who's Who in American Art.*

**Paul Sample, N.A.** (1896-1974) Born: Louisville, KY; Studied: Dartmouth College, Otis Art Institute (Los Angeles); Member: National Academy of Design, American Watercolor Society, California Water Color Society. Paul Sample attended Dartmouth before serving in the United States Navy in World War I. He studied art in New York with Jonas Lie for four years. In 1925, he moved to Los Angeles and became an art instructor at the University of Southern California for the next ten years.

Throughout this period he was part of the small group of artists that developed the California Style of watercolor painting. He often chose to paint busy cityscape scenes which often included local people in their everyday environment. These watercolors were shown in the California Group traveling exhibitions and in Los Angeles and New York.

In the later 1930s, Sample traveled to Europe and then moved to the eastern United States where he became the Artist-in-Residence at Dartmouth College. During World War II, he was an artist-correspondent for *Life* magazine. He then resumed his teaching position at Dartmouth, and contunued to produce watercolors and oil paintings which were exhibited in New York and California.
Biographical information:
*Paul Sample, Painter of the American Scene.*

**F. Grayson Sayre** (1879-1939) Born: Medoc, MO; Studied: Chicago Art Institute; Member: Pallet and Chisel Club (Chicago), Painters and Sculptors Club (Los Angeles). F. Grayson Sayre grew up in Missouri. About 1915, he moved west, spending time in California and Arizona and established a reputation as a prominent Southwestern desert painter. His early works were watercolor and gouache paintings, produced with a unique brush stroke style and pastel colors. Later, he also painted with oils and was a founding member of the Painters and Sculptors Club of Los Angeles.
Biographical information:
*F. Grayson Sayre*, Redfern Gallery, Laguna Beach (Catalog).

**Sergey John Scherbakoff** (1894-1967) Born: Kokouka, Russia; Studied: Kharkov Academy of Fine Arts (Russia); Member: San Francisco Art Association, Society of Western Artists. After studying art in Russia and living in Japan, Sergey Scherbakoff settled in San Francisco in 1922. He was primarily a watercolorist and chose to depict subjects found in Yosemite, along the the Russian River, in Carmel and other scenic spots in Northern California.
Biographical information:
*Artists in California, 1786-1940.*

**Leonard Scheu** (1904-1995) Born: San Francisco, CA; Studied: California School of Fine Arts(San Francisco), Art Students League (New York); Member: California Water Color Society, Laguna Beach Art Association. After studying art in San Francisco, Leonard Scheu went to New York for five years where he studied with George Bridgman at the Art Students League. In 1938, he moved to Laguna Beach where he produced watercolors and exhibited them with the California Water Color Society.
Biographical information:
Interview with Leonard Scheu, 1983.

**Rudolph Schmidt** (1897-1997) Born: Berkeley, CA; Studied: California School of Fine Arts (San Francisco). Rudolph Schmidt grew up in the Bay Area and after attending art school, worked as a commercial illustrator. He produced watercolor illustrations for many fruit box labels while employed at the Schmidt Lithograph Company. In addition, he painted watercolors depicting local landscape and cityscape subjects.
Biographical information:
Interview with Pat Jacobsen, 1995.

**Paul A. Schmitt** (1893-1983) Born: Philadelphia, PA; Studied: California School of Fine Arts (San Francisco), California College of Arts and Crafts (Oakland); Member: Society of Western Artists. Paul Schmitt came to California in 1903 with his family. After attending art schools in the Bay Area, he produced commercial illustrations and exhibited his watercolors in numerous shows. Schmitt was a member of the Thirteen Watercolorists group and helped found the Society of Western Artists.
Biographical information:
*Artists in California, 1786-1940*
Society of Western Artists (Catalogs).

**Palmer Schoppe** (1912-2001) Born: Woods Cross, UT; Studied: Yale School of Fine Arts, Art Students League (New York); Member: California Water Color Society. Palmer Schoppe grew up in Santa Monica. After spending a year in the Merchant Marines, he took instruction from Thomas Hart Benton and Jean Charlot at the Art Students League in New York City.

Throughout the 1930s and 1940s, he painted with both transparent and opaque watercolors. Since the early 1950s, Schoppe has concentrated on producing large oil paintings, murals and sculptural pieces for hotels, office buildings and restaurants. He was also a director of animation during World War II and has taught art at the Chouinard Art Institute (1935-1942), Art Center School (1945-1953, 1976-1980) and from 1953-1976, at the University of California (Los Angeles).
Biographical information:
Tobey C. Moss Gallery, Los Angeles, 1984.

PAUL SAMPLE  *Interlude—Castor's River*  1950  15" x 22"  Philip H. Greene Collection

PAUL SAMPLE  *Weather Vane*  1949  12" x 16"  Trotter Galleries

FREDERICK SHANE  *Beachcombers*  1947  18" x 24"  Anderson Art Gallery

JOHN SEVERSON  *The Truck Stops Here*  1970s  12" x 16"  Courtesy John Severson

**Dorner T. Schueler** (1904- ) Born: Quincy, IL; Studied: San Diego Academy of Art; Member: West Coast Water Color Society, Society of Western Artists. After attending art school, Dorner Schueler began designing movie posters for Hollywood studios in the mid-1930s. He eventually moved to San Francisco where he continued to paint and exhibit fine art watercolors, mostly landscapes and rural farm scenes.
Biographical information:
Interview with Dorner Schueler, 1983.

**Donna Schuster** (1883-1953) Born: Milwaukee, WI; Studied: Chicago Art Institute, Boston Museum; Member: California Water Color Society. Donna Schuster came to California in 1914 and lived in Monterey. She moved to Los Angeles in the early 1920s where she taught at the Otis Art Institute. She was a founding member of the California Water Color Society and served as president in 1930 and 1931. She participated regularly in their exhibitions from 1921 until the mid-1940s. She painted landscapes, still-lifes and cityscapes.
Biographical information:
Redfern Gallery, Laguna Beach, 1995.

**Frederick John Schwankovsky** (1885-1974) Born: Detroit, MI; Studied: Pennsylvania Academy of Fine Art, Art Students League (New York); Member: Laguna Beach Art Association, California Art Club, Society of Western Artists. Frederick Schwankovsky was introduced to art at an early age by his mother. He took his formal art instruction in Pennsylvania and New York City, where he worked as an illustrator and painted stage scenery. He moved to Southern California around 1917 and taught art at Manual Arts High School in Los Angeles. By 1926, he settled in Laguna Beach, where he was an active member of the local art community. Schwankovsky painted in both watercolors and oils, and wrote articles on the subject of art.
Biographical information:
*Artists in California, 1786-1940.*

**Davis Schwartz** (1879-1969) Born: Paris, KY; Studied: Chicago Art Institute; Member: Society of Western Artists, Carmel Art Association. Davis Schwartz worked as a commercial illustrator in Ohio and Los Angeles before moving to San Francisco in 1924. He exhibited watercolors in annual art exhibitions in the Bay Area and Carmel through the 1950s and was listed as a resident artist in Carmel.
Biographical information:
*Artists in California, 1786-1940.*

**David Scott** (1916- ) Born: Fall River, MA; Studied: Harvard College, Art Students League (New York), Claremont Graduate School (California), University of California (Berkeley); Member: California Water Color Society. David Scott studied art in New York with John Sloan and in California with Millard Sheets. He taught at Riverside College (1940-1942) and at Scripps College (1954-1963). Throughout the 1940s and 1950s, he painted abstract style watercolors and in 1952 was president of the California Water Color Society. Since 1964, he has been the Director of the National Collection of Fine Arts in Washington, D.C.
Biographical information:
*Who's Who in American Art*.

**Jonathan Scott** (1914- ) Born: Bath, England; Studied: Heatherly School of Art (London), Heymann Schule (Munich), Académiede Belli Arti (Florence); Member: California Water Color Society. Jonathan Scott, a resident of Pasadena from the 1930s until the 1960s, exhibited watercolors in the annual California Water Color Society shows and was the president of the Society in 1960.
Biographical information:
*Who's Who in American Art.*

**Sueo Serisawa** (1910- ) Born: Yokohama, Japan; Studied: Chicago Art Institute, Otis Art Institute (Los Angeles); Member: California Water Color Society. Sueo Serisawa first studied art with his father Yoichi Serisawa, and then attended art school in Chicago and in Los Angeles. After World War II, he exhibited his watercolors and taught at the Kann Art Institute in Beverly Hills (1947-1951), Scripps College (1949-1950), and at the Laguna Beach School of Art. He was president of the California Water Color Society in 1949.
Biographical information:
Interview with Sueo Serisawa, 1984.

**Frank Serratoni** (1908-1970) Born: Michigan. Frank Serratoni was a commercial illustrator in San Francisco during the 1930s. He worked in transparent and opaque watercolors; producing works depicting scenes of city life in San Francisco. A number of prints were produced of his work, many of which are hand colored and are often mistaken for original watercolor paintings.
Biographical information:
*Artists in California, 1786-1940.*

**Fred Sersen** (1890-1962) Born: Czechoslovakia; Studied: Portland Art Academy, Mark Hopkins Institute of Art (San Francisco), Los Angeles School of Art; Member: California Water Color Society. Fred Sersen was seventeen when he immigrated to the United States and by 1916, took up permanent residence in the Los Angeles area.

While he received a number of awards for his fine art watercolors, Sersen is best known for his work in the motion picture industry. He started as a scenic artist at the Twentieth Century-Fox Studios and eventually became head of their special effects department. Most of the large watercolors he produced for the film industry were photorealistic works which, when photographed and incorporated into the action sequences, appeared to be actual scenes. He was nominated for nine Academy Awards and received two Oscars for his motion picture work.
Biographical information:
Interview with Florence Sersen, 1982.

**John Severson** (1933- ) Born: Altadena, CA; Studied: Chico State College (California), Long Beach State College. John Severson grew up in Southern California. He began painting watercolors in the 1950s while working on his Master of Fine Arts degree at Long Beach State College. During this period, he produced Abstract Expressionist works which were exhibited in Laguna Beach art galleries. By the mid-1950s, his interest in the sport of surfing led to a series of abstract works based on waves, surfboards, figures, piers and other beach city subjects.

After serving in the United States Army, he settled in Dana Point, founded *Surfer* magazine, produced five surf movies, and continued painting fine art works. He eventually moved to Hawaii and since the early 1970s, has been shipping art to California for exhibition and sales. His watercolor abstractions are often based on surf culture subjects.

In addition to painting, Severson has also received recognition as a photographer. His photos have appeared in *Life*, *Sports Illustrated*, *Paris Match*, *Stern* (Germany) and other magazine publications.
Biographical information:
Interview with John Severson, 1978.

**Lyne T. "Bud" Shackelford** (1918- ) Born: Washington, D.C.; Studied: Chouinard Art Institute (Los Angeles), Art Students League (New York); Member: American Watercolor Society, California Water Color Society. Bud Shackelford attended the University of Alabama in the early 1930s and then moved to Los Angeles. He studied with James Patrick, Phil Paradise and Lawrence Murphy and began producing watercolors of local landscapes and cityscapes.

During World War II, he was an illustrator in the training department of the United States Army. After the war, he moved back to California and settled near San Diego.

He has exhibited his transparent watercolors on a regular basis since the early 1950s and is primarily known for his geometric abstractionist works of art.

In the 1930s, he worked at the Walt Disney Studios, producing art for feature films and a number of cartoon shorts. In the 1940s, he wrote and illustrated *As I See It*, a book about his army experiences. In addition, he illustrated children's books and became a successful commercial artist in the San Diego area. Shackelford has written two art books: *Fun with Watercolors* and *Experimental Watercolor Techniques*. He has also traveled to many parts of the world teaching art and painting.
Biographical information:
Interview with Bud Shackelford, 1983.

**Frederick Shane** (1906-1990) Born: Kansas City, MO; Studied: Kansas City Art Institute, Broadmoor Art Academy (Colorado). Frederick Shane studied art in the 1920s and was influenced by teachers Randall Davey, Thomas Hart Benton and John Sloan. He taught drawing and painting for many years at the University of Missouri in Columbia and became the Chairman of their Art Department. By the 1940s, he was exhibiting and painting on the West Coast and eventually became a resident of Southern California. Shane exhibited in numerous national exhibits, was represented by the Stendall Galleries in Los Angeles, and had a book of his drawings published in 1964.
Biographical information:
*Watercolor U.S.A., 1976* (Catalog)
*Who's Who in American Art.*

**Millard Sheets, N.A.** (1907-1989) Born: Pomona, CA; Studied: Chouinard Art Institute (Los Angeles); Member: National Academy of Design, New York Water Color Club, American Watercolor Society, California Water Color Society. Millard Sheets was a native California artist and grew up in the Pomona Valley near Los Angeles. He attended the Chouinard Art Institute and studied with F. Tolles Chamberlin and Clarence Hinkle. While still a teenager, his watercolors were accepted for exhibition in the annual California Water Color Society shows and by nineteen years of age, he was elected into membership. At twenty, even before he graduated from Chouinard, they hired him to teach watercolor painting while completing other aspects of his art education.

By the early 1930s, he was well on his way to national recognition as a prominent American artist. He was exhibiting works in Paris, New York, Pittsburgh, Chicago, Houston, St. Louis, San Antonio, San Francisco, Washington, D.C., Baltimore and many other cities throughout the United States. At home in Los Angeles, he was recognized as the leading figure and driving force behind the California Style watercolor movement.

Between 1935 and 1941, the recognition, awards, and his output of high quality art increased. He was mentioned in numerous issues of *Art Digest*, had a color reproduction in the book *Eyes on America,* and in 1935 at age twenty eight, he was the subject of a book published in Los Angeles. Sales of art enabled him to travel to Europe, Central America and Hawaii, where he painted on location. Although his watercolor painting techniques during this period varied from very tight to very loose, his personal style always came through.

During World War II, he was an artist-correspondent for *Life* magazine and the United States Air Force in India and Burma. Many of his works from this period document the scenes of famine, war and death that he witnessed. This experience also effected his post war art for a number of years. Many of his works from the 1940s, painted in California and Mexico, reflect these mood shifts, especially when he used dark tonal values and depressing subject matter. After the 1950s, his style changed again, this time featuring brighter colors and often times depicting subjects from his travels around the world.

While Sheets was a talented painter in both watercolors and oils, this was only part of his overall art career. Through his teaching at Chouinard Art Institute, Otis Art Institute, Scripps College and other institutions, hundreds of artists were taught how to paint, and then guided into an art career. He was Director of the art exhibition at the Los Angeles County Fair for many years and brought world class art to Southern California. During the Depression, he worked with Edward Bruce to hire artists for the W.P.A. Art Project. In 1946, he served as president of the California Water Color Society. In later years, he worked as an architect, illustrator, muralist, printmaker and juried art exhibitions.
Biographical information:
Interview with Millard Sheets, 1983
Stary-Sheets Fine Art Galleries, Laguna Beach, 1998.

**Margaret E. Sheppard** (1915- ) Born: Boston, MA; Studied: Massachusetts School of Art, Berkshire Summer School of Art; Member: California Water Color Society, American Watercolor Society. Margaret Sheppard moved to Laguna Beach in 1937. She studied with Eliot O'Hara at his Laguna Beach school in the late 1940s and taught for three years at his watercolor workshops. Since the 1950s, she has taught watercolor painting in Southern California.
Biographical information:
Interview with Margaret Sheppard, 1983.

MILLARD SHEETS  *Abandoned*  1932  18" x 24"  Stary-Sheets Fine Arts

MILLARD SHEETS  *Hidden Bay*  1935  22" x 30"  Stary-Sheets Fine Arts

MORRIS SHUBIN  *La Jolla Cove*  1960s  15" x 22"  Courtesy Morris Shubin

MORRIS SHUBIN  *Diving Bell*  1960s  18" x 24"  Courtesy Morris Shubin

**Morris Shubin** (1920- ) Born: Mansfield, WA; Member: American Watercolor Society, California Water Color Society. Morris Shubin grew up in Southern California and has produced art since he was in high school. He wrote about watercolor painting for various art magazines, was included in several art instruction books, and gave painting instruction to advanced students throughout the United States and Mexico.
Biographical information:
Interview with Morris Shubin, 1984.

**Burr Singer** (1912- ) Born: St. Louis, MO; Studied: St. Louis School of Fine Art, Chicago Art Institute, Art Students League (New York); Member: California Water Color Society. After studying art in St. Louis, Chicago and New York, Burr Singer went to Taos, New Mexico for several years and studied privately with Walter Ufer. She moved to Los Angeles in the late 1930s and joined the California Water Color Society. Her watercolors often depicted local people whom she felt had depth and character. Her art works were exhibited at the New York World's Fair in 1939 and one of her lithographs was included in the highly acclaimed *Artists for Victory* show after World War II.
Biographical information:
Interview with Burr Singer, 1984.

**Katherine Skeele** (1896-1963) Born: Wellington, OH; Studied: Academy of Fine Arts (Italy), Art Students League (New York); Member: California Water Color Society. Katherine Skeele studied art in Europe, taking special instruction from Andre L'Hote in Paris. She and her husband Frode Dann, settled in Southern California in the 1930s and for many years were instructors at the Pasadena School of Fine Art. She exhibited her paintings from the 1930s to the mid-1950s.
Biographical information:
*Southern California Art.*

**Dorothy Sklar** (1906-1996) Born: New York City, NY; Studied: University of California (Los Angeles), Chouinard Art Institute (Los Angeles); Member: California Water Color Society. Dorothy Sklar's family moved to Southern California when she was about four years old. She was raised in the Los Angeles area and attended the University of California with a major in the education field.

While working as a teacher in Santa Monica during the 1930s, she took instruction in watercolor painting from Millard Sheets and Dong Kingman. By the early 1940s she had quit teaching and was painting and exhibiting in art shows across the country with the California Water Color Society. Most of the time she painted right on location from the inside of her parked car. Old houses and street scenes in the East Los Angeles area were the subjects in many of these works. She was an active member of the board of directors of the California Water Color Society for many years.
Biographical information:
Interview with Dorothy Sklar, 1983.

**Helen Sloan** (active ca. 1950s) Born: Chicago, IL; Studied: Chicago Art Institute, Chicago Academy of Fine Arts; Member: Laguna Beach Art Association. Helen Sloan was a commercial artist and designer in Chicago. In the 1940s, she began working at the Walt Disney Studios. She lived in Laguna Beach for many years and exhibited her watercolors locally.
Biographical information:
Helen Sloan (Promotional Brochure).

**Charles L.A. Smith** (1871-1937) Born: New York, NY; Member: California Water Color Society. Charles Smith was a self-taught artist who moved to Los Angeles from Chicago about 1920. His watercolor paintings were included in the first annual exhibition of the California Water Color Society in 1921, and he continued to show until the early 1930s.
Biographical information:
*Southern California Art.*

**Hassel Smith** (1915- ) Born: Sturgis, MI; Studied: Northwest University, California School of Fine Arts (San Francisco); Member: San Francisco Art Association. Hassel Smith studied art in San Francisco during the 1930s and exhibited watercolor and gouache paintings of abstract figurative subjects until the mid-1940s. After that time, he became a leading figure with the San Francisco Abstract Expressionist group and received international acclaim for his innovative art works. Smith has also been an art instructor.
Biographical information:
*Who's Who in American Art*
San Francisco Art Association (Catalogs).

**Howard E. Smith, N.A.** (1885-1970) Born: Windham, NH; Studied: Art Students League (New York); Member: National Academy of Design, American Watercolor Society. In 1930, Howard Smith moved to Carmel from the eastern United States, where he had studied with Howard Pyle and worked as an illustrator for magazines such as *Harper's* and *Scribner's*. He was well known as a portrait painter and exhibited his watercolors with the American Watercolor Society.
Biographical information:
*Monterey: The Artist's View* (Catalog).

**Gene Sogioka** (active in 1940s) Studied: Chouinard Art Institute (Los Angeles); Member: California Water Color Society. Gene Sogioka was a resident of Los Angeles in the 1930s. He studied with Millard Sheets and was employed by the Walt Disney Studios as a background artist. During World War II, he was interned in a Japanese evacuation camp, where he painted numerous watercolors of camp life. Upon his release, he moved to New York City to pursue a career as a commercial artist.
Biographical information:
*Beyond Words.*

**Paul Souza** (1918- ) Born: Hawaii; Studied: Honolulu Academy of Art, Art Center School (Los Angeles); Member: American Watercolor Society, California Water Color Society. Paul Souza studied art in the late 1930s with Ben Norris in Hawaii and Stanley Reckless in California. He traveled extensively through the years and is known for his paintings of Morocco and Spain. In addition to exhibiting in the United States, he has shown his watercolor paintings in Sweden and taught at the Art Center School in Los Angeles since 1946.
Biographical information:
Interview with Paul Souza, 1984.

**Duncan Alanson Spencer** (1911-1999) Born: Los Angeles, CA; Studied: Chouinard Art Institute (Los Angeles); Member: American Watercolor Society. Duncan Spencer studied art at the Chouinard Art Institute in the 1930s, then took further instruction in watercolor painting from Arthur Beaumont. From the 1940s through the 1970s, he worked in the motion picture industry as a scenic artist. In addition, he produced California Style watercolor paintings depicting regional subjects and exhibited them in annual watercolor society shows. Spencer also produced a number of large scale background dioramas featuring landscape subjects, which were used in museum and corporate displays.
Biographical information:
Stary-Sheets Fine Art Galleries, Laguna Beach, 1997.

**Clay Spohn** (1898-1977) Born: San Francisco, CA; Studied: California College of Arts and Crafts (Oakland), University of California (Berkeley), California School of Fine Arts (San Francisco), Art Students League (New York), Académie Moderne (Paris). Clay Spohn began serious art studies when he was fourteen years old. In 1922, he traveled to New York City where he received instruction from George Luks. He then traveled to France to further his education in modern art. From the mid-1920s to the early 1950s, he was living in Northern California. During this period, he produced gouache and watercolor paintings. His style ranged greatly from fantasy and surreal works, to Dada and abstract expressionism. In addition, he produced murals for the W.P.A. Art Project and taught at the California School of Fine Arts. After the mid-1950s, he lived in New York and taught at the New York School of Visual Arts.
Biographical information:
*Artists in California, 1786-1940.*

**Edgar Starr** (1908-1971) Born: Imperial, CA; Studied: California College of Arts and Crafts (Oakland), Pennsylvania Academy of Fine Arts, Chouinard Art Institute (Los Angeles); Member: California Water Color Society. Ed Starr studied watercolor painting with Millard Sheets and drawing with Lawrence Murphy. He was employed as an artist at the Walt Disney Studios during the 1930s and exhibited watercolors in regional art exhibitions. By 1954, he settled in Puerto Vallarta, Mexico.
Biographical information:
*Artists in California, 1786-1940.*

**Judson L. Starr** (1890-1960) Born: Los Gatos, CA. Judson L. Starr was a resident of San Francisco and employed by the Foster and Kleiser Company as a commercial artist. He produced watercolors, both for commercial use and exhibition purposes, from the 1920s through the 1950s.
Biographical information:
*Artists in California, 1786-1940.*

**Charles Walter Stetson** (1858-1911) Born: Riverton Four Corners, RI. Charles Walter Stetson lived in Pasadena during the 1890s. He primarily worked with oil on canvas, but also produced watercolors and was nationally known for his paintings of women in landscape settings.
Biographical information:
*Loners, Mavericks and Dreamers* (Catalog).

**Marjory Stevens** (1902-  ) Born: Terra Haute, IN; Studied: Privately with George Post; Member: American Watercolor Society, Society of Western Artists. In the 1940s, Marjory Stevens took instruction in watercolor painting from George Post and, briefly from Dong Kingman. By the 1950s, she was painting on a regular basis, exhibiting her watercolors professionally and working as a chiropractor in San Francisco. She also served on the board of directors of the California State Fair Art Exhibition.
Biographical information:
Interview with Marjory Stevens, 1984.

**Richard Stevens** (1892-1985) Born: Oakland, CA; Studied: Académie Julian (Paris), California College of Arts and Crafts (Oakland), Scripps College (California); Member: California Water Color Society. After studying art in California and France, Richard Stevens illustrated books and contributed commercial art to various magazines, including *Sunset*, *College Humor*, *American Artist* and *Judge*. He also painted fine art watercolors that he exhibited in galleries and museums throughout California. He lived in the San Francisco area and was the founder and an instructor at the Academy of Advertising Art in the city.
Biographical information:
*Who's Who in American Art.*

**Arthur Stewart** (active ca. 1950s) Member: Society of Western Artists. Arthur Stewart was a resident of San Francisco in the 1950s. During that period, he produced expert watercolors depicting regional views of Northern California landscape and cityscape subjects.
Biographical information:
Society of Western Artists (Catalogs).

**George Stillman** (1921-  ) Born: Laramie, WY; Studied: University of California (Berkeley), California School of Fine Arts (San Francisco), Arizona State University; Member: National Watercolor Society. George Stillman attended college in Berkeley during the early 1940s and then served in the military during World War II. After the war, he moved to San Francisco, studied art, and became affiliated with the San Francisco Abstract Expressionist group. Some of his works from this period were produced using gouache on paper. Stillman became an art teacher in Washington State and has exhibited in National Watercolor Society shows since 1970.
Biographical information:
*Paper Trails: San Francisco Abstract Expressionist Prints, Drawings and Watercolors.*

**James Strombotne** (1934-  ) Born: Watertown, SD; Studied: Pomona College (California), Claremont Graduate School (California). James Strombotne, began exhibiting his abstract figurative paintings in the mid-1950s while still in college and by 1963 was receiving national acclaim. His works of the 1950s and 1960s were often angry responses to the social and political corruption of that era. Since then, he has continued to produce innovative works based on figurative and still life subjects. In addition, he has been an influential art teacher at the University of California, Riverside.
Biographical information:
*Who's Who in American Art.*

DUNCAN ALANSON SPENCER  *Riverbed*  1940s  15" x 22"  Stary-Sheets Fine Arts

DUNCAN ALANSON SPENCER  *Boatdock and Fishermen*  1950s  15" x 20"  Stary-Sheets Fine Arts

DONALD TEAGUE  *Sol y Sombre*  1960s  20" x 30"  Thomas Nygard Gallery

DONALD TEAGUE  *Ambush*  1973  20" x 30"  Thomas Nygard Gallery

**Jan Stussy** (1921-1990) Born: Benton County, MO; Studied: Art Center School (Los Angeles), University of Southern California, University of California (Los Angeles); Member: California Water Color Society. Jan Stussy grew up in Southern California and attended Long Beach City College. In 1941, he entered Art Center School in Los Angeles and studied watercolor painting with Barse Miller. This was followed by additional instruction from Stanton MacDonald-Wright and figure composition classes with Francis de Erdely. During World War II, he served in the United States Navy Intelligence Art Unit. He returned to Los Angeles after the war to resume his art career.

From 1942 until the 1960s, he actively exhibited with the California Water Color Society. During this period, he painted many abstract works which were based on still life and figurative subjects. Although Stussy is best known for his abstract works of the 1960s and 1970s, his watercolor still lifes of the 1940s and 1950s received national recognition.

Beginning in 1946, Stussy was an art instructor at the University of California, Los Angeles later becoming a full Professor. He studied art in Europe, South America and the Orient. He worked as a technical consultant in the motion picture industry and received commissions for art projects from large corporations. In addition to watercolors, he produced sculptures, oil paintings, prints and murals.
Biographical information:
Interview with Jan Stussy, 1984.

**Henry Sugimoto** (1904-1990) Born: Los Angeles, CA; Studied: California School of Fine Arts (San Francisco), California College of Arts and Crafts (Oakland), Académie Colarossi (Paris); Member: California Water Color Society, San Francisco Art Association. Henry Sugimoto was a resident of Central California in the 1930s and early 1940s. He exhibited watercolors during this period and contributed illustrations to magazine publications. By the 1950s, he was living in New York City where he produced illustrations for books.
Biographical information:
*Who's Who in American Art.*

**Charles Surendorf** (1906-1979) Born: Richmond, IN; Studied: Chicago Art Institute, Art Students League (New York), Mills College (Oakland); Member: San Francisco Art Association. Charles Surendorf was a resident of San Francisco and exhibited his watercolors and prints nationally through the 1930s and 1940s. Most of his watercolors depict landscape and rural farm scene subjects. He also worked as an illustrator and taught art in the Bay Area.
Biographical information:
*Who's Who in American Art.*

**Lewis Suzuki** (1920-  ) Born: Los Angeles, CA; Studied: Otis Art Institute (Los Angeles), Art Students League (New York). Lewis Suzuki received art instruction in Los Angeles and New York during the late 1930s and the 1940s. Since the 1950s, he has resided in the San Francisco area where he concentrates on producing cityscapes done with wet-into-wet watercolor painting style.
Biographical information:
Interview with Lewis Suzuki, 1994.

**Kango Takamura** (1895-  ) Born: Japan. Kango Takamura emigrated from Japan to Hawaii in 1912. By the early 1920s, he was a Hollywood resident working at RKO Studios. During World War II, he was interned in the Japanese relocation camp at Manzanar. During his captivity, he produced a number of watercolors depicting experiences of camp life. After the war, he continued working at RKO Studios.
Biographical information:
*Beyond Words.*

**Farwell M. Taylor** (1905-1977) Born: Conawa, OK; Studied: California School of Fine Arts (San Francisco); Member: San Francisco Art Association. Farwell Taylor worked as a commercial artist in San Francisco during the 1930s. During this period, he also began exhibiting watercolors and produced art for the Federal Art Project in the Bay Area. He was included in the *14 Bay Area Watercolorists* show at the San Francisco Museum of Art and participated in other local art exhibitions.
Biographical information:
*Artists in California, 1786-1940.*

**Donald Teague, N.A.** (1897-1991) Born: Brooklyn, NY; Studied: Art Students League (New York); Member: National Academy of Design, New York Water Color Club, American Watercolor Society. Donald Teague studied art with George Bridgman and Frank Vincent DuMond in New York City. He served in the United States Navy during World War I and while stationed in England, received additional instruction from watercolorist Norman Wilkinson. Returning to New York City, he established a career as a commercial illustrator. He produced illustrations for *The Saturday Evening Post* and signed them Donald Teague. When doing similar works for *Collier's* he signed them "Edwin Dawes". This was done because the two magazines were very competitive.

In 1938, he moved to California, first to Los Angeles, then Carmel. He continued to supply the magazines with illustrations, but also began pursuing a career as a fine artist, specializing in watercolors. Both careers went well and by the 1960s, he was exhibiting nationally in museum shows and selling works at galleries in California, New York and Texas.

His style of painting did not vary a great deal between commercial works and fine art watercolors. Both featured a tight, representational style, with great detail. Although he painted a wide variety of subjects, the ones that depict western or cowboy scenes are the works he is best known for.
Biographical information:
Interview with Donald Teague, 1984.

**Wayne Thiebaud** (1920-  ) Born: Mesa, AZ; Studied: Sacramento State College. Wayne Thiebaud, a nationally acclaimed artist from the Sacramento area, initially received acclaim for his large oil paintings exhibited in 1960s era Pop Art shows in New York City. In addition to these works, he has also produced a number of watercolors depicting cityscape and landscape subjects. Thiebaud has also been influential as an art professor and artist in residence at universities in California and the Midwest.
Biographical information:
*Who's Who in American Art*
Lecture, *Thiebaud on Thiebaud*, 1985.

**Aline Thistlethwaite** (1924- ) Born: Long Beach, CA; Studied: University of California (Los Angeles); Member: California Water Color Society. Aline Thistlethwaite has exhibited transparent watercolor paintings since the early 1960s. She is an Orange County resident, has taught art in Santa Ana, and has exhibited in Southern California.
Biographical information:
*Arts of Southern California, XVII - Watercolor* (Catalog).

**Stephen Seymour Thomas** (1868-1956) Born: San Augustine, TX; Studied: Art Students League (New York), Académie Julian (Paris), Ecole des Beaux Arts (Paris); Member: Los Angeles Art Association. Seymour Thomas was an internationally recognized portrait painter. He lived in Paris and New York before settling in Southern California in the 1920s. Thomas continued to paint portraits and landscape subjects, and exhibited them in America and Europe.
Biographical information:
*Who Was Who in American Art.*

**Walton Titus** (1907-1978) Born: Kansas City. Studied: National Academy of Design (New York), Art Students League (New York); Member: Painters & Sculptors Club. Walton Titus was a portrait painter and commercial artist in Los Angeles from the 1930s to the 1950s. Many of his watercolor and gouache works appeared on magazine covers and as commercial advertisements.
Biographical information:
Xanidu Gallery, Glendale, 1978.

**Francis Todhunter** (1884-1963) Born: San Francisco, CA; Studied: Mark Hopkins Institute of Art (San Francisco), California School of Fine Arts (San Francisco), Art Students League (New York); Member: Society of Western Artists, Marin Society of Artists. After studying art in San Francisco and New York, Francis Todhunter settled in the Bay Area. He made a career as an illustrator and art director and produced watercolors which were exhibited in art exhibitions throughout the San Francisco area.
Biographical information:
*Artists in California, 1786-1940.*

**Peter Petersen Toft** (1825-1901) Born: Kolding, Denmark. Peter Peterson Toft studied art in Denmark before sailing to San Francisco in 1850. For a brief period, he panned for gold in the Trinity River area, but eventually returned to San Francisco. He contributed art to *Harper's* magazine and produced numerous watercolor paintings depicting landscapes in Northern California, Oregon, Washington and British Columbia.
Biographical information:
*Artists in California, 1786-1940.*

**Virginia Tonetti** (1920- ) Born: Magna, Utah; Studied: Frank Wiggins Trade School (Los Angeles). Virginia Tonetti grew up in Utah and California. During the 1930s, she attended a trade school where she studied art. This led to a job at the Moore Advertising Agency doing illustration work. In 1941, she went to Douglas Aircraft in Los Angeles and helped in the war effort by producing illustrations and designs for their products. After the war, she received additional instruction in watercolor from Dorner Schueler and Jake Lee. Tonetti's watercolors depict California Scene subjects and were painted on location with transparent paints.
Biographical information:
Interview with Virginia Tonetti, 1999.

**Ernest A. Tonk** (1889-1968) Born: Evanston, IL; Studied: Chicago Art Institute; Member: Laguna Beach Art Association. Ernest Tonk settled in Glendale in 1923. After studying art in Chicago and working as a logger in Washington state, he produced art for the motion picture industry in Los Angeles. His watercolors were often painted with gouache on illustration board. Tonk was known for his depictions of cowboy and western subjects, but also painted landscape and harbor scenes.
Biographical information:
Laguna Beach Art Association (Catalog)
*Artists in California, 1786-1940.*

**Eugene Towne** (1907-1985) Born: San Francisco, CA; Member: Society of Western Artists. Eugene Towne studied watercolor painting with Eliot O'Hara, George Post and Jade Fon. He has exhibited primarily in the Bay Area and lived in Carmel.
Biographical information:
*Artists in California, 1786-1940.*

**Wing Kwong Tse** (1902-1993) Born: Canton, China; Studied: University of Southern California. Wing Kwong Tse came to California in 1922 and by the early 1930s, he was pursuing an art career in San Francisco. He primarily exhibited in the Bay Area and received notoriety for his carefully rendered watercolor painting.
Biographical information:
*Views from Asian California.*

**Dale M. Turnbull** (active in 1950s) Born: Nebraska; Studied: University of Nebraska (Lincoln), Chicago Academy of Fine Arts. Dale Turnbull grew up in Nebraska and in 1930, began working as a commercial illustrator in Chicago. He spent time in Texas, then settled in California in the 1940s, and exhibited watercolors in Southern California shows throughout the 1950s.
Biographical information:
*Widening Horizons*, 1949.

**Janet E. Turner, N.A.** (1914-1988) Born: Kansas City, MO; Studied: Kansas City Art Institute, Claremont College (California); Member: National Academy of Design, California Water Color Society. Janet Turner studied for five years with Thomas Hart Benton in Kansas and then continued her studies with Henry Lee McFee and Millard Sheets in California. She exhibited her American Scene watercolors with the California Water Color Society in the 1940s and 1950s. Her paintings often depict old dilapidated buildings and include animals and people. After the mid-1950s, she resided in Northern California and specialized in printmaking. Her works received many awards and are in major museum collections in America and Europe.
Biographical information:
Interview with Janet Turner, 1984.

WAYNE THIEBAUD  *24th Street Intersection*  1970s  11" x 14"  Private Collection

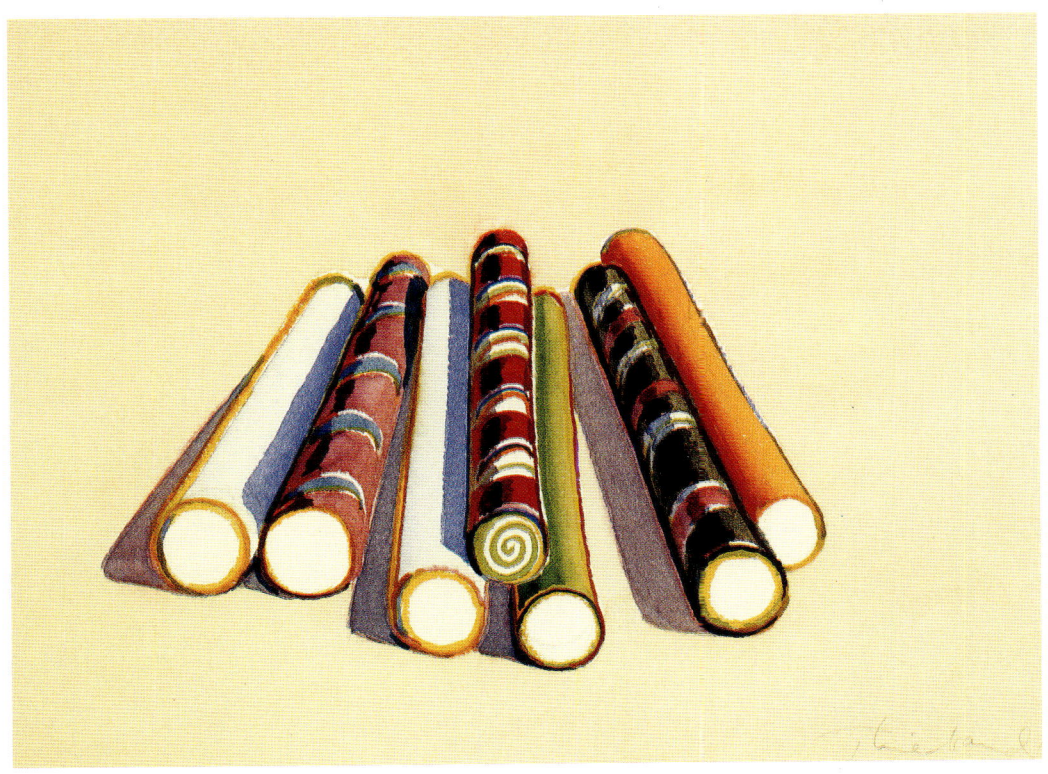
WAYNE THIEBAUD  *Candy Sticks*  1964  10" x 12"  Private Collection

JAMES VANCE  *Carmel Coastline*  1950s  15" x 22"  Dr. & Mrs. Larry Ho Collection

OSCAR VAN YOUNG  *The Old House*  1940  20" x 26"  Private Collection

**Robert Uecker** (1929-  ) Born: Los Angeles, CA; Studied: Chouinard Art Institute (Los Angeles); Member: California Water Color Society. Robert Uecker was awarded a five year scholarship to study art at the Chouinard Art Institute in the late 1940s. He received instruction from Rex Brandt, Ed Reep and Pruett Carter. Since then, he has taught art, exhibited his watercolors, and was co-owner of several art supply stores in the Pasadena area.
Biographical information:
Interview with Robert Uecker, 1990.

**Martha Underwood** (1934-  ) Born: Quincy, IL; Studied: Otis Art Institute (Los Angeles), Chouinard Art Institute (Los Angeles), Scripps College (California); Member: Los Angeles Art Association. Martha Underwood came to California as a teenager and then after high school, studied art with Millard Sheets, Phil Dike and Rex Brandt. In addition to producing watercolor and casein paintings, she has designed murals, tapestries and commercial illustrations. Underwood taught art at Chaffey Community College for 25 years.
Biographical information:
Interview with Martha Underwood, 1996.

**Albert R. Valentien** (1862-1925) Born: Cincinnati, OH; Studied: Cincinnati Academy of Art; Member: San Diego Artists Guild. Albert Valentien grew up in Ohio and became a decorative artist at Rookwood Potteries. In 1908, he moved to San Diego and was commissioned to produce watercolors depicting all types of wildflowers, native grasses, trees and cacti. He produced hundreds of these watercolors which are now in the San Diego Museum of Natural History and the State Capital Building in Sacramento.
Biographical information:
*California Design, 1910.*

**James Vance** (1919-  ) Born: Los Angeles, CA; Studied: Art Center School (Los Angeles), Chouinard Art Institute (Los Angeles), Art Students League (New York); Member: American Watercolor Society, California Water Color Society. James Vance grew up in the Los Angeles area and began studying at Art Center while still in high school. After additional studies in watercolor painting in Los Angeles and New York, he began exhibiting his works nationally.

Vance has lived in California most of his life and worked as an illustrator, designer and art director for the motion picture and television industries. In addition, he has taught watercolor painting at the Kansas City Art Institute.
Biographical information:
Interview with James Vance, 1985.

**Lucretia Van Horn** (1882-1970) Born: Louisiana; Studied: Art Students League (New York), Académie Julian (Paris). Lucretia Van Horn grew up on the East Coast and studied art with John Henry Twachtman. Just after the turn of the century, she continued studying art in France and then moved to Berkeley in the late 1920s. She worked as a designer and illustrator while exhibiting her fine art paintings in Bay Area group exhibitions.
Biographical information:
Art Exchange Gallery, San Francisco.

**Loli Vann** (1913-  ) Born: Chicago, IL; Studied: Chicago Art Institute; Member: California Water Color Society. Loli Vann grew up in Chicago and studied art with Sam Ostrowsky. She and her artist-husband, Oscar Van Young, moved to Los Angeles in the early 1940s and have lived there ever since. During the 1940s, she painted and exhibited watercolors which often depicted mother and child themes.
Biographical information:
Interview with Loli Vann, 1984.

**Frank Van Sloun** (1879-1938) Born: St. Paul, MN; Studied: St. Paul School of Fine Arts, Art Students League (New York), Chase School (New York); Member: Internationale des Beaux Arts et des Lettres, San Francisco Art Association. Frank Van Sloun received art instruction in Minnesota. At the turn of the century, he went to New York City where he studied with Robert Henri. By 1911, he had settled in San Francisco, where he became a well-respected artist and teacher. He worked with watercolors and gouache and while this was not his primary medium, the works he did produce were exceptional.
Biographical information:
*Artists in California, 1786-1940.*

**Oscar Van Young** (1906-1993) Born: Vienna, Austria; Studied: Art Academy Odessa (Russia), Academy of Fine Arts (Chicago), California State University (Los Angeles); Member: California Water Color Society. Oscar Van Young grew up in Vienna. In 1919, he received a scholarship to study art in Odessa, Russia, but after several years of instruction, fled the country because of political unrest. After traveling around Europe, he immigrated to the United States and settled in Chicago, where he continued his art education and began to exhibit his works. In 1940, he moved to California to live in Los Angeles.

Throughout the 1940s and 1950s, he produced and exhibited watercolors depicting local Los Angeles street scenes. In addition, he was an art instructor at the Otis Art Institute and various universities. He also worked as a printmaker, producing limited edition fine art lithographs, and painted large abstract oil paintings.
Biographical information:
Interview with Oscar Van Young, 1983.

**Hilda Van Zandt** (1892-1965) Born: Henry, IL; Studied: University of California (Los Angeles); Member: California Water Color Society. Hilda Van Zandt became a member of the California Water Color Society in 1926. She lived in San Pedro and traveled to many parts of the world including South America, Europe and Alaska.
Biographical information:
*Who's Who in American Art.*

**Alberto Vargas** (1896-1982) Born: Peru. Alberto Vargas studied art in Zurich and Geneva, Switzerland. From 1916 until 1934, he lived in New York City, working as a fashion illustrator and as a commercial artist. In 1934, he settled in Hollywood and produced art work for the motion picture industry. By the late 1930s, he had fully developed his unique style of painting glamorous women, some clothed and others nude. *Esquire* featured these "Varga Girls", (he dropped the

"s" from his name for *Esquire* commissions) and it established Vargas as an internationally known artist. He continued producing similar works which were featured in *Playboy* magazine and is recognized as one of the formost artists of this genre.
Biographical information:
*Great American Pin-Up.*

**Archie J. Vazquez** (active ca. 1930s). Archie Vazquez was the son of immigrants from the Basque region between France and Spain. He worked between 1910 and 1950 as a commercial illustrator in Los Angeles, designing fruit box labels and posters. These and other exhibition works were painted with watercolors or gouache.
Biographical information:
Interview with Dario De Julio, 1978.

**Hernando Villa** (1881-1952) Born: Los Angeles, CA; Studied: Los Angeles School of Art and Design. Hernando Villa was born, raised, and spent most of his life in Los Angeles. He worked as a commercial artist and sold easel paintings through local galleries. Many of his commercial works done for the Santa Fe Railroad, Southern Pacific Railroad and Southern California magazine publications were painted with watercolors. Other works depicting missions and landscape subjects were watercolors, mixed with ink and pastels. Villa also produced many oil paintings, some of which were reproduced and sold as art prints in the 1930s.
Biographical information:
*California Design 1910.*

**Herman Volz** (1904-1990) Born: Zurich, Switzerland; Studied: Commercial Art School (Zurich), Academy of Fine Arts (Vienna); Member: California Water Color Society. Herman Volz immigrated to America in the 1930s and was listed as a resident of Los Angeles, then San Francisco. He exhibited watercolors and lithographs in annual art exhibitions on the West Coast and produced a mural for the 1939 Golden Gate Exposition.
Biographical information:
*Who's Who in American Art.*

**Bernard Von Eichman** (1899-1970) Born: San Francisco, CA; Studied: California College of Arts and Crafts (Oakland). Bernard Von Eichman grew up in Northern California and in the 1920s, exhibited his colorful, modern works with the Society of Six. During the Depression, he moved to New York and then returned to California during World War II. Throughout his career, Von Eichman produced watercolors and occasionally exhibited them.
Biographical information:
*Artists in California, 1786-1940.*

**Edouard Vysekal** (1890-1939) Born: Kutna Hora, Czechoslovakia; Studied: Chicago Art Institute; Member: California Water Color Society. Edouard A. Vysekal immigrated to the United States in 1907 and studied at the Chicago Art Institute. About 1922, he moved to Los Angeles and settled there. Vysekal began teaching at the Art Students League of Los Angeles and exhibited with a group of local modern artists called the Group of Eight. In 1921, his paintings were in the first California Water Color Society exhibit. He taught life drawing and painting at the Otis Art Institute from the mid-1920s to the late 1930s.
Biographical information:
*Southern California Artists (1890-1940).*

**Elmer Wachtel** (1864-1929) Born: Baltimore, MD; Studied: Art Students League (New York). Elmer Wachtel came to California from Illinois in 1864 and settled in Los Angeles. By the 1890s, he was producing watercolors and line drawings for the *Land of Sunshine* magazine, published by Charles F. Lummis. At the turn of the century, he went to New York where he studied with William Merritt Chase, followed by a year of study in London. He eventually returned to California and occasionally produced watercolors. He ultimately became known for his oil paintings of Southern California landscape subjects.
Biographical information:
*Plein Air Painters of California.*

**Marion Kavanaugh Wachtel** (1876-1954) Born: Milwaukee, WI; Studied: Chicago Art Institute; Member: California Water Color Society, New York Water Color Club. Marion Kavanaugh Wachtel studied art with John Vanderpoel at the Chicago Art Institute and with William Merritt Chase in New York City. For two years, she taught art at the Chicago Art Institute and then in 1903, traveled to Northern California. She continued her studies there with William Keith and began exhibiting watercolors in the San Francisco Art Association exhibitions.

By 1904, she was living in Southern California and was married to artist Elmer Wachtel. Their home was in an art community near the Arroyo in Pasadena, a favorite location for landscape painters of that era. There were beautiful oak, sycamore, and eucalyptus trees lining the valley, and a clear view of the Sierra Madre Mountains. These local scenes became the subjects for many of her watercolors.

Both of the Wachtels were pursuing careers as full-time fine art painters so they were able to take extended painting trips to remote areas of California. Often they camped out and explored areas near the coast and inland valleys, seeking out California's beautiful landscape and unique natural light. The works of art they produced on these excursions were sold at art galleries in Los Angeles.

By the 1920s, she had developed a personal style of watercolor painting and mastered a technique of slowly building transparent washes of color. After the paint dried, she went back into the work with pastels to blend shapes, soften edges and add highlights. This was to be the height of her career and at this time she was one of the premier watercolorists in Southern California.

When the California Water Color Society formed in 1921, she was a founding member. Her works were often singled out for special mention in reviews of the period, particularly those published in the *Los Angeles Times*. When her husband died in 1929, she stopped exhibiting for several years, then began showing oil paintings and watercolors after the mid-1930s. She continued to produce watercolors and teach painting into the early 1950s.
Biographical information:
*Who's Who in American Art*
*Plein Air Painters of California.*

MARION K. WACHTEL  *The Western Sky*  1914  20" x 28"  Knowles Collection

MARION K. WACHTEL  *View Over Upper Ojai*  1920s  20" x 28"  Knowles Collection

JOSEPH WEISMAN  *Verena in the Arroyo*  1930s  16" x 22"  Michael Johnson Collection

JOSEPH WEISMAN  *Purple Duck Cafe*  1939  17" x 22"  David & Sally Martin Collection

**William Wallett** (1907-1987) Born: Milwaukee, WI; Studied: University of Southern California; Member: California Water Color Society. William Wallett grew up in Pasadena. After high school, he received art instruction in watercolor painting from Paul Sample and Dan Lutz.

Prior to World War II, he worked at Universal Studios on pre-production art and at the Walt Disney Studios painting watercolor background for animated films. During the war, he produced technical aviation illustrations at Lockheed Aircraft. After the war, he continued to work at Lockheed and at North American Aviation.

Throughout this period, he produced watercolors depicting Los Angeles regional subjects and exhibited them in the annual California Water Color Society exhibitions.
Biographical information:
Interview with William Wallett, 1982.

**Juan Buckingham Wandesforde** (1817-1902) Born: England; Member: San Francisco Art Association, Bohemian Club. Juan Buckingham Wandesforde grew up in England where he studied with John Varley, one of England's premier watercolor artists. He moved to New York, then to Montreal, Canada in the 1850s, before settling in San Francisco in 1862. Wandesforde produced expert watercolors depicting landscape views of expansive Northern California scenery. In addition, he taught art, was a founding member of the San Francisco Art Association, and worked as a portrait artist.
Biographical information:
*Artists in California, 1786-1940*.

**Nell Walker Warner** (1891-1970) Born: Nebraska; Studied: Los Angeles School of Art; Member: California Water Color Society. Nell Walker Warner studied art with Nicolai Fechin and Paul Lauritz. During the 1920s and 1930s, she exhibited watercolors in many Southern California art shows. After, she concentrated on oil paintings of still life subjects.
Biographical information:
*Who's Who in American Art*.

**Howard Warshaw** (1920-1977) Born: New York City, NY; Studied: Pratt Institute Art School (New York), National Academy of Design (New York), Art Students League (New York). Howard Warshaw moved to California in the early 1940s and settled in Los Angeles. He spent several years producing art for animated films, while developing a career as a fine artist. Through the support of actor and art collector Vincent Price, he was able to leave the studio job and spend more time painting and drawing. He established gallery connections in New York City and Los Angeles and began teaching at the Jepson Art Institute with his close friends William Brice and Rico Lebrun.

Warshaw's big break came in 1949 when his gouache painting, *Wrecked Automobiles*, received a top award at the Los Angeles County Museum of Art's show *California Centennials*. *Time* magazine made mention of the work in their review and *Life* magazine reproduced a picture of it and listed Warshaw as one of the nation's top nineteen young artists. He was an expert draftsman and many of his works look more like colored drawings than like paintings. This style lent itself well for producing the dark, mysterious looking works he chose to produce. In the 1960s and early 1970s, he taught art at the University of California, Santa Barbara.
Biographical information:
*Drawings and Illustrations by Southern California Artists* (Catalog)
*California Centennials* (Catalog).

**Kenneth Washburn** (1904-1989) Born: Franklinville, NY; Studied: Cornell University (New York); Member: American Watercolor Society. Kenneth Washburn graduated from Cornell University and from 1928 until 1950, taught art at that institution. In the early 1950s he moved to California and settled in San Carlos. He then became the co-founder of the Washburn-White Art Center and sent his work east to American Watercolor Society exhibitions.
Biographical information:
*Who's Who in American Art*
American Watercolor Society (Catalogs).

**William C. Watts** (1869-1961) Born: Philadelphia, PA; Studied: Pennsylvania Academy of Fine Arts, School of Industrial Arts (Philadelphia); Member: California Water Color Society, Philadelphia Sketch Club. William Watts grew up in Philadelphia and received his art instruction there. After traveling extensively throughout Asia, Africa and much of Europe, he settled in Carmel in 1915 and became an active member of the Monterey Peninsula art community. He continued to paint and exhibit watercolors until the late 1950s.

From 1924 until the early 1930s, Watts exhibited his works with the California Water Color Society. He was best known for his watercolors, but also painted with oils on canvas.
Biographical information:
*Monterey: The Artist's View* (Catalog).

**Rene Weaver** (1897-1984) Born: Pocatello, ID; Studied: University of Idaho; Member: Society of Western Artists. Rene Weaver grew up in Idaho. After serving in World War I and attending university, he moved to the West Coast, settling in Portland, Oregon. He received formal art instruction there from Emil Jacques and began producing both fine art watercolor paintings and commercial illustrations. In 1934, he moved to San Francisco and became the Art Supervisor for the Pacific Coast offices of the J. Walter Thompson Advertising Agency.

Throughout the 1940s and 1950s, Weaver was a member of the Thirteen Watercolorists group and became president of the Society of Western Artists. He also taught art and lectured on various techniques of watercolor painting.
Biographical information:
Interview with Rene Weaver, 1983.

**Joseph Weisman** (1907-1994) Born: Schenectady, NY; Studied: Chouinard Art Institute (Los Angeles); Member: California Water Color Society. Joseph Weisman moved to California in the 1920s and studied watercolor painting with Clarence Hinkle, Barse Miller and Millard Sheets.

From the 1930s, he painted and exhibited watercolors depicting regional scenes while working as a commercial artist, portrait painter, and as a scenic artist for the motion picture industry. He was also an art instructor in Los Angeles.
Biographical information:
Interview with Joseph Weisman, 1983.

**Mary Fraser Wesselhoeft** (1873-1971) Born: Boston, MA; Studied: Boston Museum School; Member: California Water Color Society. Mary Wesselhoeft was an illustrator who primarily painted with watercolor. She worked in Massachusetts and New York City before settling in Santa Barbara in the mid-1920s.
Biographical information:
*Artists in California, 1786-1940.*

**Glenn Wessels** (1895-1982) Born: Capetown, South Africa; Studied: California College of Arts and Crafts (Oakland), University of California; Member: California Water Color Society, San Francisco Art Association. Glenn Wessels came to Northern California with his family about 1902. After high school, he went on to earn a Bachelor of Fine Arts and a Master of Fine Arts degrees. He then went on to study in Europe with Andre L'Hote, Karl Hofer and Hans Hofmann. In the 1930s, he toured America with Hans Hofmann on a lecture circuit. He eventually settled in Northern California and became a Professor of Art at the University of California, Berkeley. Throughout his career, he painted and exhibited watercolors in West Coast museum shows.
Biographical information:
*Who's Who in American Art.*

**Eileen Monaghan Whitaker, N.A.** (1911- ) Born: Holyoke, MA; Studied: Massachusetts College of Art; Member: National Academy of Design, American Watercolor Society, California Water Color Society, Philadelphia Water Color Club, Connecticut Watercolor Society. Eileen Monaghan Whitaker studied art in Boston. For the next fifteen years, she worked as a commercial illustrator, producing watercolor sketches with fashion themes. In the 1940s and 1950s, she earned a reputation as an important American watercolorist by having her work shown in major museum exhibitions. Since moving to California, she has continued showing on a national level, contributed to books on watercolor painting, and presented one-woman exhibitions in the San Diego area.
Biographical information:
Interview with Eileen Monaghan Whitaker, 1985.

**Frederic Whitaker, N.A.** (1891-1980) Born: Providence, RI; Studied: Rhode Island School of Design; Member: National Academy of Design, American Water Color Society, Audubon Artists, Providence Watercolor Society, Royal Watercolor Society (London). Frederic Whitaker grew up on the East Coast. In the 1920s and 1930s, he was a successful silversmith having worked for several well-known companies including Tiffany. In the 1940s, he began exhibiting watercolors. By the late 1950s, he was a nationally recognized watercolorist and a member of over thirty art organizations. He served as president of the American Watercolor Society, vice president of the National Academy of Design, and was the founder of the Audubon Artists. Having earned the title "Mr. Watercolor," Whitaker wrote two books on watercolor painting, wrote eighty-five articles on art for magazines, and also contributed sections on watercolor painting to nine publications. He and his artist-wife Eileen, became California residents in the early 1960s.
Biographical information:
Interview with Eileen Monaghan Whitaker, 1985.

**Gunnar Widforss** (1879-1934) Born: Stockholm, Sweden; Studied: Institute of Technology (Sweden); Member: California Water Color Society. Gunnar Widforss immigrated to San Francisco in the early 1920s and began traveling through California and Arizona on painting excursions. He had a unique watercolor style and worked in a larger format than most artists of his time. While he produced excellent works depicting Yosemite, the California desert and other regional subjects, he became most famous for his dramatic depictions of the Grand Canyon.

Although Widforss lived in the Southwest for only thirteen years, he received a great deal of national attention during this period. Reproductions of his watercolors appeared on the covers of popular magazines, on a special postcard series featuring fine art, and as book illustrations.
Biographical information:
*Artists in California, 1786-1940.*

**Max Wieczorek** (1863-1955) Born: Breslau, Germany; Studied: Karlsruhe Art Academy (Germany), Weimar Art Academy (Germany); Member: American Watercolor Society, California Water Color Society. Max Wieczorek moved to the United States from Germany in 1893. For about fifteen years, he worked for Tiffany designing stained glass windows and in 1908, settled in Los Angeles. He became a founding member of the California Water Color Society in 1921 and exhibited his paintings, mainly portraits and figurative studies of local people, until the 1930s. He continued to exhibit with the American Watercolor Society until the mid-1950s.
Biographical information:
*Southern California Artists (1890-1940).*

**William T. Wiley** (1937- ) Born: Bedford, IN; Studied: San Francisco Art Institute. William T. Wiley grew up in Washington State, then attended art school in San Francisco. By the 1960s he was teaching at the University of California, Davis and exhibiting his art nationally. He has explored a variety of mediums including painting, assemblage and sculpture, and has often combined mediums to create his art. In the late 1960s, he began producing works painted with watercolors. They often included written information which was incorporated into the painted image or added in an open margin area. Art works by Wiley are in major museum collections in America and Europe.
Biographical information:
Interview with William T. Wiley, 1999.

**Mildred Pierce Wilkin** (1896-1990) Born: Kansas; Studied: Columbia University (New York), California School of Fine Arts (San Francisco); Member: California Water Color Society, Laguna Beach Art Association. Mildred Pierce Wilkin began exhibiting watercolors in the annual California Water Color Society exhibitions in 1924 and continued to do so until 1936. She also exhibited in local shows in Laguna Beach and Ontario until the mid-1940s. Most of her works were representational watercolors depicting landscape subjects near her home in Corona and the nearby desert region.
Biographical information:
*Who's Who in American Art*
California Water Color Society (Catalogs).

GUNNAR WIDFORSS  *A View of Half Dome*  1921  12" x 16"  Courtesy Butterfield & Butterfield

GUNNAR WIDFORSS  *Catalina Island*  1921  14" x 18"  George Stern Fine Arts

ROBERT E. WOOD  *Wharf Space Series*  1966  22" x 30"  Knowles Collection

ROBERT E. WOOD  *Racoon Straits*  1970s  22" x 30"  Jeff Olsen Collection

**William Harvey Williamson** (1908-1981) Born: Denver, CO; Studied: Chouinard Art Institute (Los Angeles), Art Center School (Los Angeles); Member: Society of Western Artists. William Harvey Williamson studied art in Los Angeles with F. Tolles Chamberlin and Will Foster. Employed as a costume designer in the motion picture industry, he also produced sketches for several major mural projects. Later, he moved to Carmel and exhibited his watercolor paintings with the Society of Western Artists and other art associations.
Biographical information:
*Who's Who in American Art.*

**Ray Wilson** (1906-1972) Born: Oakland, CA; Studied: California College of Arts and Crafts (Oakland); Member: San Francisco Art Association. Ray Wilson studied watercolor painting with Maurice Logan in the early 1930s. For nearly ten years, he produced colorful, expressionist style watercolors of regional scenes and still life subjects. During this period, he had several one-man shows and received a number of awards from local museums and art associations.
Biographical information:
Piedmont Lane Gallery, Piedmont, 1988.

**Dorothy Winslade** (1898-1973) Born: Isle of Wight, England; Studied: California School of Fine Arts (San Francisco); Member: San Francisco Art Association. Dorothy Winslade studied art in London and Paris before moving to California in 1924. After studying art in San Francisco, she began painting and exhibiting watercolor, gouache and tempera paintings in Bay Area museum shows. She also produced commercial artwork, painted portraits, and did drafting for the United States Navy during World War II. Married to artist Oswald Kurman, Winslade used her maiden name on art works to avoid confusion.
Biographical information:
Harold R. Wilson, Jr.

**William Wintle** (1911-1970) Born: Johannesburg, South Africa; Studied: California College of Arts and Crafts (Oakland); Member: Society of Western Artists. William Wintle immigrated to the Bay Area in 1929. He became a resident of Volcano, a small town in the Mother Lode region of Northern California, and operated an art gallery that featured his California Scene paintings that were primarily painted with transparent watercolors.
Biographical information:
*Artists in California, 1786-1940.*

**Galen Wolf** (1889-1976) Born: San Francisco, CA; Member: Society of Western Artists. Galen Wolf was born in California, spent a year in Europe, and then settled in Half Moon Bay around 1926.
Biographical information:
*Galen Wolf* (Catalog).

**Tyrus Wong** (1910- ) Born: Canton, China; Studied: Otis Art Institute (Los Angeles); Member: California Water Color Society, American Water Color Society. Tyrus Wong came to California from China in 1921 and attended art school in Los Angeles. His watercolor paintings show influences of both Oriental and California styles, and while the final works appear spontaneous, they are developed from preliminary sketches. From 1937 to 1940, Wong worked on animated films at the Walt Disney Studios. From the 1940s to the 1960s, he was a pre-production illustrator at the Warner Brothers Studios. He has exhibited his art on a national level since the late 1930s.
Biographical information:
Interview with Tyrus Wong, 1984.

**Paul Wonner** (1920- ) Born: Tucson, AZ; Studied: California College of Arts and Crafts (Oakland), University of California (Berkeley). Paul Wonner grew up in Arizona and eventually attended art school in Oakland during the late 1930s. He served in the United States Army from 1941 to 1946 and afterward, moved to New York City until 1950. Throughout the 1950s, he lived in Northern California, became known as part of the Bay Area Figurative group, and received national acclaim for his abstract paintings based on figurative subjects

In the 1960s, he lived in Southern California and taught art at the University of California, Los Angeles and the Otis Art Institute while pursuing a career in painting. Although many of his major works are oils on canvas, Wonner has also produced innovative works using watercolor and gouache on paper. His paintings are in major museum collections and have been featured in shows world-wide.
Biographical information:
*Who's Who in American Art*
*Bay Area Figurative Art.*

**Robert E. Wood N.A.** (1926-1999) Born: Gardena, CA; Studied: Pomona College (California), Claremont Graduate School (California); Member: National Academy of Design, American Watercolor Society, California Water Color Society. Robert E. Wood grew up in Southern California. Just after World War II, he began seriously studying watercolor painting and was influenced by Rex Brandt and Phil Dike. By the late 1940s, he was in a graduate program and already exhibiting watercolors in museum and gallery shows. His works from this period often depict regional subjects found near Claremont, where he was attending college, and harbor subjects near Corona del Mar and Newport Beach.

By the early 1960s, he was acknowledged as one of the premier California Watercolorists to emerge during the post-war era. The personal style for which he become well-known, was clearly developing. While most of his works have been painted with transparent watercolors, he also freely incorporated opaque colors or other complimentary mediums if they improved a specific work of art. His paintings often balance areas of pure abstraction with stylized, but recognizable subject matter. Throughout his career, he divided his time between painting outdoors and working inside his studio.

Wood also established a career in teaching watercolor painting. He taught at the University of Minnesota, Otis Art Institute, Scripps College and the Brandt-Dike Summer School of Painting. Beginning in 1961, he held the position of Director of the Robert E. Wood School of Painting in Green Valley Lake, located in the San Bernardino Mountains. His book, *Watercolor Workshop*, was published by Watson-Guptill in the early 1970s and has been reprinted three times. Wood also taught traveling watercolor workshops in Russia,

Sweden, France, Japan, Tahiti, Jamaica, Ireland and many other countries.

In addition, Wood exhibited his works in New York City at the National Academy of Design and in commercial art galleries. He was also an active member of the American Watercolor Society and served as their vice-president. On the West Coast, he exhibited regularly with the California Water Color Society, West Coast Watercolor Society, and in galleries. He presented over eighty one-man shows since 1950.
Biographical information:
Interview with Robert E. Wood, 1984.

**Stanley Wood** (1894- ) Born: Bordentown, NJ; Studied: Drexel Institute (Philadelphia); Member: California Water Color Society. Stanley Wood came to California in the mid-1920s and settled in Carmel. Known for his watercolors, drawings and lithographs of the California landscape, he exhibited and sold his works in the Bay Area. During the 1930s and 1940s, his watercolor illustrations appeared regularly in *Fortune Magazine*.
Biographical information:
*Who's Who in American Art*.

**Francis Woodcock** (1906-1983) Born: Oakland, CA; Studied: California College of Arts and Crafts (Oakland); Member: Society of Western Artists. Francis Woodcock grew up in Oakland. After high school, he took art classes in Oakland and San Francisco under the instruction of Perham Nahl, Xavier Martinez and Maurice Logan. At this time, he began to produce fine art watercolor paintings, most of which depict rural landscape subjects in Northern California.

In the 1940s and 1950s, he exhibited these works in annual museum shows in the Bay Area as well as with the Thirteen Watercolorists group. He was vice-president of the Society of Western Artists and the president of the West Coast Watercolor Society.

In addition to working as a fine artist, Woodcock was employed as a commercial illustrator and poster designer. His pen and ink line illustrations of figurative subjects were popular with book and magazine publishers.
Biographical information:
Interview with Francis Woodcock, 1982.

**James Couper Wright** (1906-1969) Born: Kirkwall, Scotland; Studied: Edinburgh College of Art; Member: American Watercolor Society, California Water Color Society. James Couper Wright grew up in the Orkney Islands. After attending the Edinburgh College of Art, he went to France and Germany on a scholarship to study the design of stained glass windows. While studying this art form, he worked with transparent painting mediums and became particularly interested in watercolor painting. He came to California in 1930 and settled in Pasadena.

Transparent watercolors were his favorite medium, and while he often went out on location to sketch, he preferred to paint his final works in the studio. As an art instructor, Wright taught at the Otis Art Institute, Occidental College and Coronado School of Fine Arts. He also conducted private classes in watercolor painting for many years.
Biographical information:
California Water Color Society (Catalogs).

**Bernard Wynne** (active ca. 1940s) Born: Indianapolis, IN. Bernard Wynne grew up in Southern California and studied art with Ejnar Hansen, Stanton MacDonald-Wright and Norman Rockwell. He was a resident of Sierra Madre by the 1940s and produced watercolors and commercial art.
Biographical information:
*Bernard Wynne* (Catalog).

**Sidney Yard** (1855-1909) Born: Rockford, IL. Sydney Yard studied art in New York City in the 1870s, then continued his education in England. There he received instruction in watercolor painting from Sutton Palmer. During the 1880s, he moved to California and worked in the photography business in Palo Alto and San Jose. In 1904, he moved to Carmel and for five years, operated a newspaper business. Yard was an expert watercolorist and often chose to paint landscape views of the Monterey Peninsula.
Biographical information:
*Artists in California, 1786-1940*.

**Karl Yens** (1868-1945) Born: Altona, Germany; Studied: Private study in Europe; Member: California Water Color Society, California Art Club, Laguna Beach Art Association. Karl Yens grew up in Germany and studied art with Max Koch in Berlin and with Constant and Laurens in Paris. He settled in Laguna Beach about 1918. He exhibited his watercolors in the first California Water Color Society show in 1921 and continued to exhibit in its shows until the early 1930s. In addition to painting, Yens was a printmaker.
Biographical information:
*Southern California Art*.

**Richard Yip** (1919-1981) Born: Canton, China; Studied: California College of Arts and Crafts (Oakland), College of the Pacific (California), University of California (Berkeley), Member: California Water Color Society. Richard Yip emigrated from China to America in 1931, and while still in high school received a scholarship to study art at the California College of Arts and Crafts in Oakland. During World War II, he served in the United States Air Force and afterwards settled in Stockton. Yip finished his studies at the University of California, Berkeley and began exhibiting his watercolors.

He spent much of his life teaching watercolor painting. He was an instructor at the College of the Pacific for many years and conducted private classes in watercolor painting.
Biographical information:
Interview with Roy Yip, 1985.

**Delmar Yoakum** (1915- ) Born: St. Joseph, MO; Studied: Kansas City Art Institute, Jepson Art Institute (Los Angeles), Chouinard Art Institute (Los Angeles), University of Southern California; Member: California Water Color Society, Los Angeles Art Association. In the late 1930s, Delmar Yoakum received a scholarship to study with Thomas Hart Benton at the Kansas City Art Institute. After serving in World War II, he came to Los Angeles and studied with Henry Lee McFee, Phil Dike and Rico Lebrun. He has exhibited with the California Water Color Society since the late 1940s and served as the Society president in 1961.
Biographical information:
Interview with Delmar Yoakum, 1984.

RICHARD YIP  *Untitled*  1930s  15" x 22"  Courtesy Roy Yip

JAMES COUPER WRIGHT  *Mexico, Hillside*  1950s  22" x 30"  Courtesy Greg Young

MILFORD ZORNES  *Laguna Shoreline*  1957  22" x 30"  Courtesy Greg Young

MILFORD ZORNES  *Winter at Mount Carmel*  1970s  22" x 30"  Pat Zornes Collection

**Ruth Ann Younglove** (1909- ) Born: Chicago, IL; Studied: University of California (Los Angeles); Member: American Watercolor Society, California Water Color Society. Ruth Ann Younglove grew up in Pasadena and attended college in Los Angeles. She settled in Pasadena and became close friends with Marion Wachtel. For many years she received private instruction in watercolor painting from Marion Wachtel and afterward continued painting on location with Wachtel and Orrin White. Most of her paintings, done with transparent watercolors, depict Southern California landscapes, but she also produced a series of regional works depicting industrial subjects. She was a school teacher for many years and also worked as a printmaker.
Biographical information:
Interview with Ruth Ann Younglove, 1983.

**George Louis Zacharie** (1906-1985) Born: Rhode Island. George Zacharie was a commercial illustrator in San Francisco during the 1930s and 1940s. He worked with watercolors to produce commercial works as well as exhibition pieces. The fine art works he exhibited were done with transparent watercolor and were exhibited with the Thirteen Watercolorists group.
Biographical information:
Interview with Hubert Buel, 1983
*Artists in California, 1786-1940.*

**Frank J. Zimmerer** (1882-1965) Born: Nebraska City, Nebraska; Studied: Art Institute of Chicago, Glasgow School of Art; Member: California Art Club. Frank J. Zimmerer studied art in Chicago, then continued his education in Scotland and France. He worked as a commercial illustrator, mural artist, and teacher in the East and Mid-West before settling in Los Angeles around 1924. Zimmerer often painted with watercolor and gouache, both for illustration and fine art works.
Biographical information:
Promotional Brochure
*Artists in California, 1786-1940.*

**Milford Zornes, N.A.** (1908- ) Born: Camargo, OK; Studied: Otis Art Institute (Los Angeles), Pomona College (California); Member: National Academy of Design, American Watercolor Society, California Water Color Society. Milford Zornes grew up in Oklahoma, Idaho and California. He loved to travel, so at twenty years of age, he hitch-hiked across America, worked on the New York docks, and then shipped out for Europe. By 1930, he was back in Los Angeles studying art with F. Tolles Chamberlin at the Otis Art Institute. He became very interested in watercolor painting and took additional study in this medium from Millard Sheets at Scripps College.

By 1933, he was exhibiting his watercolors and receiving awards. As a result of his art production for the P.W.A.P. Art Project, he was given a one-man show at the Corcoran Gallery of Art in Washington, D.C. One of his watercolors was selected by President and Mrs. Franklin D. Roosevelt to hang in the White House and an enormous amount of publicity followed. Within a very short amount of time, Zornes went from being a California watercolor student to being a nationally recognized artist.

Over the next few years, he concentrated on painting a number of high quality watercolors for exhibitions in California, Texas, Washington, D.C., Ohio, Kansas, New York, Illinois and other parts of America. When Lawson P. Cooper formed the California Group traveling show in 1937, Zornes was one of the twelve artists picked to represent California watercolor painting. On the West Coast, he also became known as a gifted instructor of watercolor painting. Throughout this period, he was an active member of the California Water Color Society and was president of that organization in 1942.

When World War II broke out, he was drafted into the United States Army and was assigned to be an official war artist in the China, India, Burma theater. For nearly three years, he painted on location in those countries and turned most of the art over to the War Department art collection housed at the Pentagon. He also had an art show in Bombay during this time.

After the war, he moved around California for a while, and eventually settled in Claremont. From there, he took a trip to Alaska and a series of trips to Greenland. All the while he was painting, teaching, and exhibiting nationally. Gradually, he developed the idea of traveling watercolor workshops. This combined his favorite things to do; travel, paint watercolors, and help others to enjoy the same. Zornes became one of the finest watercolor instructors in America and has been to nearly every part of the world at one time or another.

In addition to painting and teaching, he has worked as a mural artist, authored a book about his art and travels in Nicaragua, produced fine art prints, and was the subject of a book, which he co-authored, titled *Milford Zornes* published by Hillcrest Press Inc. in 1991.
Biographical information:
Interview with Milford Zornes, 1983.

**Bernice Zumwalt** (1904-1996) Born: Bakersfield, CA; Studied: California College of Arts and Crafts (Oakland); Member: Pacific Art Association. Bernice Zumwalt was raised in Oakland. From 1926 to 1966, she was an art teacher in Humboldt County and upon retirement settled in Pacific Grove on the Monterey Peninsula. She was primarily a watercolorist and often her works depict the coastal regions near her home.
Biographical information:
*Artists in California, 1786-1940.*

*Phil Dike (left) and Rex Brandt with student, Corona del Mar, 1947.*

# Artist Index & Photo Gallery

Every artist's name mentioned in this book appears in the index. Pages where biographies of the artists are given are italicized. Pages where artist's works are illustrated are given in bold face type. All photographs are from the McClelland Collection, provided by Rex Brandt, Ken Potter, Mrs. Nat Levy, Jessie Payzant, Millard Sheets and Phil Dike.

## A

Rowena Meeks Abdy  *79*
Ben Abril  *79*
Frank Ackerman  *79*
Clinton Adams  64, 71, *79*
Edward A. Adams  38
Karl Albert  *79*
James Alden  *79*
Clarence Nelson Aldrich  7, *79*
Anders Aldrin  *79*
Gladys Aller  *79*
Richard Altman  135
Ella Alluisi  *80*
John Altoon  71, *80*
Leon Amyx  *80*, **81**
Bill Anderson  61, **61**, *80*
Harry Anderson  45, 168
Thomas Anshutz  19
Arhenbach  140
Sidney Armer  *80*
Roger Armstrong  54, **54**, 61, *80*
Samuel Armstrong  *80*
Victor Arnautoff  *80*
Irma Attridge  *80*
John Ayres  41, *80*

## B

Robert Otto Bach  *83*
Standish Backus, Jr.  45, 58, **58**, *82*, *83*
William S. Bagdatopolous  *83*
Ralph Baker  *83*
Helen Balfour  *83*
Olive Barker  *83*
Dana Bartlett  27, *83*
Loren Barton  **81**, *83*, 128, 179
Jack Rivera Bates  *84*
Karl Baumann  63, **63**, *84*
John Jay Baumgartner  22, 23, **23**, *84*
Arthur Beaumont  50, **50**, *84*, **85**, 87, 111, 155, 183, 196

Robert Bechtle  **34**, 35, **35**, *84*
Rick Beck-Meyer  *84*
Lonie Bee  45, *84*
Carl Beetz  *84*, 180
Alvin J. Beller  *87*
Ritchie A. Bensen  57, **86**, *87*
Thomas Hart Benton  49, 147, 188, 192, 200, 212
Franz Bergman  *87*
Jane Berlandina  *87*
William Beynon  *87*
George Biddle  147
Albert Bierstadt  8
Walter Biggs  96
Jules Billington  *87*
Elmer Bischoff  67, 72, *87*, 187
Emil Bisttram  184
Lee Blair  32, 37, 38, 42, **43**, 46, 49, 50, *87*, **89**, 176
Mary Robinson Blair  37, 42, **42**, *86*, *88*
Preston Blair  42, *88*, 176
Peter Blos  159
David Blower  *88*
Lester Bonar  *88*
Sergei Bongart, A.N.A.  *88*, 135
Cora Boone  *88*
Cameron Booth  41, 127, 152
Edward Borein  *88*
Carl Oscar Borg, A.N.A.  **26**, 27, 28, 32, *91*
Dorr Bothwell  *91*
Cornelis Botke  *91*
Jessie Arms Botke  **32**, *91*
Ray Boynton  180
Robert Brackman  128
Howard Bradford  *91*
Alexandra Bradshaw  *91*, 95, 104
Rex Brandt, N.A.  36, 37, 45, 46, 49, **50**, 54, **56**, 57, 58, 76, **76**, 79, 80, **90**, *91*, 108, 111, 112, 115, 135, 136, 156, 159, 163, 176, 179, 203, 211
Sir Frank Brangwyn  32, 37, 84

George Braque  67
Arnold Franz Brasz  *92*
Hugh Breckenridge  163
William Brice  64, 71, *92*, 207
George Bridgman  84, 96, 107, 120, 139, 163, 164, 188, 199
Nicholas Brigante  62, 63, **63**, *70*, 71, *71*, 72, *92*
Morris Broderson  *92*
Gerald Brommer  32, **33**, 57, *92*, **93**
Alexander Brock  147
Benjamin Brown  16, *92*
Dorothy Brown  *92*
Theophilus Brown  72
George Elmer Browne  168
Edward Bruce  192
George de Forest Brush  140
Everett Bryant  95
Hubert Buel  50, 80, **94**, *95*, 152, 171, 215
Conrad Buff  95
Charles Burchfield  49
George Henry Burgess  7, *7*, 95
John Burgess  **94**, *95*
Hans Burkhardt  71, *95*
Jane Burnham  95

## C
Flavio Cabral  *95*
William Cahill  22
William Ross Cameron  46, *95*, **97**
Joseph Canzani  183
Robert Caples  *96*
Frank Capra  167
Paul Carey  45, 46, *96*
Emil Carlsen  116, 123
Jae Carmichael  *96*
Ben Carre  42, *96*
Albert Ross Carter  *96*
Pruett Carter  38, 87, 88, *96*, 99, 100, 107, 123, 140, 156, 160, 175, 203
Roscoe Carver  *96*
Andre Cassandre  183
Paul Cezanne  37, 63, 67
Frank Tolles Chamberlin  37, 83, *96*, 100, 107, 119, 123, 136, *139*, 147, 152, 160, *172*, 175, 192, 211, 215
Jean Charlot  116  156, 160, 188
William Merritt Chase  16, 23, 24, 83, 95, 123, 131, 204
Howard Clapp  75, *99*
Homer Clark  99
Ted Clark  *99*
Walter Clark  99
Samuel Clayberger  99
Paul Clemens  124
John Coakley  99, 136
Claude Coats  **98**, *99*
Lois Green Cohen  99
Eleanor Colborn  99
Sam Colburn  99
Gale Cole  *100*
Dorothea Cooke  **98**, *100*
Constant  92, 116, 212
Colin Campbell Cooper, N.A.  23, **24**, **25**, *100*
Lawson P. Cooper  46, 215
Mario Cooper, N.A.  *100*
Edward Corbett  67
Earl Cordrey  106
John Cotton  27, *100*
Alexander Cowie  144
Merle Cox  *100*
Whitson Cox  *100*
Willard Cox  45, 46, **46**, **98**, *100*, 132
Thomas Craig  37, 46, 50, 99, *100*, **101**, 128, 167, 176
Watson Cross, Jr.  50, **51**, 92, **102**, *103*, 147
Keith Crown  64, 68, **68**, 71, *103*
Leonard Cutrow  *103*
David Cytron  *103*
Lois Cytron  *103*

## D
Robert W. Daley  *103*
William Swift Daniell  20, *103*
Frode Dann  *103*, 195
Edwin Dawes  45, 199
William S. Darling  *103*

Paul Darrow  64, 71, *104*
Randall Davey  192
Don David  *104*, **105**
Ken Decker  *104*
John De Cuir  *104*
Francis de Erdely  64, 92, 96, *104*, 176, 199
Stephen De Hospodar  *104*
Dario De Julio  204
Henri de Kruif  27, 63, *104*
Annita Delano  *104*
Sonia Delaunay  79
Paul De Longpre  **14**, 15, **15**, *104*
Joseph De Mers  45, 46, **105**, **106**, *107*
Cecil B. DeMille  124, 136
Al Dempster  *107*
Albert De Rome  *107*
Harry Diamond  *107*
John Reed Dickinson  **11**, *107*
Charles Dickman  *107*
Eva Dickstein  *107*
Richard Diebenkorn  **66**, 67, 72, 112
Phil Dike, N.A.  36, 37, **38**, 42, 45, 46, **48**, 54, 57, **57**, 58, 76, **76**, 80, 91, 96, 104, *107*, **109**, 135, 136, 155, 156, 163, 167, 176, 179, 203, 211, 212
Walt Disney  176
James Budd Dixon  *108*
Lafayette Maynard Dixon  20, 24, *108*, 115, 151
Henry Doane  61, *108*
Arthur Dodge  *108*
Richard Dodge  *108*, **110**
William Dole  *108*
Helen Dooley  *108*
Jack Dudley  *108*
Raoul Dufy  87
Frank Vincent DuMond  107, 120, 128, 139, 163, 164, 199
Darwin Duncan  *111*
Hugh Duncan  58, **58**, 61, **110**, *111*
Harvey Dunn  100

## E

Eyvind Earle  111, **113**
Ferdinand Earle  111
Harrison Eastman  7, 8, 11, *111*
Leonard Edmondson  64, 68, **69**, *111*
El Greco  67
Duval Eliot  *111*
J. Milford Ellison  *111*
Jules Engel  **64**, 68, *111*
Verna Scott Evans  *111*
Edgar Ewing  71, *112*

## F

Justin Faivre  *112*
Edward M. Farmer  *112*
Alfred Villiers Farnsworth  11, *112*
Jerry Farnsworth  120
Nicolai Fechin  164, 207
Lyonel Feininger  63, 67, 164
Lorser Feitelson  71, 108
June Felter  **74**, 75, *112*
Eva Scott Fenyes  *112*
Jean Leon Ferris  80
Blair Field  *112*
Ernest Fiene  160
Keith Finch  68, *112*
Mary L. Finley  *112*
Mary Stevens Fish  *112*
George Fisher  143
Hugo Anton Fisher  *112*
James Fitzgerald  *112*
Flamm  140
Frank Morley Fletcher  143
Russell Flint  37, 84
Jade Fon  57, 61, **61**, *114*, *115*, 131, 200
Gordon Onslow Ford  64
Henry Chapman Ford  112, *115*
James Harrison Forman  46, *115*
Harndon Foster  95
Will Foster  211
Erwin J. Fox  *115*
Robert Frame  *115*
Sam Francis  76, 77, *115*
Alfred Frankenstein  41

Marshall Frantz  *115*
Michael Frary  64, *116*
Will Frates  *116*
Priscilla Frazer  *116*
James Fuller  *116*
Karoly Fulop  *116*

## G

Jane Greene Gale  *116*
John Gamble  *116*
Bernard Garbutt  *116*
Julian E. Garnsey  *116*
Frank Gavencky  **117**, *119*
William Gaw  96, *119*
August Gay  176
Ted Geisel  167
Robert George  *119*
Milton Gershgoren  *119*
George Gibson, N.A.  32, **32**, 42, 61, **118**, *119*, 136, 144
Robert Gilberg  *119*
Selden Conner Gile  63, *119*
Giotto  67
John Giuliani  *119*
William Glackens  19, 24
J. Duncan Gleason  23, **26**, **27**, 42, 45, *120*
Gerald Gleeson  *120*
Albert Gleizes  180
George Henry Goddard  7, 11, *120*
Karl Godwin  152
Ralph Goings  35, **35**, *120*
Leon Goldin  *120*
Fred Gordon  *120*
Henry Gorham  *120*
Arshile Gorky  63, 95
Virginia Belle Gould  41, *120*
Elsie H. Grace  *123*
Charles S. Graham  11, *123*
Don Graham  99
Hardie Gramatky, N.A.  32, 36, **37**, 37, 38, 42, 45, **45**, 111, **121**, *123*, 147, 175
Charles Henry Grant  115
Gordon Grant, A.N.A.  *123*
Ed Graves  *123*

Percy Gray  20, **20**, **21**, 23, 24, **122**, *123*
James Green  **124**, *125*
Michael Green  124
Lucille Brown Greene  124
Herald Gretzner  46, 57, 61, *124*, **125**, 171
John Grillo  67, *124*
Daniel Sayre Groesbeck  124
George Grosz  63, 79, 179

## H

Richard Haines  99, *124*, 147, 176, 187
John Haley  38, **40**, 41, 67, **67**, 80, 91, 120, **126**, *127*, 135, 139, 159, 167, 168
Clem Hall  42, *127*
William Haines Hall  *127*
Frank Hamilton  *127*, *129*
James Hamilton  164
Leah Rinne Hamilton  41, **67**, *127*
Armin Hansen  24, 96, 151, 176
Ejnar Hansen  *127*, 164, 212
Herman W. Hansen  **10**, 11, *127*
G. Powell Harding  *127*
Henry Gifford Hardy  *127*
Hazel Harper  *127*
Sam Hyde Harris  79, 88, 111
Herrica Hartmetz  *128*
Childe Hassam  24
Charles Hawthorne  104
Roger Hayward  *128*
Bessie Ella Hazen  *128*
William Randolph Hearst  183
Frederick R. Heckman  *128*
Frederick Heidel  *128*
Z. Vanessa Helder  *128*, 179
Dale Hennesy  *128*
Joseph Henninger  32, 107, 111, 127, *128*
Robert Henri  19, 24, 92, 104, 163, 203
Paul Blaine Henrie  *128*, **130**

Caesar A. Hernandez  *128*
L. Francis Herreshoff  95
Susan Lautman Hertel  75, *131*
Albert Herter, A.N.A.  80, *131*
Henry Melton Hesse  *131*
Forrest Hibbits  *131*
Floyd Hildebrand  *131*
Thomas Hill  8
Lawrence Hinckley  *131*
Clarence Hinkle  24, 37, 63, 100, 107, 123, *131*, 160, 167, 175, 192, 207
Lucile Hinkle  *131*
Karl Hofer  208
Hans Hofmann  67, 91, 104, 112, 116, 127, 140, 208
Jane Hofstetter  *131*
Robert Holdeman  *132*
Ralph Holmes  164
Winslow Homer  37
James R. Hopkins  184
Edward Hopper  49
Winfield Scott Hoskins  *132*
Thelma Speed Houston  *132*
Charles Howard  64, *132*
John Langley Howard  *132*
Robert B. Howard  132
James Hueter  *132*
Therman Huett  57
Ray Huffine  *132*
Virginia McAllister Huffman  *132*
Louis Hughes  46, **46**, *132*
Ralph Hulett  42, 45, 54, 111, *132*, **133**
La Verne Hutchings  *135*
Mabel Hutchinson  *135*
William Rich Hutton  *135*

## I

Alex Ignatiev  *135*
Joan Irving  57, **134**, *135*
Robert Irwin  *135*
Miyoko Ito  *135*
John Ivey  154, *136*

*Paul Sample instructing a watercolor class in Vermont, 1940.*

*Millard Sheets (sitting) instructng watercolor class at Los Angeles Harbor, circa 1950.*

*Ken Potter painting on location in San Francisco, circa 1963.*

## J

Everett Gee Jackson 46, *136*
Gordena Parker Jackson *136*
Robert L. Jackson *136*
Neil Jacobe *136*, **137**
Emil Jacques 207
George James 57, **57**, *136*, **137**
James Jarvaise *136*
William Jekel 45, 54, **54**, *136*, **138**
Robert Jensen 53, *136*
Herbert Jepson 99, 135
Edward Alden Jewell 54
Addison Johnson *139*
Doris Miller Johnson 41, *139*
Reginald Johnson *139*
Stan Johnson *139*
Ynez Johnston 68, 71, *139*
Chuck Jones 167
Dorothy Jordan *139*
Christian A. Jorgensen 12, **13**, *139*, **141**
William Lees Judson 15, 83, *139*
Paul Julian *140*

## K

Edward Kaminski 135
Vasily Kandinsky 63
Karl Kasten 41, **67**, *140*
Ted Kautzky 168
Arthur L. Kaye **72**, *140*
Elizabeth Emerson Keith *140*
William Keith **6**, 8, 16, 24, *140*, 164, 204
Henry Keller 143
Richmond Kelsey *140*
Robert H. Kennicott *140*
Ada Howe Kent *140*
Lenard Kester, N.A. 64, *140*
Edward Kienholz 75
Atsushi Kikuchi 143
Charles Kinghan, N.A. 143
Dong Kingman, N.A 32, 38, 41, 46, 49, **52**, 53, 57, 87, 96, 116, **142**, *143*, 151, 159, 180, 195, 196

Paul Klee 63
David Klein *143*
Earl Klein 71, *143*
Herbert Klynn *143*
Joseph Knowles *143*
Gerd Koch 68, *144*
Irene Koch *144*
Max Koch 212
Josephine Kopenhaver *144*
Emil Kosa, Jr., N.A. 37, 42, **44**, 46, 49, **49**, 54, **54**, **55**, 57, 76, 136, *144*, **145**
Peter Kotov 88
Peter Krasnow *144*
Leon Kroll 172, 184
Yasuo Kuniyoshi 164
Roger Kuntz 71, 75, *144*
Frank Kupka 76, 144
Oswald Kurman *147*, 211
Dorothy Browdy Kushner *147*
John Kwok **72**, *147*

## L

Diana La Com 32, *147*
Wayne La Com 58, **58**, 61, **72**, **146**, *147*
Irene Lagorio *147*
Robert Landry 61, **146**, *147*
Art Landy *147*
Frank Lane *148*
Mildred Lapson *148*
Lorenzo P. Latimer 12, **12**, *148*
Jean-Paul Laurens 84, 92, 116, 119
Pierre Laurens 144, 212
Paul Lauritz *148*, 207
Dillon Lauritzen *148*
Harry Law 27, **27**, *148*
James A. Lawrence *148*
Sydney Lawrence *148*
Jack Laycox 53, *148*
Rico Lebrun 64, 71, 91, 99, 103, 136, 147, *148*, 172, 175, 207, 212
Chee Chin S. Cheung Lee *148*
Jake Lee **149**, *151*, 200
John Leeper 68, 71, *151*
Fernand Leger 136, 180

Frank Lenfest *151*
David Levine *151*
Hilda Levy 68, *151*
Nat Levy 45, 46, 47, **150**, *151*
Harry Emerson Lewis 31, *151*
Tom E. Lewis 46, 49, 63, 100, *152*
Andre L'Hote 91, 183, 195, 208
Jonas Lie 188
Orson Alf Linn *152*
Phillip H. Little *152*
Maurice Logan, N.A. 37, 38, 45, 46, **46**, 53, 61, 119, 124, 132, *152*, **153**, 171, 211, 212
Arthur Lonergan *152*
Stanley Long *152*
Rene Lopez *152*
Erle Loran 38, **40**, 41, 67, 80, 135, *152*, 167
Janice Penney Lovoos *152*, 175
George Luks 24, 107, 196
Charles Lummis 112, 204
Helen Lundeberg 71
Dan Lutz 49, 80, 99, 116, **154**, *155*, 187, 207

## M

Jack Macartney *155*
Stanton MacDonald-Wright 62, **62**, 63, 71, 84, 92, 124, 147, 148, *155*, 167, 199, 212
Constance Macky 179, 180
Spencer Macky 84, 148, 167, 180
Louis Macouillard *155*, **157**
Robert Majors *155*
Grace Elizabeth Mallon *155*
John Marin 24
Carl Marr 140
Reginald Marsh 99, 147, 183
Albert Marshall *155*
Fletcher Martin, N.A. 45, 49, 50, *155*, 164

Sandy Martin *156*
Marciano Martinez *156*
Xavier Martinez 12, 16, 176, 179, 212
Roy M. Mason, N.A. *156*, **158**, 168
Arthur Mathews 11, 12, 16, 79, 80, 131, *156*, 159
Lucia K. Mathews 12, 24, *156*
Paul Mays 46, *156*
Douglas McClellan *156*
Francis McComas 19, **19**, 24, **24**, 31, *159*
Betty McCoon *159*
James McCray 64, **65**, *159*
William T. McDermitt *159*
Dixie McElroy *159*
Henry Lee McFee 80, 103, 115, 119, 132, 144, 200, 212
Robert J. McIntosh 64, **68**, *159*
William McIlvaine 7
David McKay *159*
Marcelle McKusik *160*
Richard McLean **34**, 35, *160*
Elizabeth Baskerville McNaughton *160*
Henry Meier *160*
Fred Meiers *160*
Robert Hiram Meltzer *160*
Daniel Marcus Mendelowitz 53, *160*
Knud Merrild *160*
Ben Messick *160*, **161**
Jean Metzing 180
Othello Michetti **161**, *163*
Harold Miles *163*
Barse Miller, N.A. 32, 36, 37, **37**, 38, **38**, 46, 49, 50, 54, 57, **78**, 99, 104, 107, 108, 111, 123, 124, 128, 135, 148, **162**, *163*, 164, 184, 188, 199, 207
Kenneth Hayes Miller 99
Richard Miller 119
Frank Millet 96
Arthur Millier 37, *163*
Paul Mills 72
Theodore Modra *163*

Claude Monet 24
Thomas Moran, N.A. 8, 11, *164*
Mary DeNeale Morgan 19, 24, *164*
Joseph Emil Morhardt 32, **32**, *164*
Grace Morley 63
Julon Moser *164*
Joseph Mugnaini *164*
Lawrence Murphy 37, 87, 107, 135, 140, *164*, 167, 192, 196
Darwin Musselman *164*
Louis Myljarack 136

# N

Perham Nahl 212
Alexander Nepote 38, 53, 71,72, **73**,136, **165**, *167*, 176
Hanne-Lore Sutro Nepote *167*
Ethel Pearce Nerger *167*
Maurice Noble 42, *167*
Ben Norris 46, 50, 164, **166**, *167*, 195
Crandall Norton 57, **59**, 61, *168*
Gordon Nunes *168*
Vernon Nye 45, 57, 61, *168*, **169**

# O

N. Eric Oback *168*
Chiura Obata 53, *168*
Helen G. Oehler *168*
Eliot O'Hara, N.A. 54, 83, 95, 127, 155, *168*, 179, 192, 200
Miné Okubo 41, 53, *168*
Otis Oldfield 167, 180
Nathan Oliveira 72, *171*
Joseph M. O'Malley 42, **170**, *171*
Don O'Neill **60**, 61, *171*
Ruth Powers Ortlieb *171*
John O'Shea *171*
Don Osterloh *171*
Sam Ostrowsky 203
Alfred Owles *171*, 176

# P

Horace S. Page 53, **60**, 61, *171*
Alton Painter *172*
William Pajaud *172*
Abraham Palansky *172*
Sutton Palmer 19, 212
Phil Paradise, N.A. 37, 49, 103, 104, 135, 136, 148, 155, *172*, **173**, 192
Maxfield Parrish 19
David Park 67, 72, 115, 167, *172*, 187
Cort Parkhouse 123
Stan Parkhouse 123
Douglass Parshall, N.A. 54, *172*
Richard Langtry Partington *172*
James Patrick 37, 50, **50**, 103, 112, *172*, 192
Edgar Payne 20, **31**, 79, 111, *175*
Elsie Palmer Payne 20, *175*
Charles Payzant 36, 37, 42, **42**, **43**, 111, **174**, *175*, 183
Channing Peake *175*
Bob Peck *175*
Fred Penney *175*
Albert Sheldon Pennoyer *176*
Robert Perine 57, 76, **76**, *176*
Margaret Peterson 67, 139, 167
James March Phillips *176*
Gottardo Piazzoni 148, 180
Pablo Picasso 67
George Picken 128
Rollin Pickford, Jr. *176*
Lucy Valentine Pierce *176*
William H.C. Pierce *176*
John Pike 135
Caamille Pissaro 24
Elmer Plummer 42, **42**, 46, 136, *176*, **177**
Leo Politi *179*
Pauline Polk *179*
George Polkinghorn *179*
Theodore Polos *179*
Julie Polousky **178**, *179*
Elsie Lower Pomeroy *179*
Tino Pontrelli *179*
Fritz Poock *179*
Al Porter *179*
George Post 37, 38, 41, **41**, 46, 49, 53, **53**, 57, 100, 112, 136, 156, *180*, **181**, 196, 200
Kenneth Potter 53, **53**, 61, **61**, *180*, **182**
Marshall Potter 46, 53, *183*
Maurice Prendergast 24
Clayton Price 176
Raymon Price *183*
Vincent Price 207
Wilfred Provan *183*
Hanson Puthuff 27, *183*
Howard Pyle 184, 195

# Q

Noel Quinn 87, 92, 179, *183*

# R

G.D. Arul Raj *183*
Henry Raleigh *183*
Jo Rebert *183*
Stanley Reckless 38, 107, 127, 159, 184, 188, 195
Edward Reep 50, 54, **55**, 64, **68**, 71, 79, 147, *184*, **185**, 203
Lawrence Rehag *184*
Marques S. Reitzel *184*
Auguste Renoir 24
William Rice *184*
John Hubbard Rich 23, *184*, **186**
Henry Richter *184*
Art Riley 42, *184*
Larry Rink *184*
William Frederick Ritschel, N.A. 19, 27, *187*
Paul Rivas *187*
Diego Rivera 175
Antony Rizzo *187*
Marie MacDonnell Roberts *187*
Boardman Robinson 156
Irene Bowen Robinson *187*
Cleveland Rockwell 7, **8**, *187*
Norman Rockwell 212
Louis Rogers 176
Guy Rose 24
Richards Ruben *187*
Morgan Russell 62, 155
Chauncy Ryder 156
Worth Ryder 41, 67, 120, 139, 159
Herbert Ryman 42, *187*

# S

John Saccaro *187*
Norman St. Clair 20, **27**, *187*
George Samerjan *188*
Paul Sample, N.A. 36, 37, 45, 46, 49, 83, 99, 131, *188*, **189**, 207
Birger Sandzen 27, 28, 32
John Singer Sargent 24, 37
F. Grayson Sayre *188*
Rudolph Schaeffer 96
Sergey John Scherbakoff *188*
Leonard Scheu *188*
Rudolph Schmidt *188*
Paul A. Schmitt *188*
Palmer Schoppe *188*
Dorner T. Schueler *191*, 200
Donna Schuster 23, 27, *191*
Frederick John Schwankovsky *191*
Davis Schwartz *191*
David Scott *191*
Jonathan Scott *191*
Leopold Seyffert 184
Sueo Serisawa 68, *191*
Yoichi Serisawa 191
Frank Serratoni *191*
Fred Sersen *191*
John Severson 71, **190**, *191*
Lyne T. "Bud" Shackelford *192*
Frederick Shane **190**, *192*
Millard Sheets, N.A. **32**, **36**, **37**, **38**, 38, **39**, 45, 46, 49, **49**, 50, 54, 57,

222

*Nat Levy painting on location in Mendocino, circa 1948.*

*Wayne La Com painting on location in Mexico, circa 1948.*

*Gerald Brommer, Ralph Hulett, Jae Carmichael, Robert E. Wood and Keith Crown at California Water Color Society meeting, 1965*

*George Post painting demonstration for Southern California watercolor class, 1955.*

80, 83, 87, 96, 99, 100, 104, 108, 112, 119, 124, 131, 132, 135, 136, 139, 140, 144, 155, 156, 160, 163, 164, 167, 171, 175, 176, 179, 180, 191, *192*, **193**, 195, 196, 200, 203, 207, 215
Margaret E. Sheppard 168, *192*
Roscoe Shrader 88, 179
Morris Shubin **194**, *195*
Louis Siegrist 132
Burr Singer *195*
David Alfaro Siqueiros 87
Katherine Skeele 103, *195*
Dorothy Sklar *195*
Rex Slinkard 71, 91, 92
Helen Sloan *195*
John Sloan 24, 191, 192
Charles L.A. Smith 27, *195*
Hassel Smith 67, *195*
Howard E. Smith, N.A. *195*
Henry Snell 163
Gene Sogioka 53, *195*
Paul Souza *195*
Duncan Alanson Spencer 32, 45, 136, *196*, **197**
Clay Spohn 64, *196*
Edgar Starr *196*
Judson L. Starr *196*
Earl Stendahl 31
Maurice Stern 108
Charles Walter Stetson 16, *196*
Marjory Stevens *196*
Richard Stevens 180, *196*
Arthur Stewart *196*
Clifford Still 67
George Stillman 67, *196*
James Strombotne 64, 71, 75, **75**, *196*
Jan Stussy 64, 71, *199*
Henry Sugimoto *199*
Charles Surendorf *199*
Lewis Suzuki *199*
Garner Symons 20

## T

Kango Takamura 53, *199*
Bayard Taylor 7
Farwell M. Taylor *199*

Donald Teague, N.A. 32, **33**, 45, **198**, *199*
Albert H. Thayer 140
Wayne Thiebaud *199*, **201**
Aline Thistlethwaite *200*
Stephen Seymour Thomas 23, *200*
Titian 67
Walton Titus 45, *200*
Francis Todhunter 23, *200*
Peter Petersen Toft 7, **9**, *200*
Virginia Tonetti *200*
Ernest A. Tonk *200*
Eugene Towne *200*
Wing Kwong Tse *200*
Dale M. Turnbull *200*
Janet E. Turner *200*
John Twachtman 131, 203
Dwight Tyron 96

## U

Robert Uecker *203*
Walter Ufer 195
Martha Underwood *203*

## V

Albert R. Valentien *203*
James Vance **202**, *203*
John Vanderpoel 16, 120, 204
Tony Van Hasselt 57
Lucretia Van Horn *203*
Loli Vann *203*
Frank Van Sloun 23, 115, 151, *203*
Oscar Van Young **202**, *203*
Hilda Van Zandt *203*
Alberto Vargas *203*
John Varley 8, 207
Archie J. Vazquez *204*
Hernando Villa *204*
Herman Volz *204*
Bernard Von Eichman 63, *204*
Robert Vonnoh 19
Harold Von Schmidt 151
Edouard Vysekal 23, 27, 62, 63, 128, 179, *204*

## W

Elmer Wachtel 16, *204*
Marion Kavanaugh Wachtel 15, **16**, **17**, 24, 27, **30**, 31, 83, *204*, **205**, 215
William Wallett *207*
Juan Buckingham Wandesforde 8, **8**, *207*
Nell Walker Warner *207*
Howard Warshaw 64, 71, 75, *207*
Kenneth Washburn *207*
Crafts Watson 27, 28
William C. Watts **18**, 19, **19**, *207*
Rene Weaver 45, *207*
James Weeks 72
Joseph Weisman **206**, *207*
William Wendt 20, 24
Mary Fraser Wesselhoeft *208*
Glenn Wessels *208*
James Abbott Whistler 140
Eileen Monaghan Whitaker, N.A. 32, 156, *208*
Frederic Whitaker, N.A. *208*
Orin White 215
Gunnar Widforss 28, **28**, **29**, 31, *208*, **209**
Max Wieczorek 27, *208*
William T. Wiley *208*
Mildred Pierce Wilkin *208*
Norman Wilkinson 32, 199
Virgil Williams 116, 123, 139, 164
William Harvey Williamson *211*
W. Marsden Wilson 100
Ray Wilson 83, *211*
Dorothy Winslade *211*
William Wintle *211*
Galen Wolf *211*
Hamilton Wolf 171, 180
Tyrus Wong 49, *211*
Paul Wonner 72, 74, *211*
Grant Wood 49

Robert E. Wood, N.A. 57, 58, 61, 92, 156, 179, **210**, *211*
Stanley Wood 37, **37**, 180, *212*
Francis Woodcock 46, *212*
James Couper Wright 46, 123, 168, *212*, **213**
Bernard Wynne *212*

## Y

Sidney Yard 19, **20**, *212*
Michael Yarovoy 88
Raymond Yelland 123
Karl Yens 20, 27, *212*
Richard Yip 131, *121*, **213**
Delmar Yoakum *212*
Ruth Ann Younglove *215*

## Z

George Louis Zackarie *215*
Frank J. Zimmerer *215*
Milford Zornes 37, 46, 47, 49, 50, **51**, 57, 61, 99, 147, 156, 168, 171, 179, **214**, *215*
Bernice Zumwalt *215*

# General Bibliography

Ainsworth, Ed, *The Cowboy in Art*, Bonanza Books, New York, 1968.

Albright, Thomas, *Art in the San Francisco Bay Area, 1945-1980*, University of California Press, Berkeley, CA, 1985.

American Federation of Arts, *Who's Who in American Art (Vol. 1948-1970)*, R. R. Bowker, New York, NY, 1948-1970.

*American Watercolor Society*, Catalogs

*Anders Aldrin*, Zeitlin and Ver Brugge, Los Angeles, CA, 1970.

Anderson, Nancy K., *Thomas Moran*, National Gallery of Art, Washington, DC, 1997.

Anderson, Susan M., *Regionalism: The California View*, Santa Barbara Museum of Art, Santa Barbara, CA, 1988.

Anderson, Timothy J. and Eudorah M. Moore and Robert W. Winter, editors, *California Design, 1910*, California Design Publications, 1974.

Armstrong, Richard, *David Park*, Whitney Museum of American Art, New York, NY, 1988.

*Artists of Los Angeles and Vicinity*, Los Angeles County Museum of Art, Los Angeles,

*Arts of Southern California XVII - Water Color*, Long Beach Museum of Art, Long Beach, CA, 1966.

Boas, Nancy, *The Society of Six - California Colorists*, Bedford Arts Publishers, San Francisco, CA, 1988.

Brandt, Rex, *Seeing with a Painter's Eye* (2nd Edition), Van Nostrand Reinhold Company, New York, 1984.

Brown, Michael D., *Views from Asian California, 1920-1965*, Michael Brown, San Francisco, CA, 1992.

*California Water Color Society*, Catalogs 1921-1966.

*California National Water Color Society*, Catalogs 1967-1974.

Dawdy, Doris Ostrander, *Artists of the American West, Vol. 1*, The Swallow Press, Inc., Chicago, IL, 1974.

Dawdy, Doris Ostrander, *Artists of the American West, Vol. 2*, The Swallow Press, Inc., Chicago, IL, 1981.

Enman, Tom K., *Six Decades*, Laguna Beach Museum of Art, Laguna Beach, CA, 1978.

Falk, Peter Hastings, editor, *Who Was Who in American Art*, Sound View Press, Madison, CT, 1985.

Gesensway, Deborah and Mindy Roseman, *Beyond Words, Images from America's Concentration Camps*, Cornell University Press, Ithica, NY, 1987.

Hagerty, Donald J., *Desert Dreams, The Art and Life of Maynard Dixon*, Gibbs-Smith Publisher, Layton, UT, 1993.

Harrison, Alfred C., Dr., *William Keith - The Saint Mary's College Collection*, Hearst Art Gallery, Moraga, CA, 1988.

Henstell, Bruce, *Los Angeles: An Illustrated History*, Alfred A. Knopf, New York, 1980.

Henstell, Bruce, *Sunshine and Wealth: Los Angeles in the Twenties and Thirties*, Chronicle Books, San Francisco, CA, 1984.

Hughes, Edan Milton, *Artists in California, 1786-1940*, Hughes Publishing Company, San Francisco, CA, 1989.

Jackson, Joseph Henry, *Gold Rush Album*, Charles Scribner's Sons, New York, 1949.

*Jepson Art Institute*, Jepson Art Institute, Los Angeles, 1945.

*Karl Baumann*, Maxwell Galleries, San Francisco, 1989.

Kovinick, Phil and Marian Yoshiki-Kovinick, *An Encyclopedia of Women Artists of the American West*, University of Texas Press, Austin, TX, 1998.

*The Land of Sunshine*, Vol. VII, June to November 1897, Land of Sunshine Publishing Co., Los Angeles, CA.

Loran, Erle, *Cézanne's Composition*, University of California Press, Berkeley, 1946.

Lovoos, Janice and Edmund F. Penney, *Millard Sheets - One-Man Renaissance*, Northland Press, Flagstaff, AZ, 1984.

*Rex Brandt instructing student at Balboa Bay, 1955.*

*Barse Miller, Joan Irving Brandt, Rex Brandt and George Post at Brandt's "Blue Sky Studio" in Corona del Mar, California, 1960.*

*California Water Color Society group photo, 1948. (back row) Ejner Hansen, Douglass Parshall, Noel Quinn, Frode Dann, Sueo Serisawa, Phil Dike, Watson Cross, Emil Kosa, Jr., David Scott, (front row) Rex Brandt, Michael Frary, Mary Finley Fry and George Gibson.*

Maltin, Leonard, *The Disney Films*, Crown Publishers, Inc., New York, 1973.

McGrath, Robert L. and Paula F. Glick, *Paul Sample, Painter of the American Scenel*, Dartmouth College, Hanover, NH, 1988.

*Monterey: The Artist's View (1925-1945)*, Monterey Penenisula Museum of Art, Monterey, CA, 1982.

Moure, Nancy Dustin Wall, *California Art: 450 Years of Painting and Other Media*, Dustin Publications, Los Angeles, 1998.

Moure, Nancy Dustin Wall, *Drawings and Illustrations by Southern California Artists Before 1950*, Laguna Beach Museum of Art, Laguna Beach, CA, 1982.

Moure, Nancy Dustin Wall, *Loners Mavericks & Dreamers: Art in Los Angeles Before 1900*, Laguna Art Museum, Laguna Beach, CA, 1993.

Moure, Nancy Dustin Wall, *Scenes of California Life, 1930-1950*, The Dorian Society, Bakersfield, CA, 1991.

Moure, Nancy Dustin Wall, *Southern California Art*, Dustin Publications, Glendale, CA, 1984.

Newmark, Maurice and Marco R., editors, *Sixty Years insouthern California, 1853-1913*, Zeitlin and Ver Brugge, Los Angeles, CA, 1970.

Orr-Cahall, Christina, editor, *The Art of California: Selected Works from the Collection of the Oakland Museum*, The Oakland Museum, Oakland, CA, 1984.

Perine, Robert, *Chouinard, An Art Vision Betrayed*, Artra Publishing, Inc., Encinitas, CA, 1985.

Perine, Robert, *The California Romantics: Harbingers of Watercolorism*, Artra Publishing, Inc., Encinitas, CA, 1986.

Peters, Harry T., *California on Stone*, Doubleday, Doran & Company, Inc., Garden City, NJ, 1935.

*Production Design*, Vol. 2, No. 7, The Society of Motion Picture Art Directors, Beverly Hills, CA, July 1952.

Redfern, Ray, *F. Grayson Sayre*, Redfern Gallery, Laguna Beach, CA, 1987.

Reed, Walt and Roger, *The Illustrator in America, 1880-1980*, Madison Square Press, Inc., New York City, NY, 1984.

Reep, Ed, *A Combat Artist in World War II*, The University Press of Kentucky, 1987.

Reich, Sheldon, *Keith Crown Watercolors*, University of Missouri Press, Columbia, 1986.

Schaad, Bentley *The Realm of Contemporary Still Life Painting*, Reinhold Publishing Corp., New York, 1962.

*Southern California 100*, Laguna Beach Museum of Art, Laguna Beach, CA, 1977.

*Southern California Artist: 1890-1940*, Laguna Beach Museum of Art, Laguna Beach, CA, 1979.

*Southern California Artist: 1940-1980*, Laguna Beach Museum of Art, Laguna Beach, CA, 1981.

Spangenberg, Helen, *Yesterday's Artists on the Monterey Peninsula*, Monterey Peninsula Museum of Art, Monterey, CA, 1976.

Stefoff, Rebecca, editor, *300 Years of American Art, Vol. 1 and 2*, The Wellfleet Press Edition, Secaucus, NJ, 1987.

Van Nostrand, Jeanne, *The First Hundred Years of Painting in California, 1775-1875*, John Howell Books, San Francisco, CA, 1980.

*Who's Who on the Pacific Coast*, A.N. Marquis Company, Chicago, IL, 1949.

Westphal, Ruth, *Plein Air Painters of California - The North*, Westphal Publishing, Irvine, CA, 1986.

Westphal, Ruth, *Plein Air Painters of California - The Southland*, Westphal Publishing, Irvine, CA, 1982.

*Widening Horizons: The Western Woman*, Vol.14, No. 1, Ada Wallis Publisher, Los Angeles, CA.

*Widening Horizons: The Western Woman*, Vol. 14, No. 3, Ada Wallis Publisher, Los Angeles, CA.

*William Gaw*, Maxwell Galleries, Ltd., San Francisco, CA, 1969.

# Acknowledgements

Much of the biographical information in this book came from personal interviews with the artists, their friends or relatives. These people are credited below each artists biographical entry. Additional information, help, or access to art works illustrated in this book was provided by the following people. The authors are indebted to these many individuals who were generous with time and knowledge. We wish to thank: **Susan Anderson, Terri Anderson, Dennis Askew, Susie Baron, Barbara Beretich, Robert Bijou, Paul Bingham, Ken and Mindi Blackburn, Janet Blake, Len Braarud, Joan Irving Brandt, Rexford Brandt, Gary Breitweiser, Gerald Buck, James Clark, Bolton Colburn, Chris Coleman, E. Gene Crain, John De Cuir, Coby Dahlstrom, Chris Darrow, Tom and Georgia Dillon, Diane Dodds, Robyn Dunn, Jessie Dunn-Gilbert, Sid Emerson, Kerne Erickson, Naim Farhat, Jack Ford, Robin Fuld, Whitney Ganz, John Garzoli, Roger Genser, Ed Goldfield, Alec Goldstein, Philip and Marge Greene, Rick Griffin, Alfred C. Harrison, Jr., Steve Hauk, Bob and Rhonda Heintz, Chet Helms, Mark and Jan Hilbert, Larry and Stephanie Ho, Mark Hoffman, David Howard, Sandy Hunter, Michael Johnson, Richard and Mercedes Kerwin, Bruce Kinghan, Glen and Pam Knowles, Lillian Langford, Debbie Last, Michael Latragna, Marty and Ronni Lomeli, Jim and Linda Mackie, David and Sally Martin, Dewitt McCall, Austin McClelland, Debi McClelland, Lorne McClelland, Marian McClelland, Martin Medak, Mark and Laura Mettler, Ronald Miller, John Moran, Tobey Moss, Joseph L. Moure, Nancy Moure, Richard Neville, Thomas Nygard, Jeff Olsen, Richard Opsitos, Tina O'Shea, Robert Perine, Ray Redfern, Steven Rose, Mike Rupp, Ray Sahranavard, Joan Scarboro, Joan Irvine Smith, Linda Gramatky Smith, David and Susan Stary-Sheets, George and Irene Stern, Jean Stern, Shirley Sullivan, David Tonnemacher, Mark Trout, Mike and Susan Verbal, Jim Waterbury, Shelly Walker, John and Nancy Weare, Esther Wells,** and **Greg and Lisa Young.**

While gathering pictures to reproduce in this book the authors also received a great deal of help from art galleries. We wish to thank:

*Anderson Art Gallery* - Sunset Beach, CA,
*Atelier Dore Gallery* - San Francisco, CA,
*Biltmore Galleries* - Scottsdale, AZ,
*Bingham Gallery* - San Jose, CA,
*Braarud Fine Art* - La Conner, WA,
*California Art Gallery* - Laguna Beach, CA,
*calart.com* - Encinitas, CA,
*Claremont Fine Arts* - Claremont, CA,
*DeRu's Fine Arts* - Laguna Beach, CA,
*Esther Wells Collection* - Laguna Beach, CA,
*Galeria Beretich* - Claremont, CA,
*Garzoli Gallery* - San Rafael, CA,
*George Stern Fine Arts* - West Hollywood, CA,
*Goldfield Galleries, Ltd.* - Los Angeles, CA,
*Kerwin Galleries* - Burlingame, CA,
*Maxwell Galleries, Ltd.* - San Francisco, CA,
*Michael A. Latragna Fine Art* - Rochester, NY,
*Michael Johnson Fine Arts* - Fallbrook, CA,
*North Point Gallery* - San Francisco, CA,
*OK Harris Gallery* - New York City, NY,
*Papillion Gallery* - Los Angeles, CA,
*Peregrine Galleries* - Santa Barbara, CA,
*Piedmont Lane Gallery* - Piedmont, CA,
*Redfern Gallery* - Laguna Beach, CA,
*Stary-Sheets Fine Art Galleries* - Laguna Niguel, CA,
*Studio 2 Antiques* - Santa Barbara, CA,
*Thomas Nygard Gallery* - Bozeman, MT,
*Tobey Moss Gallery* - Los Angeles, CA,
*Trotter Galleries* - Carmel, CA
*William A. Karges Fine Art* - Los Angeles, CA.

*Emil Kosa, Jr. painting on location in Newport Beach, California, 1955.*

*Charles Payzant in his studio with finished watercolor "Hay Wagon" 1948.*